CITIES ALIVE

*Jane Jacobs, Christopher Alexander,
and the Roots of the
New Urban Renaissance*

MICHAEL W. MEHAFFY

SUSTASIS PRESS

in association with

CENTER FOR THE FUTURE OF PLACES
KTH ROYAL INSTITUTE OF TECHNOLOGY

ISBN: 978-0-9893469-9-3
Copyright 2017
© Michael W. Mehaffy.

Sustasis Press, Sustasis Foundation, Portland, Oregon (USA)
In association with Center for the Future of Places,
KTH Royal Institute of Technology, Stockholm (Sweden)

Formatted by Yulia Kryazheva,
Yulia Ink (Amsterdam, The Netherlands)

Cities Alive: Jane Jacobs, Christopher Alexander and the Roots of the
New Urban Renaissance
By Michael W. Mehaffy, Ph.D.

ACKNOWLEDGEMENTS

I am indebted for the support that made this volume possible to my colleagues and hosts at the Center for the Future of Places at KTH Royal Institute of Technology: Tigran Haas, its Director, and Peter Elmlund, Board Member, and Director of Urban City Research for the Ax:son Johnson Foundation, who has provided generous funding. I owe special thanks to Yulia Kryazheva, the book's designer, who gave me crucial advice on the topic and focus of the book. I am also indebted to the many editors, collaborators and conference hosts who invited me to contribute some of the material that has been revised and re-worked for this volume. Among them I must mention: Kjersti Grut of Habitat Norway; James Brasuell of *Planetizen*; David Maddox of *The Nature of Cities*; Rob Steuteville of CNU's Public Square; my co-editors of Katarxis 3, Lucien Steil, Brian Hanson and Nikos Salingaros; Richard Hayward of *Urban Design International*; Hajo Neis of the Portland Urban Architecture Research Laboratory (PUARL) and the University of Oregon, where I have also been privileged to teach; Deependra Prashad of INTBAU India; Richard Harriss of Houston Advanced Research Center, and the Onassis Foundation, organizers of The Athens Dialogues conference in Greece; Sommer Mathis, Editor of *The Atlantic's CityLab*; Elizabeth Razzi, Editor-In-Chief of *Urban Land* magazine; Susan Szenasy, Editor of *Metropolis* magazine; Bashir Kazimee of Washington State University; my colleagues and promotors at Delft University of Technology, including Andy van den Dobbelsteen and Henco Bekkering; my long-time colleague Nikos Salingaros, with whom I co-developed many of the ideas in this volume; and last but certainly not least, Jane Jacobs, with whom I corresponded only too briefly, and Christopher Alexander, with whom I have been remarkably privileged to study and work over a period beginning in 1981 and extending to the present.

TABLE OF CONTENTS

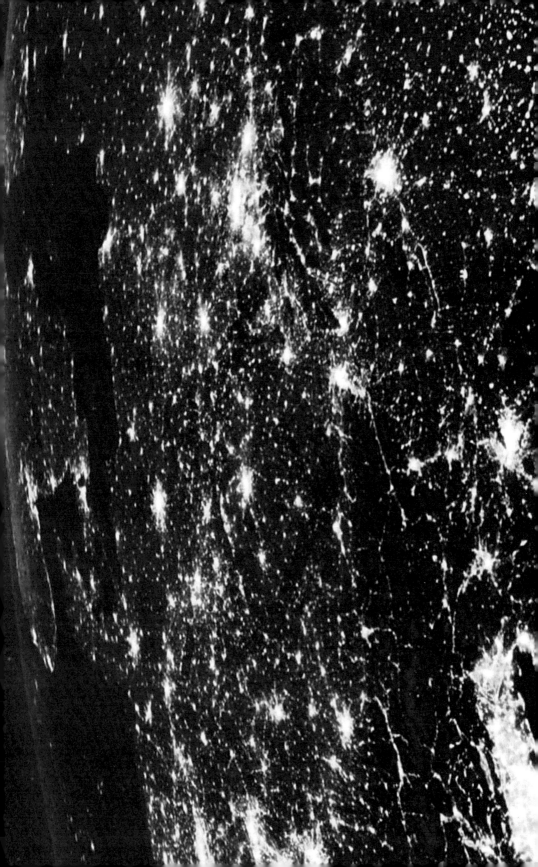

INTRODUCTION:

Why cities are the problem,
but cities are the answer too

"A growing number of people have begun, gradually, to think of cities as problems in organized complexity--organisms that are replete with unexamined, but obviously intricately interconnected, and surely understandable, relationships..."

— *Jane Jacobs,* The Death and Life of Great American Cities *(1961)*

"People used to say that just as the 20th century had been the century of physics, the 21st century would be the century of biology... We would gradually move into a world whose prevailing paradigm was one of complexity, and whose techniques sought the co-adapted harmony of hundreds or thousands of variables. This would, inevitably, involve new technique, new vision, new models of thought, and new models of action. I believe that such a transformation is starting to occur... To be well, we must set our sights on such a future."

— *Christopher Alexander,* The Nature of Order

In December 2016, the 193 member states of the United Nations adopted by consensus a document known as the "New Urban Agenda." This historic declaration, the outcome of the UN's "Habitat III" conference in October of that year, crystallizes several generations of reform in our thinking about cities and towns. It also focuses our attention on the daunting challenges ahead, in which cities and towns will play such an increasingly important role.

In a sense, the New Urban Agenda only formalizes a set of reforms that are already well under way, and that are the subject of this book. (The Agenda itself is also discussed in more detail in Chapter IV.1.) Thankfully, the benefits of these changes can already be seen in many cities and towns around the world, where once-dangerous or polluted neighborhoods are now thriving with activity; once-empty historic districts, formerly with little to offer but ugliness and despair, are now thriving and beautiful; and once-sprawling suburbs are now more diverse, more walkable, and more ecologically sustainable.

These are clear and hopeful signs that an urban renaissance is under way — a revival of our ability to make more beautiful, more

Opposite: Cities at night, seen from the International Space Station. Photo: NASA

ecological, and more successful places, from a human point of view. Moreover, there is intriguing evidence that the connection between the ecological quality of a settlement, its beauty, and its success from a human point of view, are all structurally inter-connected — a topic we will explore later in this book. Of course, much more remains to be done, and that too will be a subject of the book.

It is of course easy to focus on the many problems of cities — over-gentrification, displacement, ugly new developments, gated communities, sprawling suburbs, car dependence, pollution, habitat destruction, and all the other things we have gotten so wrong about cities in the last half-century or so. This book will discuss these things in due course. But it will do so from the perspective of what we have more recently gotten *right* about cities, with a focus on two people who have articulated these improvements with remarkable lucidity. Their work, along with many others', has paved the way for the urban renaissance that is now well under way.

Even so, from a longer historic perspective this remarkable transformation has barely begun, and its future course remains to be shaped (I hope by readers of this book, among others). As I will discuss, its achievements are far from secure, and the book will discuss some of its more notable threats, both external and self-induced (over-gentrification is a troubling example of the latter). But I aim to show that what is already happening is tapping into something deep and powerful about cities, and about human settlements in general — about the nature of life in general, and city life in particular.

So to tell the story of this renaissance, I will focus on two of its most interesting and, I think, revealing figures: the American-Canadian urbanist Jane Jacobs, and the English- American architect Christopher Alexander. I will do this for two reasons: first, each of them played a notable role in helping to bring about these changes, with highly influential works on the nature of cities beginning in 1961 and 1965, respectively. Secondly, each of them is a deep thinker about the nature of settlement, planning, design, technology — and the other related issues that we still face today. Together, their thinking has intriguing and revealing overlaps and synergies. They will serve as very good guides to our present challenges, I think.

When I speak of cities in this book, I am not only speaking of the big dense cores of major cities. Cities come in a wide range of sizes, and always have. Athens in the time of Pericles was barely 70,000 people, whereas Rome in the time of Julius Caesar was closer to one million. We focus perhaps too much of our attention on the largest cities of modernity, and especially, too much on their cores. Although these are important, so are the smaller cities and towns that have always shaped human life for a large percentage of humanity. For that reason, our purview in this book — perhaps even more than Alexander's, and certainly more than Jacobs' — will include *all* kinds of cities and suburbs and towns, large and small.

Just now almost everyone is aware that we face enormous challenges in the years ahead, including the depletion of critical resources, alarming changes in climates and ecosystems, toxic effects of production, geopolitical and economic instability, and — less obvious but no less serious — chaotic transformations in our technologies, in our cultures, and ultimately in the capacities of human civilizations. This is a daunting set of difficulties, to be sure. But human life has been full of no less existential threats, and we have persevered — even after nearing the brink of extinction, as the evidence now shows. We seem to have an innate capacity to survive, by adapting, innovating, and reforming our technology. That is a hopeful trait.

In all of our current challenges, cities — again, in the broad sense of urban settlements — loom very large. It is within the structures of these urban settlements that we consume, interact, create, and ultimately generate the impacts that now prompt such growing concern. But it is also within them that we develop as human beings and as a species — that we create, innovate, adapt and problem-solve. It is in these settlements that we create a civic framework by which we may work together on shared opportunities and challenges.

The renaissance of which I speak is ultimately just this: a revival of our capacity to live well together in settlements, to work together to adapt to our constraints, to create and develop new and well-ordered structures, to improve our quality of life, and to provide the likely basis for the vast majority of humanity to be well in the future.

The hopeful message of both Jane Jacobs and Christopher Alexander is that we *do* have the inherent capacity to grow and adapt in just this way. Their shared message is that we have a particular capacity within our settlements, our cities, that we can put to work for us, and that is far stronger than we yet realize. We have the ability to develop new solutions, combined with the genius of old and even ancient ones.

As I hinted earlier, this book will take note of one interesting and surprisingly important fact. In this renaissance, as in the more famous one half a millennium ago, the phenomenon of beauty will play an outsized role. It is the deeper beauty of a life well lived, of a street full of people and vegetables and sunlight and energy. It is something much deeper than the superficial and manipulative beauty of a consumer product or even an exotic artwork. In fact, I will suggest that the treatment of beauty as a superficial or "psychological" quality is a sign of the obstructions we have let creep into our lives — the powerful but damaging forces of industrialized, consumer-marketed built environments, and the objectivist pseudo-sciences on which they are based. As Christopher Alexander has argued, their ugliness is a sign of a much deeper structural dysfunction. But it is a dysfunction that can be repaired, a pathology that can be healed. That is what this renaissance is all about, in the end.

I will argue that this renaissance is, in fact, a transformation in the way we think of beauty, of quality, and of life. It is a determined mastery of the technological abstractions that are, on the one hand, our powerful agents, but if we are not careful — and we have not been nearly careful enough — our destructive masters. This situation compels our ethical responsibility as professionals and as citizens. But even more important, it compels our understanding, of what Jane Jacobs called "the kind of problem a city is." We could add, following historically recent scientific advancements, that we need to understand "the kind of problem that *life* is," as a form of "organized complexity." That too was a point that Jane Jacobs made, in her early and insightful observation in the brilliant last chapter of her first book, *The Death and Life of Great American Cities*.

This is a common theme for both authors, and so it will be a notable theme of this book. While both Jacobs and Alexander have celebrated and promoted the life and beauty of cities, each of them has also articulated powerful critiques of the traps we have laid for ourselves within modernity, and modern city-making. Each of them has also appealed to a rigorous, evidence-based kind of science to work our way through our challenges. Each of them has expressed a willingness to stand or fall on the evidence, to be falsified, and thereby to transcend the pseudo-scientific weakness of so much "modern" planning and design theory. (Although this point is poorly understood, and each in turn has been accused of precisely the opposite — a point we will come back to later in the book.) Both of them are confident that we *can* learn from our mistakes as we have done in the past, and that we can harness the power of cities for the future. These two aspects of cities — what is good about them, and what has also gone wrong in critical respects, and must be put right — are the twin sides of the story this book will tell. Along the way it will tell a deeper story too, about design, technology, science, and culture.

The term "iconoclast" has been applied to both Jane Jacobs and Christopher Alexander more than once, and for good reason. Both were icon-smashers within the sacred iconographies of modern architecture and urbanism, although each did so with a distinct emphasis. Jacobs opened her first and most influential book, *The Death and Life of Great American Cities* (1961), by describing it as an "attack" on conventional city planning. Alexander opened one of his most influential papers, "A city is not a tree" (1965), by noting that most non-architects, "instead of being grateful to architects for what they do, regard the onset of modern buildings and modern cities everywhere as an inevitable, rather sad piece of the larger fact that the world is going to the dogs."

Nor did either author confine their criticisms to architecture or urban planning, as this volume will explore. Each confronted broader issues of technology and culture, delving more deeply into those issues as their careers progressed — finding and reporting results that surprised even them. Both also explored deeper themes of modernity and its promises, and at the same time, both offered detailed structural critiques of the failures of modern industrial civilization, always with a focus on its systems of design, planning and building, especially the systems of city-building.

Neither, however, was an anti-modernist reactionary, or a despairing postmodernist. Both were, in an important sense, believers in the "project of modernity" — the treasury of thousands of years of philosophical reasoning and scientific advancement in understanding nature, culture, justice, and ethics, in the face of life's challenges to humanity. Both saw paths forward, rooted in science and reason, but also informed by a rich new sense of nature and its awesome, even transcendent complexities. In both cases, their iconoclasm was not an attack upon the progress of the Enlightenment, but a demand that its promises be fulfilled, that its failings and its dishonesties be confronted: that we learn and grow from our painfully evident mistakes.

It should be remembered that both Jacobs and Alexander spent their formative periods as members in good standing of the architectural establishment of their day. This is particularly easy to forget, since today they are both seen as quintessential outsiders and critics. But it was Jacobs who had been a respected journalist for *Architectural Forum,* writing admiringly about the modernist urban projects she later criticized. It was Alexander who was awarded the first Ph.D. in architecture at Harvard University, and who, as he tells it, interacted very happily with the then-elderly Walter Gropius — the man who brought the modernist architectural establishment to Harvard, and arguably, to the world.

That Jacobs and Alexander became two of the most influential critics of the same architectural establishment is an interesting and I think revealing story, with implications of great value to us even today. In both cases, they did not become critics by virtue of adopting contrarian "outsider" ideologies, but rather, by working *within* the logic of the establishment, and following their own quests for the truth within it — wherever those quests may have led them. When the result was inconsistency and evident failing, each in their own way confronted their assumptions, and each was forced by their own experiences — often painfully and slowly — to develop new ideas. That these new ideas were also at odds, often violently at odds, with the reigning orthodoxies, was clearly a surprise to them as much as to anyone.

But there is much more to the story than architectural or urban criticism. As this volume will explore, each felt compelled to develop broader ideas about history, culture, and ultimately nature — ideas with an intriguing overlap, as we will explore. In each case, the ideas have since turned out to be remarkably useful to many people outside the architecture and planning worlds. There is reason to think that much more use remains to be found in their partially overlapping, partially complementary ideas.

In a broader sense, each offers us a useful "critique of modernity" — a map of where we have begun to go wrong in our built environment, and in the cultural systems that produce it, and what we can actually do about this state of affairs. Each draws remarkably specific conclusions about what we will need for the future — the strategies, tools, habits of thinking, and notably, safeguards against the limits of reason and our common fallacies of thought and action. While each is known as a theorist — a term that has earned, in the era of modern design, a reputation as mere idle speculation — in reality each offers a most practical basis for confronting the challenges ahead.

As the philosopher Bertrand Russell put it, "there is nothing so practical as a good theory".

This book assumes a general familiarity with Jacobs and Alexander as personages without assuming detailed knowledge of their works or ideas. For those readers who already have detailed familiarity with one or both, some of the material will necessarily cover old ground. However, the goal will be to provide a sufficiently fresh enough perspective to make the book interesting for any reader, regardless of their level of familiarity.

This book will focus on the ideas of each author, and their overlapping relationships. I will not consider biographical details except as they are required to tell this story. There are a number of excellent biographies of both Jacobs and Alexander, some of them included in the "Further Reading" section at the end of the book.

Readers looking for incisive critiques of the shortcomings of these two authors (real or imagined) can also find them in a great many other books and articles elsewhere. There is surely ample material to discuss regarding their shortcomings (as with any author), but the purpose of this book is different. While not a hagiography, it will forthrightly consider what positive (and interrelated) contributions these two authors have made to our understanding of cities, and how their work has been beneficial — and may be more so in the future. If that is not your interest, this book is probably not for you.

The structure of the book will include a section to assess each thinker's ideas in detail, starting with Jacobs and then proceeding to Alexander. In some ways that allows us to start at the largest scale of cities, with Jacobs, and proceed to the scale of buildings, crafts, and the detailed shaping of human environments, about which Alexander has had more to say than Jacobs. At the same time, it should be remembered that both had considerable overlap at almost all scales, from the regional to the crucial scale of human beings and their experiences of built environments. Indeed, the connectivity of urban structure across scales is another theme that is common to both authors.

The third section will consider the philosophical implications, making the argument that both authors point to a new form of "structuralism" — that is, a deeper understanding of nature as a kind of structural network between events as we experience them, and as we apply the tool of language, both to model and to regenerate them. In some ways, this "neo-structuralism" helps us to resolve age-old dualities between the subjective and objective, "matter" and "spirit", and perhaps most importantly, "fact" and "value". This potential re-unification of the worlds of value and fact has its echoes in the writings of many other authors as well, as I will briefly discuss. No less so, their "critique of modernity" certainly has many echoes in the writings of prominent philosophers from the Enlightenment up to the present day.

The fourth section explores several key challenges and opportunities in the contemporary world considering what Jacobs' and Alexander's insights contribute to those discussions. It is here that we will explore the UN's "New Urban Agenda," the possibilities of a "new" (or revived) urbanism, the impacts of climate change, the challenges of the current rapid urbanization, and the problems of gentrification, affordability, displacement, inequality, and related contemporary issues.

The fifth section considers the practical conclusions to be drawn from both authors, and presents several practical "takeaways" for the challenges ahead. That section also includes hopeful examples of cities and towns that are demonstrating aspects of this new urban renaissance, including photos and notes. A concluding chapter makes note of some unresolved questions, and topics for further exploration.

SECTION I:

JANE JACOBS ON "THE KIND OF PROBLEM A CITY IS"

1. CITIES OF DIVERSITY

There is a quality even meaner than outright ugliness or disorder, and this meaner quality is the dishonest mask of pretended order, achieved by ignoring or suppressing the real order that is struggling to exist and to be served."

— *Jane Jacobs,* The Death and Life of Great American Cities

Jane Jacobs began her first and most influential book with these words: "This book is an attack on current city planning and rebuilding." *The Death and Life of Great American Cities* (1961) was indeed a frontal assault on then-current urban orthodoxy, and by all accounts an effective one. But the book was also a passionate defense, of human life and of the human processes that were going on in the urban places she observed. Many of these places were under grave threat in the era of "urban renewal," when the older, messier parts of cities were supposed to be replaced with fresh new "modern" environments. That benign-sounding name, "urban renewal," obscured the fact that there was very little renewal, and much more wholesale destruction of the life of large parts of cities, to be replaced by something else: an abstract idea about life, perhaps.

For that reason, it mattered a great deal whether the agents of urban renewal had sensible ideas about these parts of cities: how well they understood what was good about these neighborhoods, and how well, under their stewardship, the new projects were able to regenerate those qualities. On the evidence, it seemed that they understood these qualities very poorly indeed. As a consequence, the new projects were, in many ways, dismal failures (as extensive research literature demonstrates).

In a deeper sense, the book was an incisive critique of that era's (and perhaps still this era's too) dominant way of thinking about cities. "Functional segregation" was supposed to be the way to cure the ills of cities: sort out the tangle of problems by segregating potential conflicts from one another, with housing in one place, workplaces in another, and civic uses in still another. Create a "rationally ordered" structure, not unlike an early industrial machine. The fuel goes in

Opposite: The weekend street market in the San Telmo neighborhood of Buenos Aires draws residents from all over the city.

here, the ignition happens there, the motion happens over there, and so on. The result is smooth, orderly, predictable.

It was not a coincidence that the personal automobile, the apotheosis of the 20th Century machine age, came to dominance in this same period — or that the sleek futuristic architecture that everyone so admired in the most popular exhibit in the 1939 World's Fair was built by General Motors, the world's largest car company. Futurama held out a utopian vision of a highly ordered and powerful civilization, a kind of gigantic machine packaged in sleek minimalist design. Everyone would be whisked almost effortlessly to whatever destination they chose in their own personal car. The city itself would become a kind of machine for serving up whatever we needed or wanted. This was the well-ordered consumer paradise that awaited, like a promise, beyond the suffering and the irrational chaos of the war years.

By the mid-1950s, General Motors and other US companies were working with the government to deliver on the promise. In 1956, the year that the Federal-Aid Highway Act was passed creating the US Interstate Highway System, General Motors also ran a revealing featurette on American television called *Design for Dreaming*. It showed a couple flying along on an uncrowded freeway, over a silent nighttime city, full of fantastic lights and forms, like children's toys:

> *Tomorrow, tomorrow, our dreams will come true!*
> *Together, together, we'll make the world new!*
> *Strange shapes will rise out of the night,*
> *but our love will not change, dear —*
> *It will be like a star burning bright,*
> *lighting our way, when tomorrow meets today!*

By today's standards, that earnest featurette is laughably absurd: the jet-like tail fins on the cars, the empty freeways, the sheer naïveté of starry-eyed utopianism. A mere decade later, the real nature of the modern post-war city had begun to reveal itself: ugly monotonous development, chaotic traffic jams, relentless suburban sprawl, and the accelerated decline of once-vibrant urban cores, into cities of poverty, unrest and protest.

This was where urban renewal was supposed to do some good. Visionaries like Robert Moses, New York's powerful Parks Commissioner — later notorious for his freeway-building proposals through Greenwich Village, New Orleans' French Quarter and other treasured neighborhoods — saw the cores of cities as "slums" to be cleared and replaced with the beneficially "strange shapes" of the architects, making the world new. Everyone would have a clean and sanitary dwelling, with light and air and all the other benefits of modernity.

It didn't work, of course, and in just a few decades, once-utopian projects like Pruitt Igoe and Cabrini Green had fallen into dystopian ruin, plagued by vandalism, crime and despair. Worse, the urban fabric that had once existed, and provided an under-appreciated network of social connections, was now gone — and with it, any ideas about what could make a good place to live.

This is where Jacobs was more than a critic, and where she offered a solid idea of what made a city work for people. In place of machine-like functional segregation, she advocated diversity and mixing. In place of "loose sprawls" and "project land oozings" around towering modernist art-objects, she argued for coherent public space systems shaped by well-formed streetscapes, squares and parks. In place of super-block "projects" isolated by "border vacuums" she advocated a continuous fabric of interconnected urbanism.

The city was thus a place where contacts and connections were possible, where human presence made people safer, and where interactions between diverse people of diverse capabilities could create new opportunities. It was a kind of living tissue of urbanism, a network of people and spaces, from the most public to the most private.

Most important, this kind of city maintained a continuous level of connectivity right across its fabric, from the largest regional scales right down to the scales of sidewalks and building entries. Where an urban use interrupted this continuous fabric, it was critical to find ways to weave it back together, at a minimum spacing. That was true for rivers, railroad tracks and freeways, but it was no less true for parks, campuses and even neighborhoods.

When we allowed the city to be fragmented, the result was a phenomenon she called a "border vacuum" — a dead zone, not unlike the dead zone around a hole eaten by a caterpillar through a leaf. As the capillaries get cut off and the nutrients no longer flow, the tissue around the hole also dies. So it was for urban neighborhoods at these border vacuums: as the flow of people and goods gets interrupted — the so-called "movement economy" — the activities at the edges also decline. Businesses close, shopfronts get boarded up, and neighborhoods enter a death spiral.

This is precisely what Jacobs observed at the edges of Robert Moses' freeway projects, but also at the edges of many other kinds of single urban uses. It happened when Le Corbusier's gigantic monocultural housing projects were inserted into the urban fabric (like the aforementioned Cabrini Green and Pruitt Igoe). It also happened when the City Beautiful advocates created monocultural "civic campuses" composed of government buildings, libraries, museums and the like. And it also happened when the Garden City advocates created suburban "new towns" with segregated "wards" of housing here, commercial there, workplaces over there.

In all these cases, functional segregation — and the disruptive effect it had on mixing across scales, down to the finer grains — had the effect of fragmenting the parts of the city, creating discontinuities and border vacuums. In all the cases, the answer was to restore the continuous urban fabric, and the diversity of mixing that it allowed and supported.

For Jacobs, diversity was the crucial ingredient of all great cities: diversity of people, of activities, of building ages and types, of kinds of contact and interaction. The structure of the city needed to support this diversity, by supporting physical connectivity and access at all scales, at a minimum threshold of compactness, with a minimum scale of connectivity across relatively small blocks.

At the same time, many people had responsibility, at different scales, to shape the growth of the city — from mayors to local shop owners. Their actions had to support and encourage urban diversity, as a process as well as a product. This overlapping system of stewardship would later be called "polycentric governance" by the economist Elinor Ostrom. Formal government, in this view, needs to be supplanted with many other forms of governance, formal and informal, across many scales. They might include overlapping government jurisdictions, but also NGOs, neighborhood associations, business districts, business owners, and residents, all acting at a variety of scales to support the health of their neighborhoods and cities.

This process is hardly harmonious, of course. Cities are full of conflicts, as Jacobs pointed out, just as humanity is full of conflicts. Our actions in meeting our own needs frequently come into conflict with others' actions. Cities are especially prone to these conflicts because of their concentration of diversity. We disturb one another with noise; we crowd one another out; we block one another's access to light, air, view, free movement.

These things have to be sorted out, so that there is a reasonably equitable and just mediation between these conflicting freedoms of access, manifested in the built form of the city. In that sense, the structure of the city itself manifests a just (or as just as possible) mediation between conflicting freedoms (as my friend Paul Murrain has put it). This is, in fact, the political system of the city, the *polis*.

We go to the considerable trouble of making this arrangement because cities offer us something extremely important. It is commonly supposed that cities attract people because "that's where the jobs are." But that begs the question, *why* the jobs are in cities. Why is all employment not scattered across the countryside, as, say, agricultural employment typically is? This question consumed a large portion of Jane Jacobs' later work on cities, and she concluded that the city was far more than a cluster of convenience. Her answer was, in essence, that cities extend to the people within them a very special capacity for creative interaction and human development. This capacity has to do primarily with the kinds of networks of interaction that people can establish, rooted in the spatial networks of the city, and especially, its public spaces.

It is the opportunity that such spatial networks afford us that looms especially large in Jacobs' later work on economics.

2. CITIES OF OPPORTUNITY[*]

"Lowly, unpurposeful, and random as they may appear, sidewalk contacts are the small change from which a city's wealth of public life may grow."

— Jane Jacobs, The Death and Life of Great American Cities

It is a remarkable phenomenon, bordering on miraculous, that a city like, say, 19th Century New York, can take penniless immigrants from Ireland or Italy or Poland, and in the space of a few decades, turn them (or their children) into shopkeepers and factory owners and lawyers and senators — and poets and artists and professors. This is what ultimately draws people to cities: not simply to secure "jobs" but to develop as human beings, which is to say, to improve health and well-being, to increase opportunities for women and (often smaller) families, and to expand the creative capacities and the wealth of human culture.

This is not a random process. Education is surely a part of it, but so is the expansion of opportunity within physical networks of potential collaboration. This human development can happen because there is something in the network of connections within cities that allows these opportunities to occur, manifested within real physical space occupied by real people. That physical space includes, at its most fundamental level, the public space of the city: its streets, squares, parks and plazas, where friends, strangers and (importantly) near-strangers can encounter one another.

Jacobs' observations about how successful cities actually worked led her inevitably into the subject of urban economics. How do people create new knowledge, and new work? What is it about cities that makes this possible? Her answer was that people develop and exchange knowledge with one another within cities — not only with people they know well, in their own industries, but with other people they know less well, in other businesses or other entire industries. The subject of her work in this field came to be known as a "knowl-

---

* *Portions of this essay were drawn from an essay written for the Congress for the New Urbanism blog "Public Square". I am grateful to editor Rob Steuteville for his assistance.*

Opposite: *A woman tends her small shop on the street in Hanoi. Many shops are part of "shop houses" where shop owners live in the relatively affordable residences above.*

edge spillover," and her particular observation is now known in economics as a "Jacobs spillover."

It was this, she found, that lay at the heart of the capacity that cities have to support the growth of knowledge exchanges and combinations, producing innovation and economic growth. This is how a city like 19th Century Detroit, for example, could become a new hub of economic expansion in the early 20th, in the entirely new and unheard-of field of automobile manufacturing.

In her book *The Economy of Cities* (1969), Jacobs noted that Detroit had two things going for it. One, the city was already a center of a diverse network of businesses related to of shipbuilding, which meant there was a great diversity of enterprises that would serve the new automobile industry well — makers of motors, wheels, pulleys, carriages and the like. Two, just as important, the city had a network of spatial connections between all these individuals and enterprises, not only within the existing companies, but outside of them. Workers could meet up and form new connections within a broad range of urban spaces, both private and public. This "mixing network" provided fertile conditions for the growth of new enterprises, and even a new industry — which is precisely what happened in due course.

Earlier, in *The Death and Life of Great American Cities*, Jacobs had spent a lot of time talking about "lowly" sidewalks, and their importance for creating safety, assimilating children, and providing the essential contacts on which the life of the city is built. It was not that sidewalks were the only place for making such contacts, but that sidewalks form an essential strand of what Robert Putnam has referred to as "multi-stranded" social connections.

This understanding of diverse networks, built on human-scaled public spaces including sidewalks and their edges, is the foundation on which her economic work was built. At heart, hers became an economic vision of the city — an understanding of the "organized complexity" of human activities and creations of wealth that the city makes possible. As we now understand from network science, this system gets its power not from a "command and control" approach from the top, but from a broadly interconnected, partly self-organizing network.

In essence, she argued, most of the economic benefits for the city are not generated by any kind of concentrated power center, but are actually the result of a broad form of socio-economic interaction all across the city network, involving many small and mid-sized businesses and as well as start-ups. (And yes, a few big businesses too — though if they become too dominant the city can stagnate.) The many small-scale innovations within this mixing network compound to generate the wealth of the city, in part by replacing imports and eventually creating new exports, and in part by making possible creative synergies that are often unexpected.

It is this capacity that offers opportunity for many different people at many different scales — and not only at the top, in the form of either big companies or big government programs. (These large extremes dominate the attention of today's most prominent "right" and "left" ideologies, but for Jacobs, both of these ideological fixations miss the deeper point.) This inherent dynamic of cities can, if we put it to work for us, take penniless immigrants (as it did, say, in the example of New York that I gave earlier) and turn them into middle-class shopkeepers and manufacturers and professors and artists — and all the other economically and culturally creative people of the city.

It is true that much of the wealth of a city is temptingly visible at the top — and often in the city core, especially of late — but that does not mean it is wholly or even mostly generated there. But over-concentration of attention at the top, and in the core, not only fuels the wealth gap and the dynamics of gentrification, it distracts from the real engine of urban growth, according to Jacobs. The result is likely to be stagnation, loss of affordability, increasing segregation by income, declining quality of life, and a spiral of urban failure and re-crimination. I will have more to say about this problem later in the book.

For Jacobs, however, the real engine of growth is powered by many diverse people interacting within the continuous fabric of physical spaces of the city, including the crucial public realm — the sidewalks and other spaces where people encounter one another, share information, pass along contacts, and create the "knowledge spillovers" that are essential to innovative expansion. Within this continuous fabric, private social spaces are important too, of course, but the "glue" that binds them all together is the critical public realm. Cities are, in effect, "socio-economic reactors" that generate wealth, in the broadest sense of the term (including cultural wealth).

This is a more diffuse and less visible form of wealth production, but it is ultimately a more powerful one. In fact Jacobs argues that this is the real wellspring of human development. Simultaneously, it is a way of increasing resource efficiency (because efficiency is financially rewarded) and reducing ecological impacts. This efficiency-trending dynamic goes a long way to explaining why compact mixed use cities can be, on a per capita basis, so much "greener" than more sprawling places, as my own research and many others' has shown.

There is another, related implication. Of course it is possible, up to a point, to replace the diversified, continuous public realm of urbanism, and the catalytic growth it produces, with a system of segregated, machine-like capsules: automobiles, isolated offices and campuses, suburban housing monocultures, and the like. It is possible, in other words, to trade away a "natural human-capital city," for an artificial kind of city that is nonetheless economically productive, at least in the short term. Indeed, we can see many examples in the US and other countries.

But this economic development is only possible with massive injections of resources — notably fossil fuels — at unsustainable rates. We could think of this this model as the "crack cocaine" of urban development: it will certainly produce a very quick and intense high, but one followed by a disastrous (in this case planetary) hangover.

This is the urban crisis that we now face. The world is rapidly urbanizing according to precisely this addictive model. We are on track to produce more urban fabric by area in the first five decades of the 21st Century than we have produced in all of human history. What will be the model, if not this one? How will we avert the catastrophic collapse that seems inevitable under the current unsustainable path? Those in the urban professions will certainly be challenged to respond to this crisis (for example, in implementing the "New Urban Agenda" that has just emerged from the UN conference on housing and sustainable development).

Will we continue to stake our entire future on this economic "crack cocaine high"? Or will we take a more hopeful view, and see the city (and town) as an engine of sustainable regeneration, taking the steps needed to unleash the powerful urban dynamics on offer?

The latter choice will demand of us a more subtle, more catalytic approach to urban growth — one more focused on harnessing and directing the self-organizing capacities of cities, towns, and neighborhoods. It will demand that we avoid pursuing the latest "silver bullet" — the big employer or big sports stadium — and focus on a broader and more diversified form of urban economic development. It demands that we pay more attention to what Jacobs called "the kind of problem a city is" — and it is not the kind that we have too often supposed.

3. "TO THINK ABOUT PROCESSES..." [*]

In the case of understanding cities, I think the most important habits of thought are these:

    1. To think about processes;

    2. To work inductively, reasoning from particulars to the general, rather than the reverse;

    3. To seek for "unaverage" clues involving very small quantities, which reveal the way larger and more "average" quantities are operating.

                     — *Jane Jacobs*, The Death and Life of Great American Cities

In her last chapter of *The Death and Life of Great American Cities*, Jacobs summed up the previous arguments in the book by articulating a broader conception of "the kind of problem a city is." It was an argument that we need a more relevant, clear and useful framework of thought for confronting our urban problems. Without it, we are doomed to repeat the same mistakes, and to make no progress — indeed, to compound our problems, as we have evidently done.

In essence, Jacobs observed that we were thinking about cities as the *wrong kind of problem* — a problem that we thought was amenable to silver bullets and command-and-control techniques, working solely from the top of the urban pyramid downward. This wrongheaded approach, while it could seem effective in the short run, could only result eventually in a slow stagnation and over-exploitation of essential resources, causing a cascading series of human and ecological casualties. The book, and especially the last chapter, proposed an entirely different kind of approach. It was far from libertarian — a misunderstanding that too often occurs in thinking about Jacobs — but rather, it was a different kind of *strategic* approach.

It was known that at the time of her writing the book that her editor Jacob Epstein was advocating that she should drop this last chapter, and that she should talk about the problem of race instead. That problem was of course an urgent urban issue at that time, and it certainly seemed natural to speak of it. But Jacobs knew that, outside of the context of this new framework of thought, racism and other

---

[*] *Portions of this essay were drawn from my earlier essay on the Katarxis3.com website, "The kind of problem architecture is."*

Opposite: *Vendors selling fresh vegetables in the market in Guanajuato, Mexico.*

urban ills could not be seen as they are — *as symptoms of a deeper structural disorder,* requiring a deeper understanding of the nature of the problem itself: the nature of *cities* themselves. This was what she referred to in the chapter's title, "The kind of problem a city is." It was necessary to begin here, and then one could take up other problems, like racism (as she did indeed in later books).

This is a point that is sometimes lost on some of Jacobs' contemporary critics. They want her to march with them against the injustice of racism, or perhaps class separation, or perhaps ageism, or perhaps sexism, or perhaps homophobia, or perhaps...

We can begin to see the problem. However legitimate are our concerns, it is not enough to march, or shake our fists, or write treatises. (From ivory towers?) It is not enough to play "Whack-a-Mole" — that children's game where new toy moles continuously pop up after we whack down old ones — with our urban problems. They often simply get worse, as indeed they have.

Nor is it enough to "design away our problems" (the top-down conceit of many designers). While there is certainly a place for top-down actions — and indeed, Jacobs described a number of them in the book — they must occur in the context of a well-formulated strategic approach to the *structure* of the city. And one must understand that kind of structure, and the problem it represents for those who want to modify it.

Just so, one must also understand the *processes* that occur in the city, since structure and process are two sides of the same coin. More accurately, structure shapes process, and process shapes structure — we cannot deal with one without dealing with the other. Unfortunately, too many designers deal too much with structure alone, and too many planners deal with process alone.

This issue also invokes the age-old debate between "top-down" and "bottom-up" — and it suggests that is a false duality. The City *is* a partly self-organizing system, in bottom-up fashion. It is *not* a deterministic structure, composed by designers as a kind of final ideal state. But that is not to say that there aren't important actions we can take to catalyze and direct growth, much as gardeners shape the growth of their gardens. Like gardeners, we can build trellises (infrastructure), plant good seeds (plan types), fertilize and water (incentives), prune and weed (regulations, including targeted zoning), and apply complementary planting (targeted catalysts). In that sense, we could say that "the kind of problem a city is," is one that is more like gardening than carpentry.

This is a fundamentally important point. It means that we should be less concerned with "command and control" on the one hand, or libertarian fantasies of automatic goodness flowing from deregulation on the other. We should instead be concerned with careful stewardship, applying regulation in a more agile and deft way. We should be concerned with design *for* self-organization — to facilitate, harness and direct it, rather than to replace it.

Jacobs began the last marvelous chapter of *Death and Life* with an appeal to the importance of understanding the nature of the problem we are dealing with:

> Thinking has its strategies and tactics too, much as other forms of action have. Merely to think about cities and get somewhere, one of the main things to know is what kind of problem cities pose, for all problems cannot be thought about in the same way. Which avenues of thinking are apt to be useful and to help yield the truth depends not on how we might prefer to think about a subject, but rather on the inherent nature of the subject itself.

Jacobs proceeded with a discussion of the history of scientific thought and its relation to the ways in which we think about and act upon cities. She noted how modern science really took off, around the time of Newton, when it mastered so-called two-variable problems, like linking how many houses one has over here to how many stores one can have over there. Or in physics, the laws of motion, for example, are two-variable problems.

But in the early twentieth century, something interesting had begun to happen: through statistics and probability we learned to manage very large quantities, where large numbers of variables were interacting. The interesting discovery was that one could manage those phenomena as statistical averages, without knowing much at all about the actual interactions.

This statistical science translated into the phenomenal technological power of the industrial revolution of that period. Much of our industry and the prodigious output of 20th century modernity was rooted in these powerful new statistical methods. Jacobs pointed out that the early ideas of Le Corbusier and others, and the later ideas of planners — often to the present day — rely upon this strategy of managing large statistical populations.

In this sense, the progression in science from two-variable problems to problems of statistical populations was mirrored in the progression from the neatly ordered elements of, say, Haussmann and his Parisian boulevards relating speed and location, or of Ebenezer Howard and his Garden City plans relating city and country, through to the more statistically informed plans of Le Corbusier, implemented around the world by the likes of Robert Moses and many others.

In either case the problem of cities was seen as one of devising reductive engineering schemes, seeking to isolate smoothly-functioning, easily related mechanical parts, in place of "messy" organic conditions. This more formal approach to cities was seen as advancement and modernization. But in the former case it was two-variable engineering, and in the latter case the problem of cities was also seen as one of statistical mechanics operating on large numbers. The newer science was added to the old.

Meanwhile, however, the biological sciences had moved beyond the statistical world of so-called "disorganized complexity" and had begun to understand the phenomenon that Jacobs called "organized complexity" — the area in the middle, between simple two-variable problems on the one hand, and large numbers of loosely variables on the other. Biologically speaking, that is where the phenomenon of life occurs — where a few crucial elements or variables have a crucial interrelated structure, forming a dynamic interaction. Jacobs referred to their structure as being "interrelated into an organic whole."

It turns out that the problems of the human environment are more like these problems of "organized complexity". As Jacobs wrote,

> ...While city planning has thus mired itself in deep misunderstandings about the very nature of the problem with which it is dealing, the life sciences... have been providing some of the concepts that city planning needs... And so a growing number of people have begun, gradually, to think of cities as problems in organized complexity — organisms that are replete with unexamined, but obviously intricately interconnected, and surely understandable, relationships...

She pointed out how the planning and architecture professions were at that time — 1961 — mired in the old sciences and their inappropriate models for cities:

> Today's plans show little if any perceptible progress in comparison with plans devised a generation ago. In transportation, either regional or local, nothing is offered which was not already offered and popular-

ized in 1938 in the General Motors diorama at the New York World's Fair, and before that by Le Corbusier. In some respects, there is outright retrogression. None of today's pallid imitations of Rockefeller Center is as good as the original, which was built a quarter of a century ago….

Then she summarized what she considered the lessons of organized complexity:

In the case of understanding cities, I think the most important habits of thought are these:
1. To think about processes;
2. To work inductively, reasoning from particulars to the general, rather than the reverse;
3. To seek for "unaverage" clues involving very small quantities, which reveal the way larger and more "average" quantities are operating.

She summed up the problem as follows:

As long as [we] cling to the unexamined assumptions that [we] are dealing with a problem in the physical sciences, city planning cannot possibly progress. Of course it stagnates. It lacks the first requisite for a body of practical and progressing thought: recognition of the kind of problem at issue. Lacking this, it has found the shortest distance to a dead end.

Since the book was written, the field of "complexity science" — a loose term for related developments in mathematics, network theory, biology, and other fields — has advanced a great deal, and deepened many of Jacobs' original insights. These advances have also deepened the respect that many people have for Jacobs, and in particular, the remarkable prescience of the last chapter of *Death and Life*.

Most people are now at least generally familiar with "systems theory," and with fractals, algorithms, strange attractors, network science, and the like. We now know a great deal more about these topics, and how they can help us to understand and manage a number of complex human processes. It may not be too much to say that scientific understanding is reaching a point of "consilience," as the biologist E.O. Wilson (father of "biophilia") has termed it.

In any case, Jacobs is now being considered seriously in a number of surprising places. One of them is the Santa Fe Institute for the Study of Complex Systems. Geoffrey West, past president, has said that in many ways, what they are doing today is "Jacobs with the math."

4. A "WEB WAY OF THINKING..."*

"Under the seeming disorder of the old city, wherever the old city is working successfully, is a marvelous order for maintaining the safety of the streets and the freedom of the city. It is a complex order."

— *Jane Jacobs,* The Death and Life of Great American Cities

The year 2011 — the 50th anniversary of Jacobs' *The Death and Life of Great American Cities* — saw a remarkable series of re-assessments and, in some cases, revisionisms. Planner Thomas Campanela criticized Jacobs' "evisceration" of planning, which created a vacuum into which privatizing interests rushed; economist Ed Glaeser argued that Jacobs fed gentrification with her call for preservation of some old buildings instead of all new towers; and sociologist Sharon Zukin attacked Jacobs' alleged fantasy of the "social-less" urban block. Planner Anthony Flint suggested that Jacobs was a libertarian with a mixed legacy of NIMBYism.

What I find remarkable about these accounts — speaking as an instructor who has regularly used her texts — is that in almost all cases these were things that Jacobs herself simply never said. She was clearly not against planning, but against failed planning; not against government, but against government badly organized; and not against new buildings, but against rushing monocultures of the new. She was for a deeper tactical understanding of how the "inherent regenerative force" of "self-diversification," as she termed it, can be put to work to provide more diversity of income and opportunity, as clearly has happened in cities throughout history.

She was not, let me assert, a blind theoretician or ideologue, but a good empiricist, using theory as a helpful tool along the way. This may be part of the problem. After all, the professions of planning and architecture, to which I myself belong, do not have a particularly good history when it comes to escaping ideological or ex cathedra thinking. We don't seem particularly good at learning from the evidence of our mistakes — even when they are explained to us in painfully lucid detail.

---

* *This essay is based in part on a previous essay that appeared in Planetizen in 2011. I am grateful to James Brasuell and the other Planetizen staff for the original invitation.*

Opposite: *The city of London, viewed as a spatial network through Space Syntax analysis. Photo courtesy Bill Hillier and Space Syntax.*

But I think there is a deeper explanation for the persistent mis-readings of Jacobs. She was the first to apply the dawning new human understanding of the natural world to cities — an understanding that even now is slow to be grasped by built environment professions. It's an understanding of "organized complexity," as she called it — the dynamic inter-relationships of systems, of processes, of self-organization. This was not a mysterious world, but a comprehensible one — it was just a different kind of world than we had been envisioning. A city, certainly, was a different kind of problem than we had thought. And therein she identified a huge obstacle to learning and progress, and one that is largely still with us.

Other fields of thinking and action have made great progress on these insights: ecology, biology and medicine, to name a few. There are astonishing things happening today in genetics, in network theory, and in mathematics and computer science. Even economics, a field that has historically been more dominated by ideology than most, is beginning to use more reliable evidence-based theories of how complex economic interactions actually work. Such models seem essential in learning to make more successful, more sustainable cities.

But all these fields are informed by what Jacobs called a new "web way of thinking" — employing not simple formulas or templates from above, but catalytic changes to a network of dynamic relationships.

Doctors do this kind of thing routinely when they give medicine to boost the immune system, or prescribe changes to diet — or indeed, when they recommend that a patient adopt a healthier lifestyle or environment. They are changing the dynamic mix of variables within a complex, interactive web, and to do it they are relying on a testable, refinable idea of how that will turn out.

So, too, Jacobs argued, a city is a diverse mix of people and processes, with its own self-organizing dynamic. We can exploit this dynamic by design, but this is a different idea of design, perhaps. Top-down interventions can certainly be part of this process (Jacobs mentions, for example, the use of public projects as "chess pieces" to trigger other changes) but we understand that we have to pay attention to multiple factors and multiple relationships. We have to use different tools for different conditions — "tactical" urbanism as it has been called. We have to figure out where — and how — to change the "operating system," the rules, processes and standards that constrain and corrupt our intended outcomes. We have to plan with self-organization, in a way that exploits its inherent capacity to solve our problems.

This approach may not have the compelling simplicity of big-thinking, "silver bullet" solutions; but history shows it can achieve stunning success over time, where the big plans often lead to slow unfolding disasters. History also shows this approach can be extraordinarily hard to implement by siloed professionals accustomed to specialized, linear formulas and templates. But that too is a dynamic problem, to be studied and remedied.

I think we must do so, as a matter of highest professional and civic urgency. What is at stake is simply whether we can actually learn from our mistakes — at a time we can ill afford to go on repeating them.

Let me offer up a list of what I for one believe to be Jane Jacobs' Top Ten most important — and most misunderstood — lessons for the urban professions:

1. The city needs to maintain a continuous walkable fabric that promotes "thoroughgoing city mobility and fluidity of use." This is a key to promoting diversity, and unlocking the capacity of cities as engines of mobility. This alone does not guarantee diversity, but it is a prerequisite for it. This means, among other things, that alternatives need to be found to disruptive uses, such as freeways, large parks and the various "campuses" that might interrupt this fabric.

2. The antithesis of this approach is to create isolated "projects" or project neighborhoods — large, disruptive superblocks of monocultures, featuring artfully designed, unchangeable buildings, surrounded by amorphous no-man's landscapes that she dismissively termed "project land oozings." A particularly destructive example is the Clarence Perry "Neighborhood Unit", a standardized planner model of inward-turning neighborhoods surrounded by fast car sewers. But other examples include large shopping centers surrounded by oceans of parking; large industrial users (also surrounded by parking); large hospitals; large university campuses; and other variations of the destructive "campus" model. Examples like Portland, Oregon (discussed in more detail in Chapter V.1) show that it IS possible to integrate these uses into a modern city.

3. The best way to fight gentrification is not to demolish old buildings and build high rises, but to go into other depressed areas and regenerate them. Jacobs did not say don't do new buildings, but she said to keep a diverse mix of old and new. What about

Manhattan, which is dangerously over-gentrified? Well, how about Brooklyn, The Bronx, Queens? How about other cities that could use some positive gentrification to expand life opportunities — Baltimore, Cleveland, Detroit, New Orleans, to name a few in the USA alone? There is far more suitable urban fabric in decline that can and should be repaired, before we resort to massive new waves of buildings of dubious value.

4. The city must not be treated as a work of art, or a sculpture gallery. This silver-bullet sensibility — encouraged by many architects and developers — has favored scraping away all existing context, in exchange for new, untested, and out of scale "projects." These projects are often supposed to be "sustainable", but they rely on almost no evidence of what has actually been sustained anywhere. (Indeed, they often explicitly reject it.) As Jacobs said in her characteristically pithy tone, "the method fails."

5. Zoning is not inherently bad, but should be liberal with regard to use, and prescriptive with regard to the way buildings address the street. (To a remarkable degree she pre-figured today's form-based coding).

6. Density is a valuable urban ingredient in context, but is not an end in itself. We must be wary of single variables and single-variable solutions (like "skyscraper cities"). What we value is not sheer aggregations of people massed together — or separated by "open space" — but the web of connections and ordinary encounters between people. This is what compact, walkable urbanism can give us, in a range of conditions, including big cities and smaller towns.

7. Cities are engines of knowledge synergy that create economic prosperity (through a knowledge-transfer phenomenon that economists now call "Jacobs Spillovers"). There is a physical web of relationships that starts at the pedestrian scale. "Sidewalk contacts are the small change from which a city's wealth of public life may grow," she said. Very hopefully, there also appears to be a corollary in the conservation of resources, that does not come only from reduced driving and from compact buildings, but in fact, comes from the "metabolic efficiency" of dense networks of connection within cities.

8. Urban diversity (in the mix of buildings, people and activities) does not by itself guarantee avoidance of economic stratification; but lack of diversity does guarantee more stratification. Again, we should not be looking for single-variable solutions, but for an interplay of relationships. In human affairs, that interplay is best facilitated through strategies of diversification.

9. "It's the economics, stupid." We need to recognize that economic systems are feedback mechanisms for the values we seek, and we must treat economics as such — recognizing that there is as much danger in "money floods" as in "money droughts." Our job is to select the right tool for the job, and make sure that things are working optimally. They do not do so by themselves, but only with an active citizenry and a lively culture.

10. The capacity to solve our problems rests mostly with the informal web of creative and regulatory relationships we have — our culture — and less so with specialized "experts." To rely too much on experts in silos is to reinforce their siloed condition, which threatens us all. Certainly, this does not mean that there is no role for experts, or for government. It does mean that this role must be more catalytic, more "bottom-up" — more with the grain of culture, than against it.

In the end, Jacobs' message was a hopeful one. We "broke" cities — we created the profound damage in our built environments, in the era of sprawl — and it is in our power to repair them. Jacobs shows (as history shows) that we do have the power to make walkable, thriving cities and towns, and to erase the disastrous course of suburban fragmentation we set ourselves on several generations ago. The "kind of problem a city is," is one that can, in fact, be dealt with successfully — if we understand it, and learn from the many lessons it presents.

5. TOWARD AN "AGE OF HUMAN CAPITAL"*

"In creating city success, we human beings have created marvels, but we left out feedback. What can we do with cities to make up for this omission?"

— *Jane Jacobs,* The Death and Life of Great American Cities

In 2016 we saw a welcome reassessment of Jane Jacobs' work, on the occasion of the 100th anniversary of her birth. Unlike previous re-assessments (e.g., on the 50th anniversary of *The Death and Life of Great American Cities*, as noted in the last chapter) this reassessment did not seem to have much of a revisionist momentum. Instead it seemed to take seriously the idea that there is still a lot more to unpack, and to take forward.

In part, this may be because the occasion of her birthday was an unseemly moment to join in the ill-informed revisionism that had previously painted her as a libertarian ideologue, or a quixotic warrior against inevitable "modern" progress, or a closet racist, or an elitist who happily encouraged gentrification— depictions that were all pernicious fantasies spun by the targets of her own past criticisms. (I commented on these issues earlier.)

Perhaps, though, the greater insight on offer this time reflects a genuine maturing of the discourse, recognizing some commonality in our understanding of the nature of our challenges today, and Jacobs' helpful role in clarifying them. In this consilience we can see strong parallels to the works of many others, including Christopher Alexander, whose work we will take up in the next section. One can also find (as I have noted elsewhere) parallels to Bruno Latour, René Thom, Alfred North Whitehead, Henry George, and a number of others.

To that list we should make the notable addition of Elinor Ostrom, whose work on commons-based economics (and culture) won her a Nobel Prize, among other accolades. Her model can best be described as a network of polycentric organizations whose business is managing a resource commons. There are strong parallels to

* This essay is drawn in part from a "virtual roundtable" that I participated in, hosted by The Nature of Cities group in 2016. I am grateful to David Maddox for the invitation.

Opposite: *A local market in Fresno, California designed and built by Christopher Alexander and his associates.*

Jacobs' "web way of thinking" and to Christopher Alexander's attack on modernist planning for creating "cities as trees", mathematically speaking. (I will discuss this idea in much more detail in the next section.) Following Alexander's work, we might summarize Ostrom's insights as "commons governance is not a tree".

Ostrom did express a debt to Jacobs' insights for her own work, and the philosophical connection between them is easy to see. Aside from the web-network approach to problem-solving, both acknowledged that economic productivity is not simply about the linear transformations of inert resources within a commons, but about how human beings interact within that physical and urban commons to create and manage the transformations, whose structure is quite complex, intricate and differentiated. Jacobs' less well known books on that economic topic are marvels of insight, building on the more directly urban insights of *Death and Life*.

Ostrom, too, pointed to the dangers of an overly rigid approach, a model of "governance as a tree," and its increasing institutional, economic, and ecological failures. Like Jacobs she articulated some of the failings of current economic theory as an underlying problem for other fields — cities for Jacobs, resource commons management for Ostrom. Both of them pointed to the need for a more web-like, "polycentric" approach to governance, not only top-down, and not only bottom-up, but also "side to side" as it were, and overlapping too. This is what I discussed earlier as the "web way of thinking", and acting. Each of us is a responsible steward of our environment, but none of us has sovereign power. On the contrary, we must share this power, and allow it to overlap at times. Occasionally it will conflict with others' power — and then we will have to sort things out, patiently and often repeatedly.

Here is an example from a city. On a given city street, a police officer may apply top-down govern*ment* by enforcing laws and citing offenders — say, a young person who is in the process of vandalizing property. But a shop owner might also be providing gover*nance* by chastising the same young person and reminding them that their parents might be informed of the misbehavior. Still other young people might bring peer pressure to bear, reminding their friend not to misbehave. The person in question might also have some reservations about the actions being considered, a form of self-governance.

All of these actions are overlapping forms of governance: formal and informal, top-down and bottom-up. At the same time, all of them are exercises of responsibility by the people involved — complementary, shared, aiming for the improvement of the condition of the parts of the city. It is the exercise of responsibility because it is literally the *ability to respond* — to take action as agents of the welfare of the city, at various subsidiary (and often overlapping) levels.

Jacobs argued that this kind of "polycentric governance" (Ostrom's term) goes on all the time in cities. It is at the heart of the way a street or a neighborhood functions, forming a tissue of governance as well as interaction. Of course this kind of overlapping process is not without conflict, and it can be messy — and often is. But it is an effective process that in part relies on the spontaneous self-organizing actions of the people involved, with the aim of solving local problems and adapting to local needs. While there is an important place for top-down formal actions, that is only the beginning of the story. (I also discussed this point in the last chapter.)

This kind of overlapping structure is visible within economic processes too, as both Ostrom and Jacobs observed. The influences on the price of a good might include (overlapping) national, state and local tax structures, local market demand, demand from export markets, the capacity of local suppliers, and of course, the competition from other suppliers. Some of these actions are purely local assessments of value by purchasers and consumers. Others are broader assessments by communities and political entities — tax policy, for example. Again, these factors form an overlapping network of valuations, from which emerges a "price" at a point of exchange, i.e. within a market.

To these factors we could add so-called "externalities," that is, costs or benefits (or other impacts on our assets) that aren't taken into account in the current price structure, but impact someone else at some other time. Negative externalities might include future maintenance costs, government servicing costs (police, fire, streets, infrastructure etc.), damage to ecosystems, the impacts of resource depletion, impacts of pollution and greenhouse gas emissions, and many other negative impacts.

The study of externalities and how they might be better reflected in transaction costs is an enormous subject, and a very important one. It is also an old subject, going back at least to the political economist Henry George in the 19th Century. George argued that resources like land should be held in common, and their use should be taxed according to the impact on the community (i.e. the externality cost). On the other hand, human creativity should be rewarded, implying a shift away from taxation on creativity and greater taxation of resources like land. The result, many "Georgists" argue, would be to penalize depletion and waste, and reward doing more with less.

One implication is in the phenomenon of sprawl, or low-density, car-dependent development. At present, sprawl development carries many unaccounted externality costs — ecological impacts, pollution, greenhouse gas emissions, and much else. Yet the current set of economic incentives and disincentives actually rewards this sprawling form of development, and in part this results from the fact that externality costs are not taxed.

A developer who tries to redevelop, say, an urban parking lot, facies an immediate disincentive in the increased property taxes on the value the developer creates — whether or not the project returns any profit. On the other hand, a developer who goes out to the suburban fringe where land is cheap faces a much lower tax burden, and hence a lower risk. The result is that the urban parking lot stays, and the new development occurs in the (artificially cheap) suburban site. The externality costs are not well represented.

For Jacobs, this was a matter of establishing accurate feedback within the system. As she said in *Death and Life*, we have "left out feedback" — and this was a crucial omission. The result was that we were too focused on dead-end approaches on systems that are incapable of renewal and revitalization — systems that destroy the basis of their own ability to endure. This was, in a word, unsustainable.

Before she died, Jacobs was known to be working on a book with the subject of "the coming age of human capital". By that she seemed to mean, an age in which we will replace the stripping of massive quantities of natural resources out of the Earth at unsustainable rates, with a no less prosperous time—indeed a *more* prosperous time, because it will focus on true prosperity: the ability to live a fulfilling life of creative richness, which is no longer coupled to an endless cycle of dead-end consumption. This was possible, she was convinced, because we now understood the processes required to bring it about.

The apparent optimistic tone of this work was in stark contrast to the gloomy outlook of what would stand as her last book, *Dark Age Ahead.* In that earlier volume (2004) she warned of the dire consequences of a technocracy run amok, and a slow collapse of the problem-solving capacities of critical human institutions. In their place would come ideologically driven retreats into simplistic approaches that were doomed to fail. This was a prophecy, but not a fatalistic one: Her point was that we do have a choice of the path ahead. But first we must understand it.

SECTION II:

CHRISTOPHER ALEXANDER ON WHY "A CITY IS NOT A TREE"

1. NOTES ON THE GENESIS OF WHOLES*

"In the last two decades, physicists and other scientists and philosophers of science have begun to discover that a wholeness-based view of the world is essential to proper understanding of the purely physical universe....The conception, experimental techniques, and even the way to modify our essentially Cartesian view, so that it can admit self, "I", and feeling — are extraordinarily difficult. Yet they are necessary for the progress of science. They are necessary, too, for the progress of architecture."

— *Christopher Alexander, "Some sober reflections on the nature of architecture in our time,"* Katarxis3.com

As I noted in the introduction, Jacobs and Alexander are complementary in a very useful way, namely, while their work has considerable overlap, each of them focuses more deeply on aspects of cities that the other does not. Each of them also takes up different parts of the professions that deal with cities, and finds them wanting.

If Jane Jacobs was always primarily concerned with the actions of planners and how well they succeeded or failed in making better cities, it could be said that Christopher Alexander was always primarily concerned with architecture and urban design, and how well those professional fields succeeded or failed in making successful environments from a broader human point of view. In the same way, Alexander was more directly focused on the formal structure of human environments — the "architecture" in a more general sense — and how these forms arise, at least in part, from human design. (Indeed, this concern with the details of environmental structure is captured in the name of Alexander's long-time research office, the Center for Environmental Structure.)

Certainly, both authors were concerned with the successes and (too common) failures of architecture and planning. As I noted in the introduction, Jacobs was no stranger to the concerns of architecture, having served previously as a staff writer at *Architectural Forum* before taking on *The Death and Life of Great American Cities*. But it was Alexander who, in *Notes on the Synthesis of Form* — his first book,

---

* *Portions of this essay first appeared in Urban Design International in 2007. I am indebted to then-editor Richard Hayward and the reviewers for its development and editing.*

Opposite: *Interior of one of the buildings at the Eishin School near Tokyo, by Christopher Alexander and associates.*

in 1964 — described how environmental architectures were often created through history, in what he termed an "unself-conscious process." He went on to describe how this form-creation had changed in the modern era, taking on more "self-conscious" but still rather inadequate aspects, with important and sometimes destructive implications for the design professions. (I will have more to say about this important set of observations later in this section.)

There were other notable differences in their backgrounds. While Jacobs was an independent journalist and polymath, Alexander was a Cambridge, England educated mathematician, physicist and architect, who went on to develop many of his seminal ideas in the Cambridge, Massachusetts of the late 1950s. That was an academic environment populated by the likes of the architectural pioneer Walter Gropius, and the cognitive psychology pioneer George A. Miller, both of whom Alexander knew at the time. For Alexander, cognitive psychology in particular offered crucial insights into how we perceive our environments and shape their forms, for better or worse.

Half a century after the beginning of his career, Alexander's dramatic and sometimes controversial contributions to the field had not abated. In 2003 he began publishing the first of his four-volume magnum opus, *The Nature of Order: An Essay on the Art of Building and the Nature of the Universe*. It too was concerned with the problem of form, or the particularly well-adapted variety of it that Alexander called "order". Central to his understanding of this kind of order was the phenomenon he called "wholeness" — a concept I will discuss in more detail in this chapter.

The grand title of this last major work, and equally grand and dense text, fueled a perception in some quarters that Alexander's career somewhere derailed from his earlier, rigorous scientific path, into an impenetrable world of mysticism, solipsism or worse.

But the truth is more interesting, and more promising. Alexander's career is in fact a straight line from the Cambridge (UK) physics student of the 1950s, dealing with precisely the same topic throughout: the relation of parts to wholes — the ancient topic of *mereology* in philosophy — and the search for useful new design tools to aid in their genesis and transformation. Along the way Alexander surprised even himself with the increasing philosophical complexity of his conclusions — but he never deviated from the scientific methods that brought him there.

Furthermore, his career has revealed as much about the modern history of planning and architecture, and the philosophical issues scarcely yet confronted, let alone resolved, as it does about one individual's remarkably diverse, idiosyncratic, but (as I will argue) coherent corpus.

Alexander, the first PhD student in architecture at Harvard, made a dramatic impact as an influential new thinker with his PhD dissertation (later became his first book, *Notes on the Synthesis of Form*). Its considerable influence extended far beyond the world of architecture and planning: it was said to be a required reading for researchers in computer science throughout the 1960s, and reportedly influenced major software innovations of the 1970s including object-oriented programming. It was no less an influential text for the generation of architectural theorists that included Lionel March and Horst Rittel.

Like the remarkable polymath Herbert Simon's classic paper of that era, "The Architecture of Complexity", *Notes* took up anew the age-old philosophical question of the relationship between parts and wholes (again, *mereology*) but in a specific modern form. Both Alexander and Simon wanted to know the precise mathematical structure of that relationship, and of its development and transformation over time. Alexander was interested more specifically in the designer's challenge. As he formulated it then: how does a designer synthesize a coherent and successful form out of the elements of a design program?

Like Simon, Alexander made the basic structural observation that parts tend to relate to wholes in hierarchies, roughly speaking. The phrase 'roughly speaking' turned out to be key: there are subtle but significant areas of overlap and redundancy, and in that fact there is something profoundly important. These overlaps may seem accidental or trivial, but they are not: they are essential attributes of what we would today recognize as network structures, and they occur in very particular ways. Alexander quickly recognized, perhaps even more than Simon, that these areas were somehow of fundamental importance.

That insight was the salient point of his widely cited 1965 paper on the failures of that era's new towns — and by extension, modern urban planning as a whole — "A City is Not A Tree". The tree he referred to was a mathematical kind of structure, a neat hierarchical system of nested sets and subsets.

> Whenever we have a tree structure, it means that within this structure no piece of any unit is ever connected to other units, except through the medium of that unit as a whole. The enormity of this restriction is difficult to grasp. It is a little as though the members of a family were not free to make friends outside the family, except when the family as a whole made a friendship.

He contrasted that structure with a semilattice, a more complex kind of structure with overlap, ambiguity and mutual interaction. This characteristic was a key aspect of the architecture of complexity.

The city is full of these overlapping and ambiguous systems, Alexander noted, and they are responsible for a great deal of its complexity and richness:

> It must be emphasized, lest the orderly mind shrink in horror from anything that is not clearly articulated and categorized in tree form, that the idea of overlap, ambiguity, multiplicity of aspect and the semilattice are not less orderly than the rigid tree, but more so. They represent a thicker, tougher, more subtle and more complex view of structure.

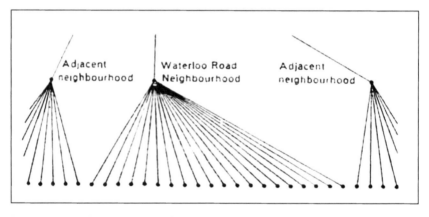

Figure II.1.1. A 'tree', or hierarchy, segregates its elements into neatly branching categories, or sets. Entirely self-contained neighborhoods might be examples of 'tree' structures within cities.

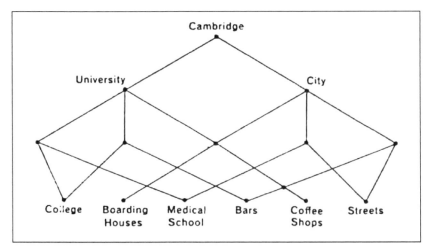

Figure II.1.2. A 'semilattice', or network, has overlapping sets. While it may seem messier, it is actually a more complex kind of structure, with more internal connectivity — and more like many natural structures, including cities. This example shows the overlapping uses between the city and the university in Cambridge, England.

And yet, as he showed, much of modern planning exhibited this tree-like structure. He argued that the rational mind inevitably defaults to these neater, more easily managed categories of thought.

> It is for this reason — because the mind's first function is to reduce the ambiguity and overlap in a confusing situation and because, to this end, it is endowed with a basic intolerance for ambiguity — that structures like the city, which do require overlapping sets within them, are nevertheless persistently conceived as trees.

But the result of this can be devastating:

> ...the city is not, cannot and must not be a tree. The city is a receptacle for life. If the receptacle severs the overlap of the strands of life within it, because it is a tree, it will be like a bowl full of razor blades on edge, ready to cut up whatever is entrusted to it. In such a receptacle life will be cut to pieces.

"A City is Not a Tree" quickly took on the status of a landmark critique, joining the ranks of Jacobs' *The Death and Life of Great American Cities* in shaping that era's seminal criticisms of modernist planning. With other critical texts of that era, it helped to put a brake on the rush of new towns and 'urban renewal', and set the stage for a more circumspect, asset-based approach to planning.

Yet 50 years later, we can ask whether the implications of this seminal work were ever fully realized. Today a new generation of planners and architects seems to have forgotten — or never learned — Alexander's elegant mathematical analysis. New towns following the old model are springing up around the world, notably in the developing world, and new infill projects are proposed for rapidly growing cities. There is a greater emphasis on mixed-use and interaction, but not much difference in the fundamental planning methodologies or results. As Jacobs noted in 1961, the urban professions have still not made the progress of other fields, particularly the biological sciences.

Alexander next asked, if the mind inevitably tries to force complex systems into neat hierarchies, then how can designers counteract this trend? Are there methods available to overcome this limitation?

Alexander noted several hopeful sources. One was in the structure of natural languages. An entire complex system, with all its overlap, can be represented by a word or phrase, which can be interlinked to other words through grammatical rules. While following basic hierarchical rules of structure, natural language nonetheless does permit tremendous ambiguity, overlap and interactivity. Poetry, for example, is an obvious example of language that is rich in overlap and density of interrelations.

Another inspiration came from computer science. Alexander had developed his original work in the synthesis of form using computer programs, and he made an intriguing observation. Amid the unwieldy thicket of data he was generating, he saw recurrent patterns of the same elements, or the same kind of solutions. If these patterns could be abstracted, they could perhaps be re-combined in usable ways, preserving the essential network structures of the patterns. Such a 'language' itself could, like a natural language, contain overlap and network connectivity.

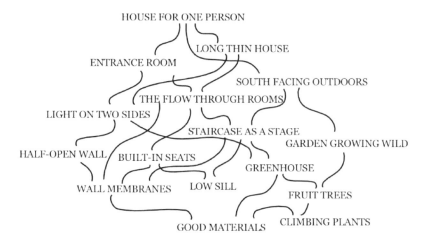

Figure II.1.3. The network structure of some of the patterns within the book A Pattern Language.

This was an enormous revelation for Alexander, and it opened his eyes to yet another revelation. He began to recognize that human beings had already been using something like a 'pattern language' in their traditional building cultures. The apparently humble structures of vernacular building were in fact extremely robust and capable of producing exceedingly complex results. Something like this pattern structure seemed to be deeply rooted in the nature of the interactions between humans and their environment. It might even be rooted in the very nature of things.

In a deeper sense, Alexander was once again wrestling with the topic of mereology, or how parts relate to wholes. Do the parts simply "add up" to the wholes? Clearly not. Are they related in some linear, sequential sense? On the contrary, they have an inter-connected web-like pattern, and this seems to be essential to their quality of wholeness. (It is also the secret to the robustness of language.)

Pattern languages were, in a real sense, a method of manipulating wholes and their parts, without disturbing the contextual structure, the "tissue" of wholeness in which they were embedded. Whereas other methods of design tended to ignore the contextual wholeness and "invent from zero," the method of pattern languages was to accept the context as an essential aspect of the problem, and to model its most salient parts.

Alexander developed this concept of a 'pattern language' through a series of tests, and found it worked sufficiently well to develop a major compendium of patterns. He began to envision a resource that any ordinary person could use to produce reasonably good vernacular buildings, in place of the unsatisfying standardized buildings that comprised the vast majority of the built environment.

Alexander and his colleagues compiled an initial set of 253 patterns, and, in 1977, published them in the book *A Pattern Language*. The book became an immediate and perennial bestseller, and a major influence on yet another generation of architects and planners. As I will discuss later in this section, there was much more to come.

...attern

Christopher
Sara Ishikawa, an
Max Jacobson, Ingri
Shlom

TOWNS · BUILDINGS

You can use this boo
...self with your fa
...with your nei
...nd neighbor
...office, or
...nd you c
...cess c
...er

69 PUBLIC OUTDOOR ROOM **

. . . the
GREEN (60
PEDESTRIAN
least some place
become possible.
one part of the comm
elaboration. Also, if no
pattern can act as a nucleus

* *

**There are very few spots along
towns and neighborhoods where pe
comfortably, for hours at a time.**

Men seek corner beer shops, where they spend
and drinking; teenagers, especially boys, choose spec
too, where they hang around, waiting for their friends. O
ple like a special spot to go to, where they can expect
others; small children need sand lots, mud, plants, and wate
play with in the open; young mothers who go to watc
children often use the children's play as an opportuni
and talk with other mothers.

Because of the diverse and casual nature of th
require a space which has a subtle balance of
yet not too defined, so that any activi
neighborhood at any given time ca
something to start from.

For example, it would b
unfinished, with the un
who live nearby, to
may need sand,
children—ADVE
seats, where
one may
into th

2. HORIZONS OF PATTERN LANGUAGES

"[A Pattern Language] could very well be the most read architectural treatise of all time, yet in the architecture schools I know, it is as if this book did not exist."

— *William Saunders, Editor,* Harvard Design Magazine

Many architects know the idea of pattern languages only through the book of 253 patterns by that name, written in 1977. A number of practitioners have written additional patterns (including this author) but they remain largely as supplements to the original primary collection. Aside from some recent work that originator Christopher Alexander himself has done, as yet there is nothing like a major new development of pattern languages in the field of architectural design. In spite of the book's perennial popularity, pattern language methods have had limited application in education and practice.

The state of affairs in architecture is in striking contrast to the software engineering world, where the same pattern language technology has had, it is fair to say, a ubiquitous and industry-wide impact. Even more telling may be the fact that most architects are ignorant of these developments.

I will argue here that this fact illuminates a major undeveloped opportunity for architects, and for others who are interested in related advances.

In a surprising disciplinary cross-fertilization, Alexander's Pattern Language technology has become the foundation for a major pattern-based movement which has spawned an enormous corpus of work, centered around so-called "design patterns" or "pattern languages of programming" — a highly influential class of object-oriented software programming methods. In turn design patterns were integral to the development of Wikis (one example of which is Wikipedia); simulation games like The Sims and Spore (and much other gaming technology); the Cocoa programming language on which iPhone apps are created; Agile software development; Extreme Programming; and others.

Indeed, in taking stock of the development of pattern languages, an astonishing fact emerges. The activity in the realm of soft-

Opposite: *Pages from the book* A Pattern Language.

ware dwarfs that of architecture — so much so that a recent Google search yielded about 250,000 hits on "pattern language," but almost 5,000,000 hits on "design patterns" (only one of the software fields). This twenty-to-one ratio is telling.

Nor is the growth in pattern language technology confined to software. Within computer science it can also be found in information management, human-computer interface, systems architecture and other related fields. Pattern language scholarly work can also be found in sociology, organization theory, economics, education, ecology, molecular biology and other fields. (This also means that the 250,000 Google hits cited above would be even smaller for architecture alone: it seems that more than half that number is accounted for by these other fields.)

Some of the most fascinating applications now being explored come from "hard" sciences like molecular biology. In one notable example, Newman and Bhat of New York Medical College proposed a "pattern language" model for the development and evolution of multi-cellular form, of the sort that occurred during the so-called "Cambrian Explosion" that gave rise to many modern animal forms. (Newman SA, Bhat R., "Dynamical patterning modules: a "pattern language" for development and evolution of multicellular form." *Int J Dev Biol.* 2009;53(5-6):693-705.)

What are the lessons for what must be, for architects, a humbling comparison?

First, there is the possibility that the real usefulness of pattern languages simply does not apply to the field of architecture. But it would seem rather unlikely that a technology developed in one field is of so little use there, but of such enormous use in other unintended disciplines. It seems more likely that something has blocked the development of pattern languages in architecture to the same degree.

Along those lines, another possibility may be that many architects have mistaken *A Pattern Language* as solely a finite set of architectural prescriptions, and failed to grasp the potential of its deeper structural logic in the way that computer scientists did. This aversion may be especially emotional among architects, because any such finite set of prescriptions, however generative in nature, is commonly assumed to place an unwarranted restriction on the designer's unfettered capacity to create novelty. Such a line of thinking can be found in some of the more acerbic criticisms of pattern languages in architecture, such as those by Alexander's Berkeley colleague Jean-Pierre Protzen, and Harvard Design magazine editor William Saunders.

Yet another possibility may be that architects — including Alexander himself, perhaps — have failed to adopt the collaborative, "open-source" methods of other disciplines. Whereas software designers immediately began sharing ideas about tinkering freely with pattern languages — even exchanging them between highly competitive companies such as Tektronix, IBM and others — architects have treated patterns as proprietary, and largely immutable. That is, either one applies the original 253 patterns, with perhaps a limited application of one or more additional patterns, or one abandons the technology altogether. But in no case does one "open the hood" and re-use the core system to develop all manner of new approaches, in the way that software designers have done with such evident zeal.

To understand the power of pattern languages — and their potential for a renewed application to the field of architecture and urban design — we must return to the core structure of patterns, and the problem it was originally meant to solve. As we saw in the last chapter, it has its roots in Alexander's first major work, *Notes on the Synthesis of Form* (1964). As he explained in the introduction to the tenth-year edition to *Notes*:

> The idea of a diagram, or pattern, is very simple. It is an abstract pattern of physical relationships which resolve a small system of interacting and conflicting forces, and is independent of all other forces, and of all other possible diagrams. The idea that it is possible to create such abstract relationships one at a time, and to create designs which are whole by fusing these relationships--this amazingly simple idea is, for me, the most important discovery of the book.

So the structure of a pattern was very simple, and yet the results of this kind of fusing of relationships could be, no less than traditional built environments often were, highly complex. This theme of simplicity-generating-complexity is echoed in much of complexity science, where simple processes can generate, through adaptive iteration, the unfathomably complex (and often irreducible) structures of the natural world. (This is seen, for example, in the highly complex patterns of fractals as they are generated by computers, and in natural formations like clouds, sand dunes, etc.)

There is a corollary with languages, which have a limited set of words, and yet produce a vast set of complex meanings. The relationships between words are not mere linear ones (as, for example, in a mere list) but rather, they form a mesh-work of complex interrelationships (as, for example, in poetry). Again, while there are nested hierarchical relationships, there are also overlaps, cross-linkages, and ambiguities.

Patterns are not needed for every structure in the built environment, or within any other design problem. In fact, their number could quickly become vast. Patterns are only needed for the most prominent configurations of needs, or what Alexander calls "forces." The pattern represents a workable resolution of the forces, as they tend to group together into strong clusters. Different patterns are only weakly related to each other, and therefore they can be combined and recombined with other patterns in a useful way.

A simple example will help to illustrate the logic. (Indeed, this example is so simple that it would not need to be articulated, and so is not included in any known pattern language.) Consider the pattern "Door". In its most common form or pattern, a door typically has hinges on one side, and a knob with a latch on the other.

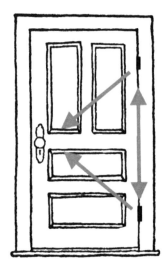

Figure II.2.1. A simple pattern "door" might consist of the pattern of relations of the two hinges and the knob and latch, and how they are required to be arranged as a set of "strong forces."

These elements are related to each other in what Alexander would call "strong forces." That means that the hinges and the knob have to be structured in a particular way, with the hinges on one side, and the knob and latch on the other. That constitutes the "pattern" of the door. We can readily see that changing this configuration would be problematic!

The pattern "Door" can also be related to sub-patterns, such as "Hinge", "Knob", "Latch" and so on. Each of these can be further related to sub-patterns, "Screws", "Pin" etc. But they are not strictly related, and we can make various flexible substitutions. It is in this sense that Alexander refers to "weak forces".

Going up the scale, we can also see that the pattern "Door" might be related to the pattern "Room" and the pattern "House" and so on. These too are "weak forces" — we might have two or three or more "Doors" within one "Room," and one "Door" might connect to two "Rooms." These are the overlapping network-like relationships between the environmental spaces of a city or a building, and between the patterns of its design.

So a pattern is just this — the cluster of "strong forces," within a larger network of weaker forces. The clusters themselves form the patterns, and then these patterns can be combined and organized within larger collections, but keeping the essential connections of forces that resolve the problems.

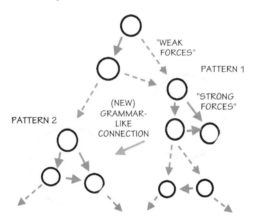

Figure II.2.2. The "patterns" are the clusters of "strong forces" that are embedded in a larger network of "weak forces" — just as, say, a "door" can be weakly related to another door in the room, but its hinges and knob are strongly related to each other.

For those who don't already know the book *A Pattern Language*, I recommend that you peruse the book if you can, and this structure will become much more self-evident. In the meantime, for our purposes, I attach here photos of one of the patterns from the book, showing how it works in an urban context.

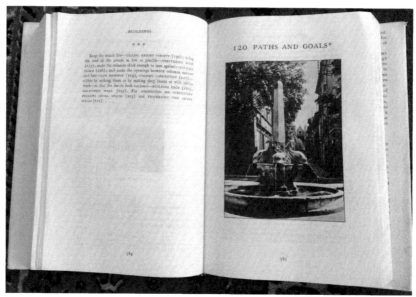

Figure II.2.3a. The pattern "Paths and Goals" begins with its title, and an iconic photo to set the context.

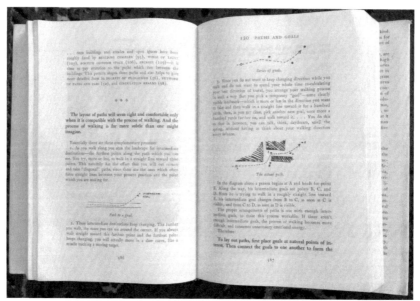

Figure II.2.3b. Next the pattern lays out the context of "upward patterns" with titles that serve as "hyperlinks" (although not literally so, of course, since the book has only appeared in print, and was made before computer hyperlinks were in common use). It then defines the problem, followed by a section that explores the structural nature of the problem as a system of elements. This section can include references to other works, analytical sketches, or other materials.

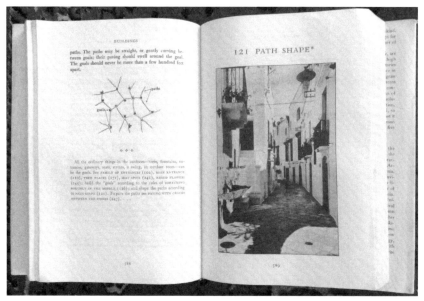

Figure II.2.3c. Finally, the pattern states a conclusion with the essential elements of the resolution of the "forces" as a structural configuration. Below the conclusion is another section of "hyperlinks," this time to "lower" patterns, i.e. those at smaller scales, or that occur as sub-problems to the pattern.

The structure of a pattern, then, is a straightforward one:

- Pattern title
- Iconic image: conveys the nature of the configuration, adding a qualitative dimension to the quantitative analysis
- Upward hyperlinks: connect the pattern to "upper" patterns that may contain it and others
- Problem-statement: gives the configuration of the problem
- Discussion: assesses of the associated issues to be treated
- Solution-statement: gives the configuration of the solution, together with any procedures to be followed
- Diagram: a cartoon of the solution, with simple notes
- Downward hyperlinks: connect the pattern to "lower" patterns that it may contain

The upward and downward hyperlinks establish any given pattern within a nested hierarchical structure. But crucially, once again, this structure is not rigidly hierarchical, but also allows overlap.

As the patterns are combined into a system, these overlapping relationships create the "thicker, tougher, more subtle and more complex" kind of structure that Alexander observed in natural cities.

Alexander's critique of conventional practice — and its implications

As I discussed in the last chapter, Alexander's innovations were aimed, from the beginning of his career, at the chief failing that he saw in conventional practice: the inability to create successful adaptations to the natural overlapping complexity of actual design problems. Yet as he argued in "A City is Not A Tree," this is a perennial problem in modern planning, whose designs do exhibit a damaging tree-like structure. This was because, he argued, the rational mind inevitably defaults to these neater, more easily managed categories of thought. In this sense, pattern language technology was aimed very directly toward plugging a very real gap in modern design — one that amounted to a major technological shortcoming of modern methods.

It is not so surprising, then, that since Alexander was dealing with design as a broad topic, and not merely with architectural design, his solution did indeed have great relevance for other fields of design too, notably software design. These designers, too, needed to translate a very serial, hierarchical kind of process into a more usefully networked one. As software pioneer and Wiki inventor Ward Cunningham has documented, he and his colleague Kent Beck quickly realized that Alexander was onto something that they needed. It required extensive adaptation and customized structuring for their needs, but the gist of it was very much what their challenge required.

In software as in architecture, the goal was to preserve the context, the aspect of wholeness or "gestalt" in which the problem is embedded, the better to resolve the real problem and not create new problems along the way. (This is a common "unintended consequence" of many design activities: just when one problem is solved, another one pops up.)

The book *A Pattern Language* was the first major demonstration of pattern languages in architecture, and it was an enormous bestseller. (As William Saunders noted, it "could very well be the most read architectural treatise of all time.") The book certainly had a great appeal, and clearly evoked a broader feeling of what the human environment can give to us.

More poignantly, it had the ability to evoke *qualitative* aspects of the built environment, at precisely the same time that it spelled out *quantitative* aspects. Make the balcony at least *this many* feet deep. Make the public space *this* wide. And so on.

This was a remarkable feat: it united the quantitative and the qualitative, within a manageable network of design actions and structural relationships.

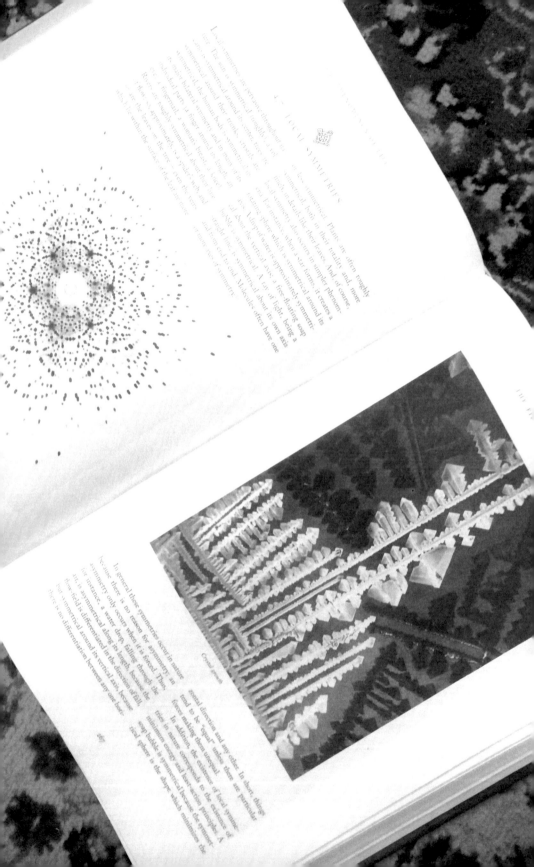

Local symmetries are pervasive throughout our lives. We are symmetrical, roughly; the symmetry of our trunks and our limbs is symmetrical about an axis... Plants are often roughly symmetrical both in their totality and, more obviously, in their leaves. And of course, left-right symmetry dominates the living world...

In general these symmetries occur in nature because there is no reason for asymmetry — symmetry only occurs when it is forced. For instance, a water drop falling through the air is symmetrical along its length because the flow field is differentiated in the vertical axis, but is symmetrical around its vertical axis, so there is no differentiation between any one face...

Crystals grown

3. LEARNING FROM "THE NATURE OF ORDER"

"In the past century, architecture has always been a minor science — if it has been a science at all. Present day architects who want to be scientific, try to incorporate the ideas of physics, psychology, anthropology in their work, in the hope of keeping in tune with the "scientific" times. I believe we are on the threshold of a new era, when this relation between architecture and the physical sciences may be reversed — when the proper understanding of the deep questions of space, as they are embodied in architecture, will play a revolutionary role in the way we see the world and will do for the world view of the 21st and 22nd centuries, what physics did for the 19th and 20th..."

— Christopher Alexander, "The interaction of science and architecture,"
www.katarxis3.com

For Christopher Alexander and his colleagues, the popularity of *A Pattern Language* was certainly remarkable, and gratifying — and in particular its evident success with non-architects seeking to design and build for themselves. (Its perennial bestseller status suggests it is still a major influence among this group.) But Alexander and his colleagues were disturbed to find that many of the designers inspired by the book produced crude work that lacked the simple dignity of older vernacular buildings. Clearly they had not succeeded in replacing the robust traditional pattern languages of vernacular building with an equivalent new technology. What was missing from the methodology?

Alexander came to believe that he had not sufficiently dealt with the detailed problem of geometrical form. Returning to the problem of the relation of parts to wholes, he asked, what is it about the particular geometries of the built environment that we find most satisfying — not just on the basis of one narrow problem-solving criterion or another, but more broadly, on the level of a whole system? What characteristics do they have, and what detailed processes actually created them, in nature, and in traditional societies? What can we learn from them to improve our own methods and results?

Opposite: Pages from Christopher Alexander's book The Nature of Order, showing an x-ray scattering pattern from a beryllium atom, and a pattern of self-organizing crystal formation. Alexander wanted to find out what we can learn from natural processes and their resulting geometric structures.

Answering this question, and documenting the ideas for his readers, was the task that would occupy him for the next 25 years, culminating in his magnum opus *The Nature of Order*, subtitled "An Essay on the Art of Building and the Nature of the Universe."

Taking his cue from nature, Alexander studied the processes of morphogenesis in biology and other natural phenomena, and the characteristic geometries that resulted. Working phenomenologically rather than reductively, he grouped them into a series of categories, eventually distilling them down to 15 "properties". They range from familiar ones like "boundaries" and "alternating repetition" to more esoteric-sounding ones like "not-separateness". Even so, as always, the structural logic of even the esoteric-sounding ones is rigorous.

In addition to these geometric properties, Alexander also looked at the processes that shape them. He made an intriguing observation: each of the 15 properties has a corresponding kind of step-wise transformation that gives rise to it — and this goes for human acts of creation as well. These transformations do not create structure from scratch, but instead preserve some aspect of the previously existing structure. Hence Alexander referred to these as "structure-preserving transformations."

The compounding of results through such a sequence of stepwise transformations turns out to have some surprising characteristics, as mathematicians like Stephen Wolfram have shown. What seems to be a straightforward linear process of steps turns out to produce, through the multiplication of pattern, astonishing complexity. One can think of the surprising results of just a few artful Origami folds, or the way two cooking ingredients can mix initially very crudely, but in just a few steps of kneading, can take on new properties. Compounding of the interrelationships creates some surprisingly transformative results.

This was a crucial finding. Our contemporary methods of technology have relied upon much more atomic processes of standardization, replication and combination. In architecture, they had their analogue in the technical act of "composition" — the assembly of parts to form pleasing wholes. This has been a powerful and productive strategy for humans in the modern era. But it is generally not the way that nature works to produce its bounty of successful, sustainable, beautiful structures. Rather, natural systems rely at least as much upon such stepwise processes of differentiation, transformation and articulation.

In natural processes, the whole characteristics of the system do not arise anew from the mere aggregation of parts. Rather, there is a wholeness at some level that is always present, at every step. It is merely transforming as the steps go forward, and the structure unfolds, often into a more elaborate configuration.

In Book One of *The Nature of Order*, Alexander refers to a famous series of photographs of a milk drop by the photographer-scientist Harold Edgerton. One can readily see that this very ordinary, simple process results in a remarkably elaborate structure with a deep interrelation of all the parts — a deep wholeness of the structure. Moreover, this is not occurring through only one logical step, but it is occurring continuously through a complex set of sequential transformations in time.

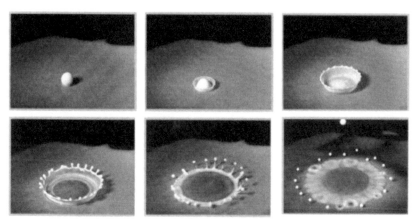

Figure II.3.1. A series of Harold Edgerton's famous milk drop photographs.

Note that it is never true that at any stage the parts "went together" in any conventional sense. The parts did not "make" the whole. Rather, the parts were differentiated out of the process, and changed their structure and their relationship to one another, as the whole went through each transformation. In fact, it would be more accurate to say that the whole made the part! There was always a whole structure, at every step: the milk drop, and then the splattering form, then the deformed ring, then the articulated bumps, then the little arm-like appendages, then the emerging smaller spheres, then the cell-like regions at the bottom, and so on.

It now seems apparent that the process of morphogenesis in nature works very much like this, with structures responding to natural physical forces of this kind — articulating, extruding, mirroring, and carrying out similar "structure-preserving transformations." Nor are such processes strictly confined to biological systems: indeed, it appears that many other natural phenomena undergo similar processes.

A second, closely related point is that at any point, each region or center is in some way closely fitted to all the others, and to the whole. They are always in some sense part of a deeper order, and the act of creation is not to bring together an aggregation of atomic parts, but to orchestrate a transformation of parts that already existed within a whole. (For this reason, Alexander later referred to "structure-preserving transformations" as "wholeness-extending transformations.")

Put differently, a local action can contribute most to the global structure when its already existing, embedded relationship to that global structure is acknowledged and strengthened.

For Alexander, it followed that it is impossible to talk about the structure of a built environment and its effect upon the human user, without facing squarely the human users themselves, and the qualitative nature of their experience as an *a priori* condition that must be accommodated. One could pretend that qualitative experience didn't matter, and only quantitative analyses and "facts" mattered. But it was increasingly clear that this omission was precisely the source of much of the current grief, and the reason that progress had begun to grind to a halt. In fields that had taken this "positivist" approach. Meanwhile, progress continued in fields like neuroscience, artificial intelligence and other subjects of complexity, precisely because these fields had recognized the necessity of facing the phenomenon of subjectivity, and the subjective experience of value.

As Alexander noted, value is the unwelcome guest at the party, simply because it is so hard to define in quantitative terms. It is the ultimate holistic, emergent phenomenon. And yet, Alexander noted, value *is* a sharable phenomenon, and a discussable one. There are straightforward scientific methodologies that can indeed reliably find large areas of shared value. Moreover, these shared areas turn out to have a surprisingly definable relation to structure itself.

When it comes to living organisms, and apparently, when it comes to the built environment, value is rooted in the structure of things.

For some design theorists and critics, this was treacherous, alarming stuff — the makings of totalitarian design, or an enforced blandness of "average tastes". But for Alexander, there was no alternative but to face it squarely. While some things are variable, not everything about value is entirely relative or "subjective". Indeed, there seems to be something more like a continuum, from the personal to the universal. Our job as scientists is to tease this apart carefully, using rigorous scientific methods.

In this respect, Alexander saw no problem whatever applying the rigor of science to subjective and qualitative phenomena. Indeed, he saw them as necessary allies in confronting the current challenge of the built environment.

A biological perspective may help to put a more comprehensible perspective on the situation. Clearly there are matters of individual taste and preference in the built environment, but equally clearly, matters of shared valuation. (To illustrate the point with one extreme example, car exhaust is likely to be universally regarded as an undesirable feature of built environments, whereas, say, fresh air is generally regarded as desirable.)

There are structures within the built environment that affect human health and well-being, and for Alexander, it is the business of built environment professionals, not unlike doctors, to diagnose and prescribe more healthful and more desirable conditions. There is certainly art to it; but there is equally science, to be applied to the professional care of the well-being of others.

While some architects see Alexander's work as idiosyncratic, many in other fields see familiar insights and ready opportunities for collaborative development. As noted, there are strong correspondences with the insights of much complexity science, notably in the understanding of complex generative processes, adaptive algorithms, cellular automata and the like. There are resonances with biology, and the processes of morphogenesis. There are resonances with studies of wholeness in other disciplines, as for example in quantum physics. There are echoes of the insights of neuroscience and the study of artificial life, in the study of qualitative phenomena and the surprising relation of living systems to non-living ones.

As Wiki inventor Ward Cunningham has noted, many of the problems Alexander has explored are indeed inter-disciplinary in nature. Hence the interest of him and other computer scientists in this work. For example, the topic of generativity is a very important one in computer programming, and Alexander has explored it very directly, and in a way that Cunningham and others have clearly found useful.

Yet these inter-disciplinary topics have not been much explored by very many architects, except perhaps as devices to generate expressive ideas. This may be, again, because the emphasis in architectural design is on the abstract expressive qualities of the work, as opposed to its adaptive problem-solving power.

Alexander's work also shares strong correspondences with other reformers in the planning and urban design fields. For example, we already noted Jane Jacobs' extensive writings on the topic of "organized complexity" and the importance of its insights for the design of cities. She also spoke of the generative capacity of cities, and the responsibility of designers to facilitate this capacity. She warned about the practice of sweeping away context and composing from scratch, and she also argued that the best cities continuously generated their qualities of life from their existing ingredients, however humble.

More recently, members of the New Urbanism movement (which we will discuss in more detail later) have campaigned for greater mixed use and diversity in development, and more use of existing contextual patterns. A number of prominent academics and practitioners within the New Urbanism tradition have also explored Alexander's ideas.

All of these collaborators have shown a willingness to work in an "open-source" format with Alexander and other colleagues, and to find new insights that will benefit architecture as well as other fields. At the same time, many of those from other disciplines have also expressed some bemused perplexity at the apparent isolation of many architects, and at Alexander's "prophet without honor" status in his own ranks.

Still, *The Nature of Order* was a treatise, not a manual of applied technology in the style of *A Pattern Language*. While it gave a number of methods for design using its insights, it left a number of topics for further development, which I will consider in more detail in the next two chapters. Among these we could include:

1. Generative codes. How does one operationalize "structure-preserving transformations?" What are the steps that one can take to incorporate qualitative and diagnostic procedures within a stepwise methodology of this kind?

2. Collaborative development. What can we learn from the success of those in the software community for greater progress? How can we incorporate more "open- source" methods into the work ahead? Given that Alexander has been at work for over a half-century, how will this work be taken forward?

3. The remaining opportunities with pattern languages. As we have seen, the software community has also achieved much more success with pattern languages as a robust technology. What can we learn from them? What can we learn from Alexander's own later work, which was meant to address the perceived weaknesses of pattern languages? What opportunities remain to return to pattern languages, and infuse them with useful new capabilities in architecture?

4. **"Massive process difficulties."** Alexander notes that there are major constraints on the kinds of processes he describes, built into the current institutional system of design and building, and into the current flow of money and debt. As he notes, this problem needs much more work, as I will discuss further in the last chapter of this section.

   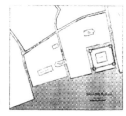

About 560 A.D.   *Latent centers*   *New building position*   *Hospice first phase c.700*

About 700 A.D.   *Latent centers*   *New building position*   *First basilica built 832*

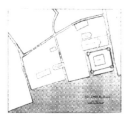   

About 832 A.D.   *Latent centers*   *New building position*   *The Campanile built 976*

 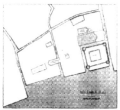  

About 976 A.D.   *Latent centers*   *New building position*   *Cruciform St. Mark's, 1071*

  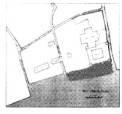 

About 1071 A.D.   *Latent centers*   *New building position*   *Piazza extended c. 1100*

Each row represents one four-step cycle in the process: 1 context, 2 latent centers, 3 possible action, 4 new construction.

4. THE UNTAPPED POWER OF "ADAPTIVE MORPHOGENESIS" IN MODERN DESIGN[*]

"In a structure which is differentiated, the structure will not, in general, be made by small piecemeal acts happening in random order. Rather, each step creates the context for the next step in the whole, and allows the process as a whole to lay down, next, what has to be laid down next in order for an orderly unfolding to occur."

— *Christopher Alexander,* The Nature of Order

Underlying his specific interest in architecture, throughout his career Christopher Alexander was always searching for a more intelligent kind of *technology* — more adaptive, more integrative of the wisdom gained over centuries, more enduring and sustainable. For him, technology was nothing other than the original Greek idea of *techne + logos*, knowledge of making. At heart, what are we making, from a human point of view, and how do we ourselves know and understand its impacts? What are the "rules of the game," so to speak, and how do we change those rules to create a more intelligent and wiser human future?

Like Jacobs, Alexander found reasons to be hopeful about the answers, particularly those beginning to emerge from the "new sciences" of complexity. It seems many of the answers are indeed to be found in nature, including human nature. Some surprisingly modern lessons are also to be found in the rich "collective intelligence" of human history and its traditional knowledge — a point we will come back to.

Hence Alexander believed his work had to deal more directly with the problem of process. What is the process by which a pattern

* *This chapter is drawn from several sources, including a talk given at the launch of the India chapter of INTBAU, the International Network for Traditional Building, Architecture and Urbanism, generously sponsored by the Nabha Foundation. A version of the talk later appeared in the conference proceedings, New Architecture and Urbanism: Development of Indian Traditions, edited by Deependra Prashad. I am grateful to Deependra and the Nabha Foundation. Other portions are drawn from my own drafts of papers I combined with Nikos Salingaros in a series of posts that ran at the Metropolis POV website. I am grateful to Susan Szenasy and Nilos Salingaros for the development of these ideas.*

Opposite: *A drawing by Christopher Alexander showing the transformation of Venice over about four centuries.*

language is actually used effectively to create form? What are the steps one must go through? Whereas pattern languages were about the structure of things, offering a kind of library of combinable fragments of that structure, perhaps his newer work must be about the process of creating that structure. The library this time might be of recombinable fragments of steps, rather like the steps in a recipe, that tell you how to get from one stage of form to the next.

Alexander's insight came again from the observation of traditional cultures and their remarkable adaptive sophistication and success, as it so often did throughout his career. He observed that building traditions guided individuals in specific steps of building, and in how those steps should respond to their context. Often very sophisticated ancient codes functioned to do this. Often more direct linguistic concepts and "rules of thumb" guided individuals and groups, and the guidance was refined and handed down in tradition.

But in the technology of the last several centuries, this delicate contextual structure was swept away, replaced by a more powerful but at the same time cruder, much less contextual system. This system was more dependent on abstractions, and more likely to ignore or even to destroy the contextual structure — often with powerful results, but also often with disastrous unintended consequences.

As we saw in the last chapter, Alexander took his odyssey beyond human traditions, to ask basic questions about the processes of growth in nature. He made a simple, even obvious observation: nature regularly and almost effortlessly, it seems, creates a vast range of successful living forms, from astonishingly simple ingredients. These structures are exquisitely well-adapted, beautiful, sustainable. What are the processes it uses to do this? And what can we learn from those processes for our own human applications?

To answer that question, he drew on insights from many fields, including embryology, physics and others. He came to one central conclusion: nature does not use a "plan" or "blueprint" of some final end result. Rather, as we saw in the last chapter, nature acts to transform an existing whole into a new whole, and it does this repeatedly, over many cycles of evolution.

In doing so, it preserves the structure of the earlier whole, but it often amplifies, articulates and deepens it in some important way. We can see that process of transformation very clearly in the biological patterns of evolution. Alexander noted, intriguingly, that we can also see it in our own built history — in the structure-preserving trans-formations of the Piazza San Marco in Venice over 1,000 years, for example, where at every step, the whole was maintained. At no point was the piazza entirely bulldozed and rebuilt according to some ar-chitect's bold new vision. It was rather a continuous evolution, with human plans playing a disciplined role within what could be seen as a kind of "dance of the centuries."

But the steps of such a "dance" can appear deceptively simple and humble — much as a mere 26 letters cluster into words, sen-tences and soliloquies can create the complex beauty of Shakespeare. When presented with the 26 letters alone we might wonder how we could possibly create something so rich from such modest parts; but that is just what Shakespeare did.

So, too, in the process of creating form, as we see all over in na-ture, the steps can seem exceedingly simple and modest. But the key is in how they combine, how they multiply in repetition — much like the way two colors of putty will mix surprisingly quickly after just a few repeated folds, or the way a marvelous animal shape can result from just a few relatively simple steps of folding paper in Origami. There is an exponentially multiplying interaction between the parts, which manifests over repeated steps.

It turns out that this is very much how forms develop in embryol-ogy, through a very similar kind of "unfolding" process. This occurs not only in the DNA and RNA molecules, but also in the protein struc-tures that they then form, that subsequently bend, fold and interact, and form various products, including tissues. These tissues then di-vide, fold, differentiate and articulate into new structures. In addi-tion to the simple parts — just four molecules in the genetic code — all of this rich complexity comes from relatively simple steps too: combine, divide, fold, merge, and so on.

This "complexity out of simplicity" is a key to understanding the processes that create richly articulated, differentiated, living struc-ture. It is at the heart of what biologists call "adaptive morphogen-esis" — underlying the creation of thriving, stable ecosystems.

This was a major revelation for Alexander. It was not lost on him that age-old human processes share some aspects of this structure. He observed the way traditional craftspeople took relatively simple steps to gradually weave stunningly beautiful patterns in carpets, or the way traditional city-builders took small steps to position their houses and the spaces around them, gradually building up a marvelous urban structure with exquisite traits.

Our "modern" methods, he noted, are based on a very different, radical approach: creating templates and "blueprints" and "expressions" ahead of time, which can be thought of as little fully-developed models of reality. They produce powerful economies of scale because they allow for standardized repetition. But they also tend to impose rigid artificial aspects on the reality, instead of adapting to it to the very fine degree that nature requires.

Nature too uses templates, on occasion, or something like them. One might think of DNA as a kind of blueprint. But nature is much more subtle than current human technology: there is no little model of a finger encapsulated in the DNA molecule. Nature actually uses a strategy that is at once far simpler than that, and far more complex and sophisticated in its output. For every finger produced is a marvel of uniqueness, sophistication and complexity. The human version of a template methodology, though it has been enormously effective in conventional technology, is a far cruder and less elegant device. The implications of that are significant.

Perhaps an even more sophisticated, more "modern" approach, would re-integrate these other powerful processes into human methods — including the powerful if often unconscious processes of human tradition. Perhaps nothing less would be required to create the kind of well-adapted, sustainable, balanced structure that nature had done, and that was beginning to look like an essential requirement for a prosperous human future.

Alexander came to see that even his pattern language was guilty of the "template" limitation. If people used the language to come up with a design, planned in advance, without a careful generative process for adapting the form, then the form simply wouldn't have that living quality that is needed, and that was achieved by previous generations across so many cultures. The reform of our unsustainable modern processes of morphogenesis was still incomplete.

Alexander asked himself, what were the methods that people could use to apply these kinds of processes to acts of building (and other form-making) in a modern age? What insights would they be built upon, and how would they function?

Here I will outline several of the key concepts of this work.

Centers

One needs a useful diagrammatic model of the structure of things that is undergoing a pattern of growth — an analytic understanding of the essence of what is going on geometrically. For Alexander, that model is a system of centers. Every form can be understood as a system of centers in some relation to one another — one inside another, one forming part of a boundary around another, and so on.

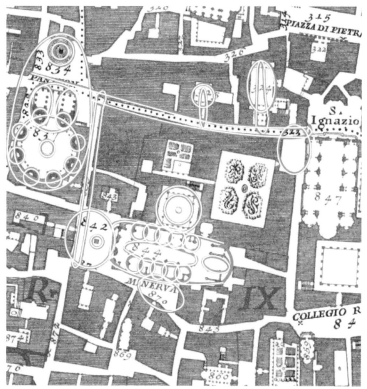

Figure II.4.1: The Nolli Plan of Rome, which can be analyzed as a series of nested (hierarchical) and overlapping (networked) centers.

A system of centers can have a hierarchical relationship, a networked or semi-lattice relationship, or some combination. It can have all of the kinds of relationship that Alexander and other theorists described, in critiquing the limitations of modern design methods.

Thus the model offers a powerful way of understanding the structure of form, and the transformations it undergoes

— and also its limitations. There are echoes of the "process" philosopher Alfred North Whitehead's "actual entities", and echoes too with theoretical physics. There is also an echo in the work of Herbert Simon and "The Architecture of Complexity". But there are also unique insights that have gone on to prove themselves useful foundations for the rest of the work.

Fifteen Properties

Alexander then made an interesting observation: in spite of the endless variety of configurations in which centers can be found in nature, he found that one can distil them down to just 15 different classes of organization, or geometric properties. Every form of structure that he was able to observe could be grouped into one of these classes. This scheme of classes turns out to be very useful in analysis and, Alexander believes, in aiding as a design tool. I will outline the 15 classes here briefly.

15 Properties of Natural Morphology

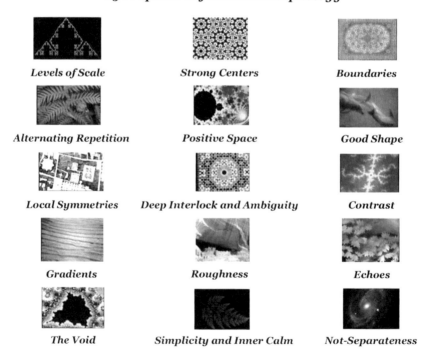

Figure II.4.2: The 15 Properties of Natural Morphology in which centers may be structured.

1. LEVELS OF SCALE: Structures of centers occur in similar configurations at different scales, often spanning a vast range of scales. This is similar to the concept of fractal structure.

2. STRONG CENTERS: Certain centers will have greater prominence than others, and may attract sub-structures around them.

3. BOUNDARIES. Centers may form linked structures that wrap around other centers, forming a boundary.

4. ALTERNATING REPETITION. Centers may form alternating pairs that are then repeated in chain-like structures around other structures.

5. POSITIVE SPACE. Where structures of centers wrap around and enclose space, that space also forms an efficient structure of centers, without crowded, wasted or asymmetrical regions.

6. GOOD SHAPE. This is in effect the inverse of the above: where structures of centers form larger clusters of centers, these larger structures are also efficient, without crowded, wasted or otherwise disordered areas.

7. LOCAL SYMMETRIES. While the configuration of centers at larger scales can be highly asymmetrical, local areas often tend to form highly symmetrical clusters. The Nolli Plan of Rome (see Figure II.4.1, above) is a particularly clear example of this.

8. DEEP INTERLOCK AND AMBIGUITY. Adjacent regions may interlock in a mutually dependent way, to the point that there is ambiguity of one form in relation to another. An obvious example is the optical illusion of a vase-face shape, in which each shape has its own coherent relation to some external structure, or can be seen ambiguously as the profile of a radically different form.

9. CONTRAST. Adjacent regions may be abruptly discontinuous.

10. GRADIENTS. Adjacent regions may exhibit a gradation between them.

11. ROUGHNESS. A region may have a complex structure at finer scales that appears chaotic or "rough": it is in fact a form of transformed structure at finer scales.

12. ECHOES. A region may exhibit partial symmetries with other entities (symmetries in the most general sense, i.e. isometric configurations).

13. THE VOID. A region may have no centers within it.

14. SIMPLICITY AND INNER CALM. A region may have deceptively few centers within it, with a surprisingly strong effect upon a viewer.

15. NOT-SEPARATENESS. Every region is linked ultimately to all other regions, including the viewer and their world, and ultimately the cosmos. The property of not-separateness exhibits this linkage to the viewer, which can evoke a profound feeling in response.

Alexander observed and reported the 15 properties phenomeno-logically, but then began to seek clues to their underlying formation and arrangement. He came to understand that they arose naturally as a result of the natural transformations in the processes of morphogenesis. That is, the process of structural development leads to these classes of order, through the workings of the transformations.

Structure-Preserving Transformations

We discussed the central notion of transformation earlier. The process of a "structure-preserving transformation" is capable of generating the different properties of natural morphology, as the result of its morphogenesis or generation of form. To see how this is so, we can go back to the famous milk-drop photographs by Harold Edgerton that I mentioned in the last chapter, and we find that even this simple process generates remarkable geometric characteristics.

On the next page is the famous series again, showing the drop of milk hitting a thin layer of milk covering a hard surface. Note the initial sphere, a simple center in the middle with no articulated centers around it. It strikes the surface, and its symmetry is immediately broken. The result is not chaos, but a new kind of organization. (This "symmetry-breaking" is a very important idea in physics.)

Specifically, notice how the displaced milk rises up and forms a ring, a boundary around the original drop. The ring expands, and as it does so it too becomes unstable — the equilibrium between gravity and velocity is exceeded — and its symmetry is broken as well. But again, the result is not chaos but the articulation of new structures

— arm-like appendages, and at their ends, like exclamation points, new "baby" spheres.

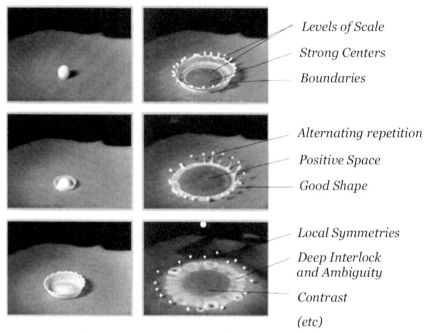

Figure II.4.3: The structure-preserving transformation of a simple milk drop, in the famous series of photos by Harold Edgerton, and showing characteristic properties of natural morphology as Alexander identified them. Photo courtesy Edgerton Digital Collections

The overall structure exhibits the features of organization, not unlike an organism. There is a unity of form without the overall composition. There is a hierarchy between the center, the ring, the appendages and the small spheres. There are interconnections between the different arms, which can be seen to slightly perturb each other. There is an irregularity too, which is intricate, varied and unique — not exactly like any other milk drop. It is not a perfectly repeated pattern, but it is a well-organized one all the same.

We can begin to see, in this simple example, how Alexander's "15 properties" can be generated spontaneously through such a process. One can see levels of scale, boundaries, alternating repetition, and so on.

What is significant is that this structure has arisen as a direct result of the steps in the transformation. The structure of the original sphere transformed into the ring, which transformed into the appendages, and finally to the little spheres. It did not simply disappear, to be replaced with a new structure inserted into the environment, assembled from parts according to a template. (That is the exceptional, limited and extreme method that is unique to contemporary human beings — producing a fundamentally limited set of geometric properties, from this perspective.)

As I noted previously, it is a remarkable fact that the structure at each stage is a complete whole — first the sphere, then the splash pattern, then the rings, then the droplets and so on. It is not a combination of separate and independent parts. Instead, at each stage, the whole is transformed and extended in some important way. This is why Alexander later used the term "wholeness-extending transformations."

Nature of course is full of far more complex examples than the milk drop — perhaps nowhere more than in embryology.

Unfolding

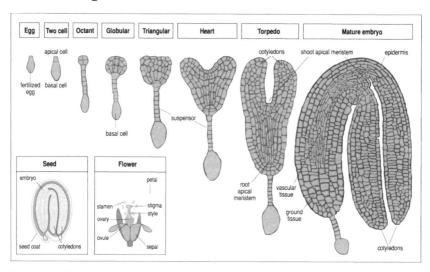

Figure II.4.4: Morphogenesis in biological processes.

What is interesting for our purposes is that the DNA in some way guides the process, like a recipe, with instructions for the various steps. A similar process can be observed in human processes, including cooking recipes and medical procedures. The steps are very simple, but their effect becomes sequentially more profound, resulting in a delicious meal, or a process of complex healing.

I mentioned previously that similar process can be observed in the function of traditional urban codes. Relatively simple rules guide builders through various steps of construction, specifying contextual responses, such as position of windows relative to previously built windows, and so on. The result is an emergent contextual form. Alexander has found that traditional building processes used a similar kind of stepwise guidance, or "rules of thumb."

In all cases, the evolution proceeds to "unfold" more and more complex, powerful, beautiful forms, not merely as a matter of "trial and error," but as a compounding characteristic of the process itself. It appears that there are capacities built into the nature of space itself, or space-time, that allow these structures to be formed as the result of their adaptations.

The lesson for human designers and planners is a simple and one. We need to return to an understanding of these basic, powerful processes of adaptive morphogenesis, in responding to the context of our designs. We need to temper our use of abstractions (including abstract ideas of art) and place primary emphasis on the human being, the human context, and the natural world, including the world of human nature.

These living places and activities are the seeds of the renaissance of cities.

5. "MASSIVE PROCESS DIFFICULTIES"

"The non-art-loving public at large, instead of being grateful to architects for what they do, regard the onset of modern buildings and modern cities everywhere as an inevitable, rather sad piece of the larger fact that the world is going to the dogs."

— *Christopher Alexander,* "A City is Not a Tree"

From the very beginning of his career, Christopher Alexander was always interested in the differences between the "modern" systems of production of cities — beginning around the early 20th Century — and what he termed the "unself-conscious" processes of designing and building that largely governed the creation of the human environment for most of human history.

As he noted in *Notes on the Synthesis of Form* (1964), there were clearly some advantages in the former system, from a human point of view. Our challenge in the modern era was, in a sense, to recapitulate these more satisfying, life-giving characteristics, now in a necessarily more self-conscious way. All of his subsequent work over the next half century or more — his work on pattern languages, generative processes and the like — can be seen as an effort to do just that.

In just the way that Alexander's entire career was, in a sense, an exploration of *mereology*, or the relation between parts and wholes — a point I have argued throughout this book — we can also see that his entire career was, in a similar sense, an exploration of human technology, and its failure to account adequately for this aspect of nature. Moreover it was an exploration of the nature of the needed correctives.

His last major published work, *The Battle for the Life and Beauty of the Earth* (2012), returned to this topic. On the surface it was an account of the development of the Eishin School in Japan, one of Alexander's most notable building projects (working with his associate Hajo Neis and others). At a deeper level, the book was an exploration again of our time in the history of design and production, the nature of our systems, and the question of needed reforms. In a sense, the Eishin project was the case study for examining this larger set of issues.

Opposite: *The construction site of the Eishin School in Japan, designed by Christopher Alexander and his colleagues.*

In the book Alexander distinguished between "System A" production and "System B" production. In a real sense, System A was the same "unself-conscious process" of his PhD thesis, and System B was the process we have today: governed by powerful but limited abstractions, by rigid template-based production, and by economies of scale and standardization. In this scheme of things, architects are just another set of specialists in their own "silos," whose job it is to cloak an appropriately alluring art costume on the whole questionable enterprise.

As my colleague Nikos Salingaros and I have written about elsewhere, there is certainly an important place in the natural world for the economies of scale and standardization, and biological systems do employ them frequently. For example, genetic seeds certainly operate on vast scales, and their components are highly standardized. But biological systems, unlike "modern" human technology, also routinely employs economies of *place* and *differentiation*. When the first two are applied without a balanced application of the second two, the results are powerful but can also be exceedingly destructive. It is place and differentiation that provide the contextual feedback, the necessary balance to scale and standardization, without which they become destructive. (There is an interesting and remarkably accurate analogy to the process of cancer in biological systems, in that cancer is a runaway process of standardized, i.e. undifferentiated, cells, that reproduce at large scales without responding appropriately to their place within the body.)

In *The Nature of Order,* Alexander referred to the root of the problem as "massive process difficulties." That is, the processes we have instituted for shaping our world in "modernity" have begun to malfunction in important ways, creating unsustainable and harmful forms of development (e.g. "sprawl," lifeless buildings and cities, etc.). This is not because we are intentionally creating such a system, but because we are making a certain kind of mistake:

> How could rules, laws and processes which generate such obviously harmful structures, have been introduced and replicated throughout modern society, unless it were on purpose? Yet of course, it is not on purpose. It is all by mistake. And it is by means of a very particular kind of mistake."

Part of the problem is that we do not yet even understand what is happening:

We, the first children of the modern age, have not yet understood the huge extent to which *the physical structure of the world is generated by its processes.* The processes do have a huge impact on the way the world is shaped. But these impacts are most often unintended, tangential. So the structure-*destroying* processes which run rampant in creating our modern environment are on the loose, uncontrolled, created by idiot processes for which no one takes morphogenetic responsibility. We have let loose a system that generates monsters. And we do not even realize that it is we who created this system of processes and we who continue to let it loose."

In *Battle,* Alexander delved more deeply into these issues. He spent a considerable amount of time tracking how the modern development process works, and the many places where it goes wrong. Most importantly, he says, the process does not allow for local adaptation. In the second chapter titled "The Crucial Importance of Local Adaptation," he started out by saying,

An environment or community will not come to life unless each place, each building, each street, each room becomes unique, as a result of careful and piecemeal processes of adaptation... Paying attention to this pervasive kind of adaptation throughout our project required mental, artistic, and procedural tools. We had to develop these tools so that adaptation could be a constant focus in each place, at many different scales, all over the Eishin Campus.

The supposedly "modern" systems of development and production did not have such tools, for the simple reason that there was no perceived need. The economies of scale and standardization were imagined to be sufficiently powerful and adequate to build a satisfactory new world. But as Alexander observed, this was a fundamental mistake.

Like Jacobs, Alexander also clearly saw the economic dimensions of the problem, and the problem of faulty feedback. For Alexander, this was a question of "the flow of money" and the processes whereby each person who handled money had a series of adaptive steps to take in applying the expenditures. This was not simply an additive combination of elements, but rather, a careful sequencing of steps and gathering of feedback for adaptation.

Of course, the money itself did not require such a careful sequencing, and it was perfectly possible — as it always is — to treat money as a purely quantitative resource, without regard to quality. However, as we have seen, this approach can produce enormous damage.

Worse, this amounts to an abdication of responsibility — and for Alexander, the central task is to revitalize the immediate responsibility of the maker, the adaptive agent, the human being. This requires two aspects — one, the recognition of our actual power, our actual ability to respond (response-ability), applied with appropriate tools, and two, the recognition of the qualitative aspects of the built environment, and of human life.

Alexander is hardly the first to note that methodologies since about 1600 have discounted the qualitative aspects of experience, attempting to relegate them to the status of "mere" psychological phenomena. As the philosopher Alfred North Whitehead and others have noted, this attempt was not ultimately sound, from a logical point of view, but it constituted a kind of "mental trick" that allowed modern thinking to progress on its then-current path, for better or worse.

This mental trick, as it were, was an extremely useful tool to dispense with highly variable and unreliable phenomena. But modern science has come up against the limits of this tool, which is in fact what Whitehead memorably called "an omission of part of the truth." As I noted earlier, in fields as diverse as neuroscience, anthropology and medicine, the qualitative experience of value has made an insistent return to the scientific purview. Perhaps nowhere does this re-integration seem more necessary than in the fields of the human environment, where "quality of life" and "the quality of a natural environment" are hardly trivial aspects of what is going on. Indeed, they are increasingly being seen as the very essence.

For Alexander, the qualitative is not some trivial psychological side-effect, nor is it some mysterious unseen realm. It is quite literally right before our eyes, in the structure of things. What we call "matter" is matter precisely because it "matters" — it has a qualitative experiential effect upon us, and only then becomes a "fact".

Just so, we cannot separate value from the world of facts, as Whitehead also pointed out. The Universe is shot through with value, and this phenomenon cannot be "psychologized" away. A corollary, as I alluded to in the introduction, is that beauty is also not a psychological effect, or a trivial source of pleasure — as it is so often regarded. It is, rather, a recognition of a deep order, of a kind that is likely to be beneficial to the perceiver. That is, it is an experience of quality and value, embedded deeply in the structures and spaces we experience. (This is one of the key insights of the topic of "biophilia," which suggests that we have naturally evolved preferences for environments that are the most likely to promote our well-being, e.g. meadows, vistas seen from safe vantage points, etc.)

This view of things must be at the root of the recovered benefits of a "System A" architecture. It is not that our current world must be swept away, replaced with some radically different world containing a radically different economic system. That would be to make the same kind of mistake we have already been making. Instead we need a "structure-preserving transformation" that preserves what is already good about our cities, and about our economic systems too. Or, following Alexander's later terminology, we need a "wholeness-extending transformation" that recognizes and builds upon the existing health, wealth, and wholeness (all related words) of cities and towns.

In that sense, we need to build on the renaissance that has already begun.

This way of thinking amounts to a return to a "structuralist" view of nature, as I will discuss in more detail in the next section. In essence, structuralism is the philosophical idea that meaning has a relation to the structures of the world, and to language, and interacts creatively with them. We make the meaning of our lives by structuring our world, and by structuring the language by which we know it and act on it.

While Alexander's is a more elaborate form of neo-structuralism than Jacobs', we can readily see the echoes of this structuralism in both writers.

SECTION III:

PHILOSOPHICAL ROOTS

1. THE ANCIENT AND CUTTING-EDGE TOPIC OF MEREOLOGY*

"First, the taking in of scattered particulars under one Idea, so that everyone understands what is being talked about... Second, the separation of the Idea into parts, by dividing it at the joints, as nature directs, not breaking any limb in half as a bad carver might."

— *Plato,* Phaedrus

I previously asserted that both Jacobs and Alexander have taken up again the ancient philosophical topic of *mereology* — the relation of parts to wholes. This topic is a central theme in both of their works: how a city serves as an inter-connected fabric, how a design problem forms a network of related elements, or how people work together in polycentric groups to manage the growth of a complex whole. In this section I will consider mereology more directly, as a topic that is overdue for a re-assessment.

In spite of modernity's radical technological and social advances—or perhaps precisely because of them — ancient questions of philosophy remain relevant, even urgent, and we would do well to revisit them. This is particularly true when we are dealing with problems of planning and design, working in groups and organizations of varying complexity. We need to be clear about our premises, our aims, and the efforts we are making individually and collectively to achieve them.

What is reliable knowledge? How do actions bring into being new structures? How can we work with others, and together as a civilization, to produce, and to sustain, a higher quality of life?

For Jacobs and Alexander, these are surprisingly dynamic questions. The old topics have certainly been informed, and transformed, by a centuries-long series of mind-boggling scientific discoveries into the structures of nature (as Jacobs described so lucidly in the

---

* *The chapters in this section are drawn in part from a paper delivered at The Athens Dialogues, a conference organized by The Onassis Foundation, Harvard University and other partners, in Athens, Greece in 2010. I am grateful for the invitation, especially by Prof. George Babiniotis of Onassis Foundation, and Prof. Robert Harriss, my session chair.*

Opposite: *Flowers blooming in the author's London garden. In spite of dramatic changes over the blooming process, the structure always displays a remarkably integrated relation of parts to wholes.*

last chapter of *The Death and Life of Great American Cities*). These discoveries have also served to reveal logically inherent weaknesses within modern technology itself and its progressive capacity for breakdown and malfunction.

Most disheartening, we have witnessed a series of unintended consequences and self-destructive outcomes, stemming directly from our own apparent best intentions and rational efforts. Instead of the hoped-for modernity of rational fulfillment, we are left with a "post-modernity" of geopolitical dysfunction, ecological devastation, and the grim specter of climate change. In this environment, the modern design professions seem to alternate between cynical despair and a manic faith in magical thinking.

And yet, as Jacobs and Alexander argued, within the logic of these scientific discoveries — particularly the more recent discoveries of organized complexity — lie the seeds of regeneration. As we begin to tease apart the secrets of living systems, we can begin to draw useful lessons indeed for the reform of our own failing technologies.

There are on offer, moreover, new ways of decomposing and analyzing the structure of our problems, the better to resolve them. As Jacobs put it, the way we think about, say, "the kind of problem a city is," must correspond to the structure of the problem sufficiently for us to get somewhere in its solution. If it doesn't — if we have made categorical errors in our own thinking — we will be doomed to a series of intractable and very possibly catastrophic failures.

Therefore, in order to get to the bottom of things, we need to ask fundamentally philosophical questions, following the principle that "as we think, we live." For planning and design are profoundly philosophical activities, at once employing teleology (aims), epistemology (the nature of knowledge), ontology (the nature of reality), and logic (the structure of truth). This is a philosophy that, as we will discuss, has been informed, and profoundly transformed, by the structural revelations of modern science — and vice versa.

Birth in a Cave

Alfred North Whitehead famously observed that the European philosophical tradition can be characterized as "a series of footnotes to Plato." Plato's idealism — his understanding of a static class of "Forms" underlying the varied appearances of form we experience — has left its deep mark on the Western intellect, and nowhere more so than in the modern design professions.

We must recognize, of course, that Plato was not the real beginning of the story, and he owed a profound debt to Pythagoras' earlier mathematical idealism. Similarly, Plato's legacy was transformed by Aristotle and others to follow. (As Bertrand Russell put it, Aristotle could be thought of as "Plato with common sense.") Nonetheless, Plato undoubtedly marks a seminal moment in the history of Western, indeed perhaps human, thought. And one metaphor stands out as most seminal.

It is, of course, the famous Allegory of the Cave, recounted by Plato in *The Republic*. We are, Socrates says, like men chained to the floor of a cave, watching only the flickering, ever-changing reflections on the wall before us, cast by unseen puppeteers behind, projected from the light of a great fire. We do not see the real, unchanging objects held by the puppeteers, nor the fire — even less, the bright sun outside the cave. Thus our knowledge of the nature of the world and its objects is derived only from a series of transitory reflections — mere instances — of the real, permanent truth, which we can only uncover slowly, through a kind of "ascent" from the depths of this cave. That ascent begins when we are freed from our chains, and are able to behold the objects of the puppeteers.

Those objects are, as students of philosophy know, Plato's *eide* or Forms: the unseen but "really real" categorical structures that create the shadowy, impermanent perceptions of everyday experience. These are, we later learn, invariant and timeless mathematical and geometric structures, carrying universal aesthetic and moral implications. (It is here that Pythagoras' earlier mathematical idealism is most keenly felt.) There is a unity to be discovered between the Good, the True, and the Beautiful.

Thus the allegory encapsulated Plato's explanation of the central problem of epistemology: the variability of the world around us, the fragmentation and apparent disorder of it, and the incompleteness and even the corruption of our knowledge of it. What we encounter in the world is only a series of reflections of a deeper but no less knowable reality — but one that is precisely ordered and fundamental.

But as later philosophers noted, Plato's idealism removed the epistemological problem to another realm, but did not get rid of it. After all, it is not clear how we will be any more able to establish the reality of the *eide* and ascertain their invariability and completeness. Even if we verify their existence, might they not turn out to be just as shadowy in their own way? (As I will discuss shortly, this was very much the sort of picture that modern science would later offer.)

Plato's student Aristotle certainly cast the situation in a very different light — though his account still owed much to his great teacher. In his hylomorphism — his theory of matter, *hylo-*, taking form, *morphe* — he was still supremely concerned to explain the fact that many objects have the same universal form — many trees all have the form of a tree, and so on. But for Aristotle, the form was not located in a transcendent or unseen realm, but inhered within the object itself, as an instance of a potential universal becoming actual — and it is this, he said, that comprises its substance.

Moreover, this was a process that could repeat at different scales: the substance at one level could become the matter at another. Thus the matter of, say, a house — its bricks — could take on the triangular form of a pediment, or the cubic form of its walls. In turn, these forms could become the constituent matter for still other forms: a house, a city, and so on.

In this rudimentary structuralist account — which, like Plato's, would become profoundly influential — Aristotle began to describe a logic of mereology: the way parts relate to wholes. This is a topic of central importance in modernity — all the more so, as the technology of modernity greatly magnifies the number of constituents, and the complexity of their relationships.

As noted, both Plato's and Aristotle's accounts owe much to the earlier Pythagoras and his mathematical "music of the spheres" — his faith that precise ratios underlay the orderly structures of the cosmos, and indeed, the order of all that is good and beautiful. Thus the mathematical properties of the forms — their proportions, their adherence to unchanging mathematical laws, and so on — were considered fundamental. In fact the five regular solids discovered by Pythagoras and his followers are now called "Platonic solids."

In Plato's case, however, such geometric forms were extrinsic, part of a transcendent reality, while for Aristotle they were intrinsic, the universal structural fundamentals of substance. This shift to the structures of daily experience is widely regarded as a watershed event in the history of philosophy, and earns Aristotle the title of "the father of empiricism." But importantly for our discussion, it was an empiricism anchored in a no less Platonic kind of "fundamentalism of form." In both cases, the categories of form (whether seen as ideals or universals) were fundamental, aggregate constituents.

This is a view of form that, in both cases, sees a particular form as reducible to simpler forms, and ultimately, to a primary and eternal set of mathematical forms and ratios. It follows that the act of creating form is the reverse: a kind of hierarchical process of applying primary structures according to correct rules of proportion, scale, fitness and so on — which, if executed correctly, delivered the Good, the True and the Beautiful, as part of a single ordered process.

Idealism and Hylomorphism in Early Modern Theory

This essentially reductionist view of structure held powerful sway over the coming tradition of Western science, and provided the mental framework to unlock a long series of astonishing secrets of nature — to say nothing of the prodigious industrial advances that ensued. But it slowly became clear that this reductionism was also, as we will discuss presently, not the entire story, and some of the minor bits left out are much more critical than we realized — a revelation that we are grappling with still today.

But in the meantime, this structural reductionism also held powerful sway over designers and architects for generations to come — and over their most influential theorists. For example, it can be seen clearly in the writings of Vitruvius in the Classical era, and his doctrine that architecture is the imitation of nature, and of its fundamental patterns — culminating in his conception of the"Vitruvian Man," later drawn by Leonardo da Vinci: the human figure, decomposed into the square and the circle. It can also be seen clearly in Alberti's early Renaissance classic *De Re Aedificatoria*, which also echoed Plato, Aristotle and Vitruvius, and described a fundamental ordering of circles, squares, and harmonic relations between them.

Indeed, the same reductionism can be seen readily from the writings of the most influential early Modernists — and in fact they took this reductionism to a remarkable extreme. Perhaps this reflected an over-confidence in the late nineteenth century, that the gifts of technological modernity, expressing the logical rigor and progressive spirit of the Enlightenment, had finally delivered on the ultimate promise of Hellenic rationality. The payoff was at hand.

Here is Le Corbusier's critique, presented in his book *Toward a New Architecture* (1924), of Gothic architecture, presenting a remarkably Aristotelian argument that, in essence, Gothicism gets its hylomorphism all wrong:

> Gothic architecture is not, fundamentally, based on spheres, cones and cylinders. Only the nave is an expression of a simple form, but of a complex geometry of the second order (intersecting arches). It is for that reason that a cathedral is not very beautiful and that we search in it for compensations of a subjective kind outside plastic art. A cathedral interests us as the ingenious solution of a difficult problem, but a problem of which the postulates have been badly stated because they do not proceed from the great primary forms.

The geometrical fundamentalism of the phrase "great primary forms" is striking. But if "a cathedral is not very beautiful," then what is beautiful, and why? For Le Corbusier, it is those structures that arise directly from the Platonic fundamentals of mathematical calculation — like American grain elevators:

> Thus we have the American grain elevators and factories, the magnificent FIRST FRUITS of the new age. THE AMERICAN ENGINEERS OVERWHELM WITH THEIR CALCULATIONS OUR EXPIRING ARCHITECTURE.

This picture is in contrast to the usual opposition of modernism to classicism. Certainly the former emphasis on ornament and decoration was stripped away, replaced by a new minimalist celebration of the logic of the machine. But the understanding of architecture as a composition of primary forms, bound by the timeless Pythagorean laws of mathematics, is consistent throughout. Indeed, modernism's central narrative of the "end of history" — its faith in an arrival beyond the messiness of happenstance, delivered by logic and reason into a new age of mechanical perfection, can now be seen for the Hellenic idealism that it is. At last, we would achieve the rational ordering of our buildings, our machines, our very culture, in a glorious flowering of rational modernity.

Incompleteness, Uncertainty, and Complexity

And yet, at precisely the moment that architects were celebrating the triumph of reason in the new modernity, scientists and philosophers were busy making new discoveries that had a devastating effect upon it. These discoveries came inexorably from the further teasing out of the complex structure of things, in fields such as biology, physics, information theory and — most disheartening for logical idealists — mathematics and logic itself.

In 1912, Whitehead and his Cambridge colleague Bertrand Russell, in their classic treatise *Principia Mathematica,* attempted to lay out a reductionist scheme for all of logic and mathematics. Their result is widely considered to be one of the most important works of mathematical logic since Aristotle. But Kurt Gödel, in an earth-shaking 1931 paper, managed the neat trick of using the machinery of Whitehead's and Russell's logical scheme to disprove itself — more specifically, to prove that in spite of their intended aim, and whatever else its merits, their work is and must be logically "incomplete." More than that, he managed to prove that any such system must be, at least to some degree, "incomplete."

The implications, developed in further papers and in philosophical work since, were staggering. There can be no perfect blueprint of nature, no reductive model to fully explain the logical structure of things. This would seem to be a powerful blow to Platonic idealism, and no less, to Aristotelian hylomorphism.

At the same time, physicists were observing very strange behavior at the subatomic level, with powerful implications for the rest of nature's structure. Far from assuring us, in Platonic fashion, of an unseen solid realm, experimental results seemed to point the way to ever more impermanence, endless variability, and even randomness. With each new discovery, the universe looked more and more complicated, more and more a cloud-like shower of energy particles (or were they waves?) that only temporarily coalesce into "things" or forms, and then fly off to coalesce into other things, following complex pattern-like rules. (This seemed to echo an earlier and decidedly non-Platonic theme in Hellenic thought, the dynamicism of Heraclitus.)

The lessons of biology were no less astounding, and humbling for fundamental reductionists. We ourselves turn out to be vast-trillion-member societies of semi-independent, cooperating micro-organisms, few of whom live longer than about seven years. (In fact every one of those cells contains two separate symbiotic organisms with separate genetic histories.) And while we do seem to be generated from simpler processes, the whole scheme is not at all the neat picture of an earlier age, but rather, one of coded transformations and interactions of stupendous complexity. The cells, rather than forming "top-down" according to neat divisions and assignments, seem to know how to "self-organize" into over-arching patterns that tend to resemble the primary forms of mathematics, but do not conform at all precisely. (For example, we have a sphere-like, but not precisely spherical, structure in our eyes, and a cylinder-like, but not precisely cylindrical, structure in our fingers, and so on).

Whitehead himself helped to articulate important outlines of a new "structuralist" (or "process") philosophy that was rooted more in the workings of processes over time — generators of endless varieties of form whose products bore the marks of this diachronic and evolutionary process. In his later work he outlined a "process philosophy" that could explain the cloud-like particulate forms of nature that were more consistent with the powerful new picture emerging from the sciences — described in books such as *Process and Reality* and *Science and the Modern World*. And he sought to explain the relation of our own ideas to these realities of process, and the dangers of confusion that lay therein, in books like *Modes of Thought* and *Adventures of Ideas*.

The postmodernist debacle

Gradually, of course, these ideas seeped into everyday life — and, ultimately, our understanding of culture, the arts, and architecture. We came to see that we live in a less than rational world, where accidental political events could result in nuclear annihilation, or unintended economic forces could result in a global depression. Worse, even our own beautiful technological structures could malfunction in horrendous but unforeseen ways, and deliver not utopia, but pollution, ecological destruction, climate change, and economic decay.

A series of disastrous failures of modernist architectural and urbanist projects — insightfully critiqued by a generation of scholars like Jane Jacobs — reached a crisis point in the 1960s and 1970s. The achievements of rationality and logic had culminated in the modern technology of city-making: but it had not delivered utopia, but a persistent fragmentation, disorder and decay. There was a flaw in the neatly ordered system — and it was not merely in its surface application, but increasingly, could be seen to reside at the logical core of it. Gödel's critique seemed to apply to the very logic of modernism: it was fatally, catastrophically, incomplete.

The ensuing counter-reaction to modernism was dubbed, of course, "postmodernism:" marked by an abandonment of the fundamentalist quest for ideals of form, and a return to the diachronic qualities of language and narrative. Architecture would now be a kind of story that a civilization tells about itself: highly symbolic, self-referential, ironic. The failure of Hellenic rationality would itself become part of the story.

The postmodernist critique of modernism was articulated particularly clearly by the architect Rem Koolhaas, in his essay, "Whatever Happened to Urbanism" (in *S, M, L, XL,* 1995):

> Modernism's alchemistic promise — to transform quantity into quality through abstraction and repetition — has been a failure, a hoax: magic that didn't work. Its ideas, aesthetics, strategies are finished. Together, all attempts to make a new beginning have only discredited the idea of a new beginning. A collective shame in the wake of this fiasco has left a massive crater in our understanding of modernity and modernization. . . Since then, we have been engaged in two parallel operations: documenting our overwhelming awe for the existing city, developing philosophies, projects, prototypes for a preserved and reconstituted city and, at the same time, laughing the professional field of urbanism out of existence, dismantling it in our contempt for those who planned (and made huge mistakes in planning) airports, New Towns, satellite cities, highways, high-rise buildings, infrastructures, and all the other fallout from modernization.

This postmodernism in art and architecture was mirrored by a post-structuralism in philosophy, built upon an empirical and even logical suspicion of the presumed powers of knowledge and reason. It, too, had its roots deep in the story of Western philosophy. It owed a particular debt to Immanuel Kant's earlier philosophy of Transcendental Idealism — itself a confrontation with the evident limits of knowledge.

Kant's Transcendental Idealism can be thought of as a kind of inversion of Plato's idealism. We do experience something roughly like Platonic forms, in a sense — in the experienced structures of words and ideas — but they are to be treated as *a priori* categories of mind, and not, in any sense deeper realities of the world — which, even if they existed, could never be understood except through the very same categories of mind. Thus, if we wanted to be logical, we must begin there in the realm of mind — and we must inevitably find ourselves trapped there. Ontology is forever bounded by epistemology.

The post-structuralists went a step farther, taking as their departure point the linguistic structuralism of anthropology. But whereas structuralists like Saussure and Levi-Strauss saw language as a malleable tool for the anchoring of an external meaning within a culturally variable structure, post-structuralists like Derrida and Foucault dispatched with external meaning altogether, and focused instead on the relative ways in which cultures and their sub-groups construct narratives of "meaning" (or reliable knowledge, or truth) as a wholly synthetic structural process. Echoing the tension between Plato and Aristotle, they dispensed with any external concept of meaning, and (if they considered it at all) saw it as something that inhered within the structure, and the structural differences, of language itself.

The post-structuralists also saw the ways that different groups use this construction process to gain political control of one another, by imposing the structural narratives by which cultural meanings are defined. Thus the task of a philosopher is now to analyze this construction, and deconstruct it into its constituents so as to expose its inner workings. We may not be able to determine the relative merits of one set of meanings over another — indeed, that would be "privileging" one group of constructors over another — but we can certainly reveal the hegemony of one group and its constructions (say, colonial powers) over the constructions of others (say, indigenous peoples).

In architecture and the arts, this philosophy expressed itself in acts of deconstruction of the narrative texts of power: exposing the constructions of power elites, so as to fuel an art of liberation. Thus we may decry the concentration of corporate power — perhaps finding it even among our own clientele, if we are architects — but we can still "deconstruct" this reality, and reveal it within our art. This kind of art may not be transcendent in any metaphysical sense — nor does it any longer claim to be. Rather, it is meant to derive an emotional power from its cathartic eloquence. If we cannot fix the world, we can at least understand its hidden structure, and celebrate its revelation.

Post-structuralism was thus a logical evolutionary step, and a useful cautionary narrative on the powers of reason. Like a good Zen *koan,* it served to break the spell of ideas over those who applied them too rigidly — in particular, the demonstrably specious claims of some philosophical absolutists (including some neo-Platonists) to have "got it right." But beyond describing these limits, it did not go very far in explaining to us what is really going on with language, and its structural relation to the emerging scientific picture of nature — and in particular, the evident phenomenon of biological intelligence.

Indeed, there are fundamental logical flaws with the post-structuralist account that leave it, at best, highly compromised in its ability to provide a useful explanation of what is going on in the structure of things—at least beyond the narrow confines of cultural creativity. In its logically purest form, its doctrine against external meaning and truth is ultimately self-contradictory, since, as Gödel showed, we are no more able to escape the problem of incompleteness within language than outside it. The illusion of escape comes from a categorical confusion, forgetting that language is just as "real" a structure in the world as any other — with all the same epistemological perils. (We will come back to this logically confusing point in more detail in the next chapter.)

This categorical confusion leaves the post-structuralists with the inability to form a coherent theory of even what they themselves are doing, and how it applies to any "thing" — even their own construction — beyond a kind of elaborate word-game. But the process of science requires that we posit a structural model of "what is going on" — and then test that model for conformance, revision, and refinement. Thus we are required to have a meta-model of fidelity, or what some call "the ring of truth" — which is not the same thing as absolute congruence with truth. Thus, in its essentially all-or-nothing form, the epistemological doctrine of post-structuralism is at best severely limited in its empirical usefulness, and at worst, fundamentally irreconcilable with a coherent scientific project. (A point of harsh criticism during the so-called "science wars" debates.)

One may deny the validity of such a scientific project, of course — or, like many post-structuralists, argue that it is merely one more constructed narrative. But that seems charmingly oblivious to the practical urgency of the situation at hand. We are rather like passengers in a car that we ourselves have made, and we are finding it unusually hard to steer. Should we now propose to stop steering altogether, because we have found error, partiality, and bias in the car's manual? This seems at best an over-reaction, and at worst, a kind of pervasive logical confusion about the useful, if imperfect, role of language. (We will discuss this "useful imperfection" in more detail below.)

Indeed, a more coherent picture of the situation is now being conveyed by fields like neuroscience and information theory, which have brought new insights into the workings of language and the brain, and their place in the structure of nature. As I will explore in the next chapter, these and other developments point toward a revived structuralist account of what is going on — bringing with it a series of profound new implications.

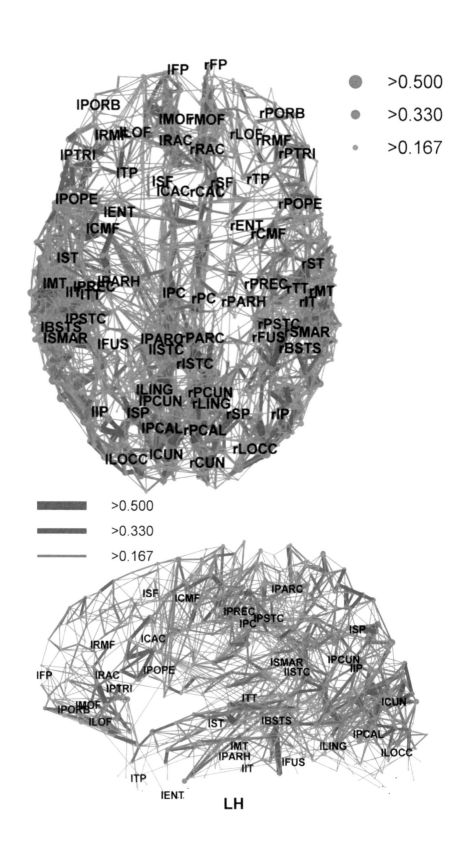

2. STRUCTURALISM RECONSIDERED

"The most incomprehensible thing about the universe is that it is comprehensible."

— *Albert Einstein*

As Einstein noted, although it may be a curious fact, the world is not an impenetrable fog, nor are we prisoners in and of our own minds. Rather, we can tease out a reliable (if always partially incomplete) account of the structure of what is really going on, to a remarkable, even astonishing, degree. It is simply the case that nature does not give up its secrets easily, and the process of teasing out what is going on is immense. But fortunately for us, this process has culminated in recent years with a breathtaking kind of consilience — and a most useful one.

Perhaps nowhere do these developments have more practical effect than in the topic of mereology. Aristotle's understanding of hylomorphism has been greatly deepened, and in some cases turned on its head, by over two millennia of discoveries into the universal atomic and molecular structure of the world. There is no real place for fundamental essence to enter the picture, nor any need for it to: the universe is perfectly comprehensible as an endless compositional structure. But this composition is not merely additive, but, in an important sense, transformative and inter-relational. We will discuss below the profound significance of this revelation.

Similarly, it is possible to make a perfectly useful description of the structure of the brain, and its relation to various problem-solving and representative functions of the animal (that is, ourselves). We can note interesting and useful structural relationships and isomorphic properties, without respect to any metaphysical or ontological assumptions.

This "new structuralism" (or it could be called "symmetric structuralism," for reasons that will become apparent) is distinguished from the original most notably in its emphasis on process, and the complex symmetric transformations that occur within it. As Jean Piaget, a notable figure in this school of thought, put it in 1968, "there

Opposite: *Illustration from the paper, "Mapping the structural core of human cerebral cortex" by Hagmann P, Cammoun L, Gigandet X, Meuli R, Honey CJ, Wedeen VJ, Sporns O (2008). PLoS Biology Vol. 6, No. 7, e159.*

exists no structure without a construction, abstract or genetic." Moreover, as we shall see, the new understanding can even find a structural home for value, meaning, agency, choice — those things that are thought of as exclusionary opposites of what had been assumed to be an inherently determinist structural perspective. But it is in the new structures revealed by modern science that things get very interesting indeed.

We begin with the neuro-structuralist's view of the human brain. What is particularly useful about this picture of things is that the structure of the brain and its activities — let us assume, the equivalent of the mind, seen from beyond our own first-person perspective — is a structure in the world like any other, and it is not necessary to posit a transcendental realm of the mind, or of ideal forms, to explain what is going on in a plausible way. Such a realm may or may not exist; it is simply unnecessary to account for it from this perspective on things.

Furthermore, the relation between this structure of the brain and that of the rest of the world can now be seen to have an important relational structure in its own right. For one thing, there is a fundamental characteristic of partial symmetry. That is, the structures of the brain do have partial isomorphic correspondences with the structures of reality. These correspondences have their origin in the transformations of structures through symmetric progressions, beginning with the most direct kinds (say, instantaneous flashes of activity corresponding to instantaneous threats in the external world) and progressing to much more speculative threats (say, evasive patterns of instinctive behavior in response to a possible threat that is more remote, such as the agitated evasions of animal herds at the mere sight of a predator).

A similar thing can be seen to be going on in a more articulated form within language, its structure, and its structural processes. Indeed, the more we understand it, the more language seems to be a form of useful "software" running on our mental hardware, and, so to speak, written in its operating code. And language, too, displays this "progressive symmetry" — from vocalizations that originally stood for the patterns of events in nature, e.g. the glissandos of expectation and curiosity, the staccatos of action) to more sophisticated symmetric verbal elements and grammars, describing progressively more complex conditions within the world (including complex philosophical discussions like this one).

Language as "the architecture of possibility"

Thus, we arrive at a notion of language as a kind of model-making activity — mirroring and modeling some part of the world that is of interest to us. But these models are not static, but in fact define the realm of our action and possibility. Moreover, in doing so, they actually generate new possibility, as a real logical feature of the structure of nature within that landscape. And in that generation are the seeds of choice, and what is generally identified as free will.

This is an important but little-appreciated point. To bring the point home, let us consider a very simple example. X informs Y that Y can catch the bus on the other side of the street, but only when the hand on X's watch passes between these two marks. Y then asks, "Can I catch another bus later?" "Yes," X reports that Y can catch another one in another hour; or Y can catch another one down that street in two hours.

X and Y have both just built a dynamic model of Y's bus-catching that is relevant and useful on that day. In constructing that model, they have defined new possibilities — and in so doing, in this exceedingly simple example, they have actually generated them.

Y has no possibility of catching a bus that Y doesn't know is coming — or more precisely, but what is virtually the same thing, Y has infinite numbers of small random possibilities, including stumbling upon that bus at that hour; but that logical possibility is, like most others, vanishingly remote. Similarly, Y can discover a network of other possibilities that can be generated only through the dynamics of language. It is only through the power of language, the power of such mental symmetries creating systemic relationships, that X and Y have defined this particular — and, for them, novel — architecture of possibility.

It is in this generative power that we have also identified an architecture of choice, and of agency. For the linguistic power to generate possibility has also generated the possibility of selection. We have arrived at the old philosophic value of free choice, set loose from its anchor in a deterministic structure.

But one might object, are not the structures of the language, like the structures of the world, determining the outcomes? Why is this no less a matter of "reading a script written in advance"? It is at this point that the new sciences of complexity offer us two very useful and related insights.

One is the notion that the complex interconnectivity of a system creates ambiguity and multiple potential — or, in more familiar terminology, freedom. An example may be helpful, in the familiar children's game, Rock, Paper, Scissors. These are three interactive elements within this system. Which is superior? Rock is superior to scissors, which is superior to paper, which is superior to rock. Any two couplings are unambiguous; but the system overall is ambiguous, because of these circular (but in fact purely structural) linkages.

This kind of ambiguity created by multiple inter-linkage is precisely what distinguishes complex systems from simple ones.

But one might object, if we know the initial state of the system, why can't we determine the next step unambiguously? If we know the current object is a rock, for example, then we also know unambiguously that the next object will be inferior if scissors, and superior if paper.

But this is the second point from the sciences of complexity: in a non-trivial complex system, it is impossible to know precisely the initial set of conditions. This is the familiar principle of sensitivity to (unknowable) initial conditions. Although it seems possible, looking in rear-view fashion, to determine a course of events based upon initial conditions, it is (probably) impossible to represent initial conditions with absolute precision. And in a deterministic analysis of behavior of any but the most trivially complex systems, absolute precision is required. But in fact, absolute precision can never be achieved.

The proof of this can be found, once again, in Kurt Gödel's 1931 paper, and a series of follow-up papers. Not only was *Principia Mathematica* necessarily incomplete — that is, incapable of representing even itself with absolute precision — but any such system must be equally incomplete. We cannot distill down to an "absolute blueprint" of the initial conditions.

In essence Gödel relied upon a kind of "Epimenides' Paradox" — showing that any such system is capable of saying, in effect, "I am lying to you now." But this is a logically untenable state of affairs, of course: if the system is lying, then it is telling the truth; if it is telling the truth, then it is lying! The problem is that in essence we are failing to account for the regressive nature of abstractions. Every abstraction is a secondary structure, only partially symmetrical with the first. It is not possible to get an abstraction that is completely congruent with its subject. This is true even if the subject is itself. This is the problem with the post-structuralists' retreat into language, as 114 discussed earlier.

Moreover, it would not be of much use even if it were. A typically wonderful Lewis Carroll story demonstrates this clearly on an intuitive level. In the children's tale *Sylvie and Bruno Concluded*, our protagonists meet a man from another country, who tells them about his country's efforts to greatly improve the accuracy of their maps. As the maps get more and more complete, they become as large as the regions they represent. Finally they make the ultimate map, as large as the country itself! But do they use it much?

> "It has never been spread out, yet," said Mein Herr: "the farmers objected: they said it would cover the whole country, and shut out the sunlight! So we now use the country itself, as its own map, and I assure you it does nearly as well."

This delightfully absurd little fable reminds us that in order to be useful, maps — abstractions, models, linguistic structures, knowledge — must be in some sense different than, and indeed, simpler than, the regions they represent. Gödel's incompleteness is not a defect of knowledge, but an essential and highly useful characteristic of it — but it is we who are already doing the selection and the omission. As Whitehead noted, "an abstraction is nothing other than an omission of part of the truth."

Moreover, there is another major fly in the ointment of initial conditions. It is nothing other than ourselves. As the physicist Werner Heisenberg noted, first in a "hard" principle of quantum physics and later as a more general epistemological principle, we can never fully write ourselves, the observers, out of the observations. Our impenetrable subjectivity, uncertainty and ambiguity are unavoidably and, *a priori* part of the initial conditions at any point.

It is here that the essence of our own agency lies, in our own irreducible, uncomputable, undecidable participation. Any valid scientific description of what is going on must ultimately take this situation into account, as an *a priori* condition. All facts are derivative of this truth: we are embedded participants.

This is not bad news; indeed, it is the best possible news. It gives us ever more choice: meaningful choice. It means that we can make useful abstractions, and abstractions of abstractions, and grand and powerful theories — and that they can be extremely useful to us, in defining, and creating, new architectures of real possibility — real, because our choices are real, and our ability to cause them to occur is real.

This also means that we must be aware of the limitations of abstractions, and their fundamental derivative nature. Furthermore, we must be aware of the dangers of their seductive accuracy (too easily confused with perfection), and the perpetual tendency to become lost in the abstractions, and fail to understand their perpetual (if often undetectable) incongruences, limitations, and derivations. We may become lost in what Wittgenstein called "the bewitchment of intelligence by means of language." As Whitehead noted in his remarkable book *Modes of Thought,* we must ensure "a right adjustment of the process of abstraction."

A (neo) structuralist reinterpretation of idealism and hylomorphism

What can we conclude now about the primary forms, going back to Plato and Pythagoras? What of proportion and harmony, and their possible echoes in the moral order of things?

It might appear that they have been destroyed for good, or at best, left as simplified constructions of language, or of the mind. But if we remember that language tends to have symmetrical correspondences with the structure of nature, we may not be so surprised to learn that oddly similar kinds of structures have returned, in a very different set of circumstances.

The new emphasis on pattern-like structures has made us aware of certain recurrent classes of structural outlines that get created as a result of certain kinds of patterning processes. A long thin structure (such as a rod) that is moving otherwise freely about a fixed length fixed at the end (relative to other structures) delimits a kind of shell structure that takes on a characteristic pattern: a dome or sphere or hemisphere. A structure moving freely along the length of a tensioned cord and around it as an axis delimits a cylinder. And so on.

We need not posit a transcendent realm of such structures, other than to say that they are patterns that are consistently created by the interactive movements of other patterns — and made comprehensible by the symmetrical patterns of our own language and thinking. They are no more "independently real" than the word "sphere" is real, except as a generative possibility modeled within language. But so are vast numbers of other structures. These are simply structures that we find of particular interest, because they have a particularly simple and comprehensible genesis.

Moreover, the power of modern biology and mathematics is in its ability to move along a progression of complexity to much more esoteric structures — which, nonetheless, can also be comprehended through such a process of linguistic symmetry-mapping.

A particularly fascinating (and representative) example is what is known as an attractor. If one graphs complex phenomena according to their variable constituents (e.g. position, density, or other characteristics) it is often observed to be the case that certain patterns form around particular regions of the graph, for reasons that are not always obvious. These "attractor basins" are in fact similar to the limits of a radius that describes a sphere, but they are often much more complex and esoteric versions of the same kind of phenomenon. Indeed, some of these are so complex and odd that they have been dubbed "strange attractors" — quite odd graphical shapes that nonetheless take on strongly defined patterns (swirls, toruses, etc).

It turns out that such attractors occur all over — and they appear to be very important characteristics of the way things work, notably in biological processes. They are in fact the structures of the characteristic patterns that form within nature as the result of complex adaptive processes.

The biologist Brian Goodwin proposed that such "structural attractors" played a key role in the formation of biological structures within evolution. A dolphin's dorsal fin, for example, took on a characteristic but very complex shape as the result of highly complex interactions of turbulence processes in water, laminar flows and so on. The dolphin was solving the problem (or more accurately, the dolphin's evolutionary process was solving the problem) with a characteristic geometry, that was defined as the limit of the solution, just as the radius of a string defines the limit of a sphere. The shark, evolving from an entirely different animal class some 300 million years earlier, produced the nearly identical structure — for no other reason than that the complexity of the problem defined a similar structural attractor.

Going back to Plato, was the shape of a dorsal fin a timeless form, existing in some unseen realm? No, certainly not: it was a pattern that formed for comprehensible reasons, but one that formed repeatedly and consistently. We could name that pattern, and find use in the naming (i.e. repeated instances of application, or characteristic symmetries). The pattern may not be decomposable — and yet, it was comprehensible, through this new lens of nature.

Such patterns also have their counterpart in what physicists refer to as symmetry-breaking. A perfectly symmetrical universe would have no pattern at all: indeed, it would be a very dull place! But introduce a tiny break in that symmetry — a kind of grit within the oyster, so to speak — and fascinating things begin to happen. (This can be seen in a simple mathematical analogue, in the computer program called "Life" — a series of cells following rules "do nothing" until one tiny change is made in one cell — and instantly, a vast pattern is created across the screen.)

In a sense, this is a return to Plato's idealism, and to Aristotle's hylomorphism — but with a very notable twist. We are not appealing to any fundamental set of forms that are at the decomposable root of things, but rather, we are identifying a set of recurrent patterns that can be classed according to their tendency to coalesce into relative simplicity, or into what we may term "order." A sphere is indeed simpler than a dorsal fin — but they are both the same kind of structure within reality. They are both generated by the interactions of ultimately comprehensible structures. (Though in the case of the dorsal fin, that takes a great deal of time and effort.)

There is even an implied resolution of the age-old mystery of the "place" of mathematics. Is it, as Pythagoras suggested, a fundamental level of reality underlying all we see? This is no longer necessary: we can see the world instead as an inter-related field of isomorphic structures transforming in time. Thus the mathematical laws and categories of order are not residing in an unseen realm, but instead, are generated simpler structures that arise from the interactions of other more complex structures. They are, in effect, limit domains of generative possibility. They are symmetrical features (exhibiting partial symmetry-breaking) within the world of structure and process. They are, in a word, patterns.

But what is the ultimate reality of such a "pattern," then, as a distinct entity with generative possibility? And what is the ultimate reality of "possibility" itself? As far as we are concerned, ultimately these are "only" abstractions within our own brains (or in our computers, or on our papers.) But these are no less "real" structures in the world. It is our participatory interest in this isomorphic relationship — and our active deletion of parts of the reality in the isomorphism, through our powers of language and thought — that creates its generative power.

It is in the categorical confusion between what is "real" as a structure at the level at which our biological interest (and *a priori* participation) is usefully concerned, and the secondary or tertiary (or beyond) levels of abstractive self-reference, that the trouble begins. The trouble is in the seductive appearance of fundamental completeness, which does not exist.

So we can finally dispense with an external, transcendent realm of *Forms*, and shift our understanding to that of patterns. But in a powerful echo of Aristotle, Plato, and Pythagoras, we can classify these forms, or patterns, usefully, and see them as primary orders within certain contexts (again, being careful that we understand these abstractions for what they are, and taking care not to make categorical or fundamentalist errors).

Certainly these forms are primary with respect to the composition of a dolphin's body, say, or a shark's. And they are primary with respect to their repetition over time, and their ontogeny within an organism. Genetically speaking, they appear to be primary with respect to certain genome or proteome sequences within embryogenesis, which express themselves in the familiar form. They appear to originate as primary patterns within these structures.

Very interesting work suggests that these genetic sequences may in fact be clusters of pattern-like genetic sequences, functioning to bud and fold and shape dorsal fin structures, not unlike the sequences of origami. For example, Newman and Bhat (2008) have proposed a pattern-based model for the genesis of the Cambrian Explosion, which seems to offer a plausible (and very intriguing) model for the hylomorphic evolution of multi-cellular form.

If we are designers making houses, we might identify a corollary. Let us describe, for example, the shape of a column. Why does it exist as it does? We can ascertain structural tensions on its base and top that call for thickening at these points. We can describe efficient shapes that call for tapering of the shafts, or stiffening using rib-like flutes. We can describe the psychological needs of human beings who are in the presence of these columns, who may find a deep and pleasing biological resonance in their tree-like structure. This description of a column can amount to a structural attractor within architecture — and indeed, we can see columns with precisely this set of characteristics in cultures around the world.

We can now turn to larger structures — let us say, a porch structure — and consider similar questions. How does it connect the building to the public realm? What relation do people have with the street when they are within it, and simultaneously with the building? Are they able to interact with other people on the street, while having a sense of safe refuge, combined with an appealing sense of prospect? Does this add to the civic quality of the neighborhood?

And do the columns of such a porch also take on the shapes described above, which add to the psychological and structural coherence of the porch? Have we defined a structural type — a structural attractor of "porch" which has certain recurrent problem-solving value?

It becomes apparent that such recurrent patterns may have great value — if seen as such — and as elements that have components (columns, say) and that in turn combine into still larger elements (buildings, say). We need not take a rigidly hierarchical view of how such forms are composed, or pose a transcendent or fundamental class, but we can still see that there is a nested relationship between these recurrent and re-usable patterns — at least partially so. It presents us with a highly useful opportunity to make adaptive transformations of whole structures.

This "symmetric structuralist" view of nature does not diminish the capacity for meaning and value within a world of structure. On the contrary, as we will discuss in more detail below, it enriches the meaning and value of structure itself. Structure is thus not some dead shell: it is the domain where the phenomenon of life as we know it arises — and along with it, the related phenomena of quality, meaning and value.

And it appears to do so through the patterning of the interconnected wholes of structure, rather than through a simply conceived atomic assembly. The latter is a derivative abstraction. The former is, quite literally, where life happens — indeed, where we ourselves, living beings, already find ourselves immersed. Meaning is structural, and structure is meaningful. And there is much to say about how all this works, and how we may apply it to our own activities.

3. CHRISTOPHER ALEXANDER: MEREOLOGY IN PRACTICE

"The core of all living process is step-by-step adaptation — the modification and evolution which happen gradually in response to information about the extent to which an emerging structure supports and embellishes the whole."

— *Christopher Alexander,* The Nature of Order

It's likely that no architect illustrates — or indeed, develops — these ideas better than Christopher Alexander. As we discussed previously, his first book, *Notes on the Synthesis of Form*, was hailed at the time, as a landmark treatise in design theory. It launched him on his life's work in mereology, his own modern exploration of the relation between parts and wholes, and the structure of wholes — and thus, "wholeness" itself, as a structurally comprehensible phenomenon.

At the time the subject was the elements of a design problem, and how they may be solved through solution configurations that he called diagrams (and later, patterns). The context was the dawning of the cybernetic age, and the manifest problem of complexity in human technology — and in nature itself. (As mentioned before, the cybernetic pioneer Herbert Simon had two years earlier written his landmark paper on the same topic, "The Architecture of Complexity.")

But the ultimate subject was none other than Aristotle's hylomorphism, updated for technological modernity. Essentially Alexander asks, do parts simply "make" wholes, in some additive or compositional sense? Clearly not: the whole is somehow greater than the sum of the parts. Moreover, the whole in a sense makes the parts as much as the reverse. (This is particularly true for biological processes. We would not say that the leaves "make" the tree — on the contrary, it's clear that through a process of differentiation, the tree makes the leaves!)

Where things get particularly sticky is in the way the parts and wholes propagate out to other parts of the environment, and come back to interact in unexpected ways — a manifestly complex affair. How can this complexity be distilled down usefully to a salient "dia-

Opposite: A small tree that was kept in the yard of the Eishin School near Tokyo, Japan, designed by Christopher Alexander and associates.

gram," without losing some essential connectivity? For designers and technologists, how can we decompose this complexity — not to assume it is merely a reductive aggregation, but rather, so as to manage it effectively?

As I discussed in Section II, what Alexander observed was that the sets of diagrams — which as noted, he later termed "patterns" — were not perfectly nested into tree-like hierarchies. On the contrary, they contained subtle but important characteristics of "semi-lattices," or redundant networks — a property he called "overlap." This relatively small feature, easy to overlook, is not an accidental defect, but a critical property of natural systems — particularly living systems. Somehow, we needed to be sure our processes of diagramming and generating — our processes of using human abstractions — engaged this structural quality.

The consequences of failing to do so could be seen when looking at structures like cities — as Alexander showed in "A City is Not a Tree." He showed that cities also display this critical property of overlap, or "semi-lattice structure". But planned cities often lack the property — which, Alexander argued, accounts for their higher rates of failure and dysfunction. He did so through a brilliant set of simple examples and analyses of catastrophic failures of modern "planned" cities — thereby providing a comprehensible structural explanation for a critical modern failure. The paper was widely hailed as a landmark, but its core message was sadly ignored by most urban designers.

But this insight had important implications for design at many levels — and an important implication for Platonic idealism. One could "nearly decompose" a design problem (to use Herbert Simon's apt phrase) to useful effect, but one could never go so far as to reduce the problem to a purely elemental scheme without losing some essential vital attributes of the system. As Gödel showed, there can be no perfect blueprint of reality.

Further work on patterns

Alexander then asked the next question: how can we create a design tool or method that explicitly incorporates these overlaps, and generates these network-like attributes? As we now know, his answer was a "pattern language" — a structure of design elements that has hierarchical properties, but also network properties and the potential for overlap and ambiguity. The reference to language is more than an analogy, since languages also have the same combination of hierarchy-like overall form with the capacity for overlap, networks of meaning, and even intentional ambiguity. Indeed, this is what marks the distinction between a mere list of facts, or grammatical statement of the ordinary, and the power of literature or poetry. But something like this happens in ordinary circumstances too, Alexander argued, in the creation of ordinary environments and the ordering of ordinary events of human life.

This kind of ordering, he argued, did proceed routinely in human affairs as a matter of instinct. But in our modern (and neo-Hellenic) effort to be rational, we could too easily strip away this complex level of order, and leave ourselves greatly impoverished. Moreover, we could experience potentially catastrophic failures in our designs, no matter how well-intended, resulting in an increasingly unsustainable condition for technology and for civilization. Alexander's design theory was beginning to take on the outlines of a critique of technological modernity itself.

Mereology, wholeness and quality

But Alexander wanted to go deeper — into the workings of life itself, and its processes of creating form. What could we learn from the new scientific insights into these processes? What could we learn about how living systems achieve complexity, sustainability, even great beauty — doing so with prodigious quantities and at prodigious scales, through the marvelous working s of self-organization? What are the implications for modern human technology? The new insights of science were offering tantalizing new clues.

As we saw in section II, Alexander concluded that living systems do not use anything like a "little blueprint" or set of Platonic forms. Rather, they use coded processes to generate form, and these function rather like step-wise recipes. Though these processes can become dizzyingly complex in their iterative compounding, at heart they are relatively simple algorithms and can be understood in a fully rational way.

But second, these processes are transformational, and cannot be "run in reverse" in most cases (except as a simplifying abstraction, which inevitably loses important parts of the story). The transformations introduce progressive differentiation through the breaking of the symmetrical states that existed previously (e.g. a round egg splits and becomes a linear structure). And as this process unfolds, all of the parts are, to varying degrees, mutually adapting to one another — including parts that are not within the same originating cluster. This creates (to often small but important degrees) the quality of "overlap," and the network of inter-connections that is characteristic of complex systems.

The process can be seen clearly in embryogenesis, where the whole organism is going through a continuous transformation that preserves the whole, but also articulates new structures (Figure One). And the process is clearly coded according to simple chemical operations at the molecular scale — but operations that quickly become vastly complex and interactive at larger scales.

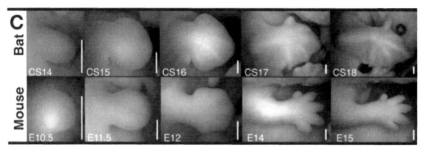

Figure III.3.1: Comparison of bat and mouse limb embryogenesis — a process of stepwise differentiation of wholes with new parts — but always preserving and extending the whole.

One can also see the same kind of process in non-living systems. For example, I previously described the simple process of a small droplet of milk striking a thin sheet of milk, in a famous series of photographs by Harold Edgerton. For this discussion I will present the images once again (Figure III.3.2). At any step of the process, there is a coherent whole with coherent parts (which indeed look strikingly like the articulation of arms and hands in embryogenesis). At each step, there is a comprehensible dynamic operating to transform those wholes and parts — at its heart, a relatively simple dynamic. But at each step, the wholes differentiate and articulate in new and often very surprising ways, giving rise to astonishing variety — even in a simple example like the milk drop.

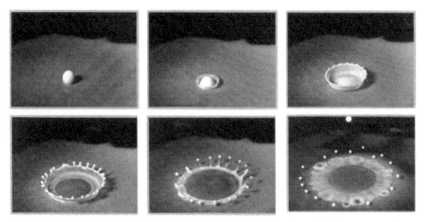

FIGURE III.3.2: Edgerton's famous series of photographs of a milk drop as it strikes a thin sheet of milk on a sheet

Again, there is a progressive differentiation, following a symmetry-breaking. There is a mutual interaction of all of the milk particles, with various forces they exert upon one another (most notably, the forces of surface tension). These forces can overlap across distinct regions, so that the motion of one droplet can pull on its neighbor through the surface tension of its arm. All of these generative processes result in distinct structural patterns, and can be identified as such. A "genetic recipe" could be created for generating just such a structure, and by varying the patterns of the initial setup (the thickness of the milk plane, say) one could vary the patterns that result.

Indeed, Alexander noted that such morphogenetic processes often give rise to the same characteristic sets geometries, whether in biology or in other natural systems: strong centers, boundaries, alternating repetition, levels of scale, local symmetries, and so on. These in turn can be tied to the detailed mechanics of the transformations, and the transformations of sets of "centers" or localized fields. This was a hylomorphism taken to a much more articulated level of description.

For Alexander, it was clear from new biological research that the processes that give rise to life are themselves natural, and can also produce structures that have equally life-like characteristics. More astounding, he concluded from this, and from his own empirical examples, that we can assess "degrees of life" in a given structure, including a human environment and, moreover, that this is no mere analogy, but a factual description of the characteristics of a given structure. (This is a controversial idea in some quarters, but seen from a new structuralist lens, it need not be: life is a kind of structural process, and it can and does occur in "precursor" forms.)

At an urban scale, a very similar kind of process could be seen at work. I previously shouwd the gradual transformation of the Piazza San Marco in Venice, which involves the same kind of transformation of wholes, the same kinds of articulations of new centers and the same kinds of differentiations of space into more articulated sub-spaces.

Philosophical implications:
The Place of value and the place of the quantitative

For Alexander, the structuralist, value can now be understood as the structure of what is living and thriving, and what promotes and enhances that structure. In this sense, what is valuable can be thought of as a kind of structural fitness to the *a priori* problem of living and thriving.

This will vary between individuals who are in competition, perhaps; they may certainly experience different value in the same outcome if it happens to benefit one but not the other, say, if a young woman chooses between two male suitors. (This example shows how Alexander can perfectly well accommodate diversity while retaining a sharable definition of value, countering a persistent claim of some critics of a pathetic fallacy or, worse, a "value foundationalism.") But, nonetheless, this value can be understood rationally as a kind of structure (in the example, the structure of courtship and family). Where individuals are cooperating, it can most certainly be shared.

But what is valuable is not exactly the same thing as what is qualitative. I may value or not value redness, but in either case I experience it as a quality. So what is this quality? What accounts for the qualitative dimension of things?

We know that in the case of redness, there is a wave pattern in the light energy emitting from a source, in the range of about 650 millionths of a meter from one wave peak to the next. If we change that frequency, the light consistently stops being red. (If we shrink the wave peaks to about 460 millionths of a meter, the light becomes "blue.") In a sense this is "all there is" to redness, but in another sense, it is only the beginning of what redness truly is.

For we can now begin to see that redness is a complex, emergent, but ultimately non-mysterious property, from the whole structural system that comprises me, my brain, my eye, the light source, the "red" object and its tendency to absorb non-red colors, and so on. The quality of redness can really only be explained as a systemic property of the whole system, that inextricably includes my body and all the other structures. It follows that to try to decompose the system into a set of simple parts is to miss the essential dynamics of the system — and its small but important connections to external components, too.

Moreover, we miss the capacity of the system to produce what we experience as "meaning," as the following example will illustrate. In a condition where some structural element of the system is not working in the same way — for those who have a very complex change in the color-processing structure of their brains as a result of a stroke, say — "redness" is not present. One could say, "Oh yes, 'red' is present, you just don't perceive it." But that is not actually true. What you have come to call 'red" as an abstraction is still present, — but not the emergent property of redness. This would be a little like saying, "Oh yes, the color "gruengepled" also exists at 5 millionths of a meter, you just don't perceive it, nor does anyone else." This would not be false so much as it would simply be meaningless. We are simply not interested in this structure, because it does not comprise a salient whole that is related to our experience. We do not call it a color, and if we describe it at all, it is for much more secondary reasons. For example, we might discover some property in the laboratory, far from ordinary experience, in which case we might name the frequency for its discoverer, but we would be very unlikely to describe it as anything so salient as a "color."

Again, to describe it as a color would be, quite literally, meaningless. And yet, we now see that describing redness as a color is certainly, by contrast, meaningful. In this way, Alexander brings us back to a comprehensible structuralist theory of meaning.

What is meaningful to us is very close to what "matters" to us as living structures, that is, what we encounter and consider important as organisms, in our *a priori* participation in the world (notwithstanding our ability to discern a partly decomposable structure to these phenomena). Indeed, "matter" is nothing other than what "matters to us," what is the matter, what is in the way, what is "material" to us. The abstractions we use are all secondary, and forever derivative of this *a priori* condition.

As Whitehead argued coherently and persuasively (in *Modes of Thought*, 1938), it is this sense of importance that is the logical antecedent of what we regard as "fact." And it is a kind of trick of the mind, or more precisely, an abstraction, to suppose the reverse is true. Abstractions are, of course, highly useful, but as abstraction, this is (again as Whitehead so effectively pointed out) an omission of part of the truth.

Again, there is surely a comprehensible biological basis to all this. Going back to the example of redness, there may be (and surely are) other structural phenomena going on, of which we may be unaware (for example, the way certain perceptual processes work, the shifts in color perception with certain adjacencies, and so on). But the important point is, we are able to take in all these (comprehensible but complex) structural conditions, and experience an emergent quality. This is very likely closely associated with the need for living systems to make rapid determinations of large fields of stimuli.

Thus I can very quickly perceive the redness of a fire raging near me, at the same time that I can perceive a blue sky in the other direction that offers escape. I can no less quickly detect the alarming smell of burning wood, which must go through a series of highly complex and subtle processes on the way to my brain. Indeed I routinely make exceedingly complex (in fact vastly complex) syntheses of what is going on structurally, and experience these complex inputs as qualitative feelings. I can then act as an organism in a way that is most likely to preserve and enhance my own structure.

Thus we also have a structuralist theory of quality, and of feeling, rooted not only in biological needs, but in the complex structure of biological wholes. I may feel well or ill, happy or sad, based upon vast numbers of complex internal and external inputs, structurally transformed. But my feeling and the quality of the things I perceive, are not simple atomic states, but vast fields of wholes, whose structure is vastly intricate, rich, and varied.

Moreover, based upon my definition of choices through the agency of thinking and language and its vast transformational powers, I can then take actions to alter them and do so with my fellows, thereby creating the very dynamic of culture and of life. But I must do so with skill and care, so as not to make categorical errors, or misuse the capacity of abstraction to tease out these useful structural insights.

If I do this with care, I find that the structures I make have a biological suitability to them that is extremely gratifying to me. I find their aesthetic character to be beautiful. I find that they gratify important biological and cultural needs which are, to varying degrees, both innate and malleable. There is a deep capacity for cultural creativity.

Again, this is seen as a natural structure at heart, though it is astonishingly vast. But this structural essence in no way reduces what it is to feel or to experience these powerful structural processes of life. It only means that we can also come to know these processes, in our capacity to "see," isomorphically, their essentially structural, and at the same time interconnected and (to us as organisms) meaningful aspects.

An example from music can make the point very well. I find Bach's Prelude Number 1 from "The Well-Tempered Clavier" to be quite beautiful, and indeed I can find a particular passage with a sudden A flat note particularly beautiful and emotionally powerful. But if I pull that A flat out of the song, it has no power by itself whatsoever. It is not an independent element that can be added to others to produce a simple cumulative compositional effect;, rather, its power comes from its place in a field of relationships. The symmetry of these relationships to parts of my own brain and to the parts of my life is deeply pleasing and beautiful.

This one small example engages the Pythagorean ratios of the musical vibrations; the physics of hearing; the high level of neuroprocessing in my brain; the evolutionary function of my perception of sound; the cultural tempering of my perception of music (including the tempering of the scale, itself a profound structural innovation); the structuring of my own appreciation for music and for this piece in particular; and so on. In just this example, we begin to see the vast complexity of everyday experience.

The universe is thus shot through with meaning, and it is shot through with structure. It is alive, and at the same time, it is structural. There is no conflict.

We will discuss the implications for designers in more detail below. But one implication is dramatic: characteristics of the built environment do carry relative value for individuals — and that value can, to varying degrees, be shared. The beautiful (like the good and the true) is not so much in the eye of the beholder, as it is in the complex structural resonance between an individual and the world around. This is a comprehensible state of affairs — one with important implications for designers.

4. JANE JACOBS: THE KIND OF PROBLEM DESIGN IS

"Cities happen to be problems in organized complexity, like the life sciences. They present 'situations in which a half-dozen or even several dozen quantities are all <u>varying simultaneously and in subtly interconnected ways</u>'.... The variables are many, but they are not helter-skelter; they are 'interrelated into an organic whole.'"

— *Jane Jacobs,* The Death and Life of Great American Cities

As should be clear by now, Jane Jacobs was another remarkable polymath with a notable structuralist line of thinking. Her seminal urban work *The Death and Life of Great American Cities* was published in 1961, around the same time Alexander was developing his PhD thesis. Like Alexander, Jacobs wanted to know how our design processes were going wrong and destroying the life and quality of modern cities. Like Alexander, she cautioned against the modern planners' technocratic habit to impose a reductive scheme on cities in top-down fashion. And like Alexander, she did not simply bemoan the state of affairs, but gave a lucid and detailed account of the structure of what was really going on — and what could be done about it.

We saw previously her remarkably lucid account, in the last chapter of *The Death and Life of Great American Cities,* of the development of modern complexity science (expressing a debt to Dr. Warren Weaver of the Rockefeller Foundation). Like Alexander, she described the mereology of many variables acting together, and the importance of understanding their web-like interconnections, beyond the simple connection of a few variables or the average behavior of many variables. This was where living systems seemed to operate, in the realm that she described as "organized complexity."

Like Alexander, she too applied the analogy of living systems — or perhaps for her, too, it was more than an analogy — to the "life" of cities. We needed to look for the subtle ways that variables of an urban system interacted, and we needed to respect the subtle and "unaverage" factors that might be accounting for much more than we might assume. (There are parallels with Alexander's "overlap" here.)

Opposite: *Jerusalem's historic market. Photo by Esther Inbar via Wikimedia Commons.*

We must understand "the kind of problem a city is," in its "organized complexity," as a kind of biological problem.

As I noted previously, one of Jacobs' most important contributions after *The Death and Life of Great American Cities* was in the field of economics. We must come to understand that economics is a dynamic system, she says, like any natural system (argued most powerfully in her book *The Nature of Economies*). However, as in any such system, the feedback within the system can become disrupted, or provide false signals. Therefore our culture can experience perverse incentives, and behave irrationally. What seems sane and rational can in fact be a kind of noise from the echo chambers of specialists.

Jacobs was of course a powerful critic of modern planners, who seemed intent upon achieving a rational order by purifying the "messiness" of urban systems — a conception of planning she scathingly referred to as "decontaminated sortings." This was an echo of Alexander's critique of the modern treatment of cities as mathematical "trees" — and the failure to understand the overlap and complexity within their structures. Instead, Jacobs argued for mixing of uses, and for much greater diversity within a given neighborhood.

Jacobs was no less withering toward architects, and particularly those who, like Le Corbusier, sought to replace the complex intrinsic order of the city with an extrinsic, purely visual order from above. A city is not a work of art, she argued, and must not be treated as so much canvas on which to express one's compositional imagination. This was a confusion that substituted real cities with simplified images of them:

> His conception, as an architectural work, had a dazzling clarity, simplicity, and harmony. It was so orderly, so visible, so easy to understand. It said everything in a flash, like a good advertisement... But as to how the city works, it tells, like the Garden City, nothing but lies.

In a sense, Jacobs was sounding a final rejection of the modernists' form of Platonic idealism, which had culminated in a particularly destructive kind of "geometrical fundamentalism." However, as should be clear by now, she was no hand-wringing, laissez-faire post-structuralist. She argued convincingly — and highly influentially — for a new approach to cities, using patient inductive methods and tools, and an inter-disciplinary approach that respected what already existed and what was already working. It distrusted simplified theories of order that masqueraded as real order and relied instead on keen observation of local differentiation and complexity. It was a pragmatic recipe that combined design with programming, sociology with economics, and theory with common sense.

Quality of life: A new pragmatism, a new structuralism

Alexander and Jacobs both represent a point of view that sees the now catastrophic failings of modernity as fully repairable — if we learn the structural lessons on hand. They both seek to learn those lessons from biological process, and from the burgeoning new sciences of complexity. They both see the inevitable qualitative aspects of the problem and its diagnosis. They both see the creation of cities and buildings as a largely emergent and self-organizing process — but one in which human valuation, and human design, play a profound role.

But "design" here is not the combinatorial hylomorphism of Aristotle, nor the abstract mathematical idealism of Plato. Rather, it is more a discipline that must make transformational steps in the inter-relation of patterns to one another — be they patterns in space or patterns in ideas. And of course, it is more accurate now to say that there is no fundamental difference between the two: the world can now be seen to contain a web of patterns that have the capacity to mirror each other in certain useful, language-like aspects. These patterns are to be found throughout the built environment, in our brains, and in other parts of the world. It is a pattern universe.

Alexander and Jacobs are but two of the most prominent of a larger number who are taking forward these insights in different disciplines, and to different degrees. Among these, the growing field of evidence-based design is well worth mentioning. It began in the patient healthcare environment, and gradually spread out into other environments where there is evidence of health impacts. (For example, so-called "obesogenic" suburban environments, where lack of exercise and dependence on drive-through cuisine are contributing to alarming rises in rates of obesity in the USA and, to an increasing extent, other countries.)

There can be dangers in trying to couple evidence too mechanically to design: if this discussion has shown anything, it is that such a combinatorial mereology does not work. But we can begin to see that by using inductive processes, provisional patterns, and then adaptive refinements, an empirical, evidence-based approach can be highly fruitful.

One of the most surprising new discoveries in the field of environmental design is in the health impacts of various aesthetic characteristics. Many researchers have noticed that certain characteristics in the built environment consistently produce beneficial health effects, while others do not. For example, Ulrich (1984) showed that patients with a view of a natural scene recovered from surgery more quickly and successfully than those who had a view of a blank wall. Other natural features, like plants, water, sunlit scenes, and the like had similar effects, so much so that there is now a major effort to retrofit hospitals with gardens and other such amenities.

This discovery of the importance of natural structures in the human environment — what has come to be termed "biophilia" — seems a promising avenue for future research. It seems very likely that there is an evolved preference for such structures. More than that, as Alexander's work suggests, it may be that such structures offer denser, richer structural wholes, which meet our needs as human beings within our environments. This may be the key to the importance of beauty in our lives.

Nor is this likely to be purely a matter of visual scenery. Indeed, some research shows that the effect from purely visual scenes fades rapidly. It seems more likely that the strongest effect comes from our ability to move through environments, interact with people, view prospects, seek refuge, frame views, experience filters of sight and sound that we find the richest experiences in the built environment.

This finding suggests that while the perception of users is critical to their well-being, the usual architects' emphasis on the composition of buildings as objects or urbanists' treatment of cityscapes as visual scenes, is highly incomplete. We must focus much more on the system of connections and the layers and filters between the zones of connection — that is, on the sequences of possible experiences — if we are to have the most robust, thriving kind of environments. Again, the logic of such sequences is a language-like structure. Again, this invokes a deeper sense of what we call beauty.

This finding also has another important implication. Built environment professionals must regard themselves as having a deep responsibility for the health of their users. They are not mere engineers of transportation networks, or artist-architects of visual or sculptural compositions. They are a kind of physician to the built environment.

THE STRUCTURALIST RENAISSANCE

"By far the greatest and most admirable form of wisdom is that needed to plan and beautify cities and human communities."

— *Plato*, The Republic

How can we sum up these scientific and philosophical lessons for designers? I would suggest that they point us toward a profound reformation of the methodologies of design — methodologies that will, in their essential outlines, be less like the creative processes of artists, and more like the diagnostic processes of physicians. (It is important to note that the artist's creativity is certainly not eliminated, but is re-integrated into a larger process.) Or, to use another useful metaphor, our design approach might be less like that of a carpenter (planning and blueprinting a structure, then milling, cutting, assembling, etc.) than that of a gardener (planting seeds, watering, pruning, weeding, building trellises, etc.) As Jacobs and Alexander remind us, we must plan for the unplanned, and design for emergence. And there is indeed a rational discipline for doing so.

Broadly speaking, we might describe the steps in such a design process as follows:

- A sequence of design actions will proceed principally as a series of rule-based transformational steps.

- That sequence must begin by recognizing and adapting to initial conditions as a whole.

- This requires a careful qualitative diagnosis of "initial conditions." (e.g. the physician begins not with a battery of tests, but by asking "how are you feeling?"

- These qualitative characteristics are "really real"—and largely sharable.

- This carries implications for the value of collaborative design strategies.

Several other important consequences flow from this as well:

Opposite: A public space in Guanajuato, Mexico.

- We must respond to the evidence of what will succeed in design, using inductive methods, rather than relying solely upon the deductive conclusions of theory;

- We cannot do so in elemental fashion, but rather, we must do so through the provisional adoption of wholes, and their adaptive modification as needed;

- These wholes can be thought of as design patterns, together with general rules for their transformation and local adaptation;

- Wholes that have gone through adaptive evolution may require further adaptation, but nonetheless are likely to be far superior to novel elemental combinations.

The last point is worth dwelling upon. For several generations we have taken a largely reductionist, *tabula rasa* approach to design, imagining that we can "start from scratch" and "use our imagination" and assemble elemental structures to compose wonderful, functional, effective designs. But we can now see this for the dangerous fallacy that it is. We can see that we have relied too heavily upon only one of the principal strategies of design synthesis — that of reduction and re-combination — and we have failed to understand the power of induction and differentiation.

There is another, related danger of the modern fundamentalist method. It is in the inherent danger of abstractions, to lure us away from the discipline of rigorous adaptivity, and into the enchanting realm of pure abstract synthesis. Alfred North Whitehead touched on this theme often, and nowhere better than when he noted, in his 1938 book *Modes of Thought*:

> Mankind is distinguished form animal life by its emphasis on abstractions. The degeneracy of mankind is distinguished from its uprise by the dominance of chill abstractions, divorced from aesthetic content.

Or, we might add, it is distinguished by abstractions that provide their own derivative aesthetic qualities, which can be dangerously disconnected from the immediate realities of place and life.

There are many other implications awaiting further development. We summarize several of the most notable here:

- Design is not principally a process of creating novel compositional objects, but principally of creating new fields of relationships between existing structures.

- These relationships are of central importance in their potential to provide sequences of experience for human users, and sequences of relationships.

- At the urban level, these relationships will meet human needs, and thus likely include: degrees of high or low social interaction; degrees of high or low activity versus tranquility; degrees of admittance of sight, sound, smell, through a series of layered zones; degrees of public or private, semi-public or semi-private space.

- The zones in which these factors vary have definable geometric properties, which can be identified from the largest urban scales, down to the smallest architectural and detailed scales. Their qualities must contain a continuous interrelationship, even as they contain contrasts and high variability.

- These geometries can in fact be coded into algorithmic processes, as is demonstrated by natural morphogenesis, and the high degree of adaptive coherence that emerges through such a process. There are similar processes within existing traditional design systems, and within their repositories of patterns, which are available for useful adaptation and transformation.

- This opens the door to an exciting new class of "generative code," able to achieve some of the adaptive coherence of previous traditional settlements—but without necessarily requiring the same set of social and political conditions. (Including conditions now thought to be reactionary or otherwise inappropriate.)

- More broadly, this opens the door to new kinds of cultural processes, which are themselves subject to the same principles of "design." Indeed, such processes are increasingly integral to the design activity.

- Such cultural processes include more responsive and adaptive economic, political, and social processes, incorporating new insights into the dynamics of game theory, feedback theory, open-source processes, and much other exciting recent work that carries forward and implements these insights.

This discussion is by necessity the briefest overview of a vast and burgeoning subject. But we hope it does suggest the progress that awaits, and the many avenues that are available for further development.

Moreover, as we hope this discussion has shown, we now stand at a critical kind of culmination, and, we can hope, the beginning of a new chapter, of a very long historical dialogue on mereology, hylomorphism, and idealism. In a sense, we have not strayed far from Hellenic culture — and indeed, in modernity we find that we have returned to our own philosophical origins, where, in the words of T.S. Eliot, we "know the place for the first time." We have come back to Plato's idealism, in the patterns and the structural attractors of modernity; and we have come back to Aristotle's hylomorphism, in modern complexity science, and in Alexander's structure-preserving transformations. And yet, we have also taken important steps to transcend them, and to resolve age-old apparent paradoxes between matter and value, and form and life. If this is true, then it may free us from the prison of our former ideas, and place us on the edge of a veritable renaissance of structural and qualitative possibility, within our technology, and within our culture. May that much-needed renaissance begin.

SECTION IV:

OPPORTUNITIES AND THREATS

1. TOWARD A NEW URBAN AGENDA

"In general, the urban community has become lost in strategic planning, masterplanning, zoning and landscaping ... All these have their own purposes, of course — but they don't address the principal question, which is the relationship in a city between public space and buildable space. This is the art and science of building cities — and until we recover this basic knowledge, we will continue to make huge mistakes."

— *Joan Clos, Secretary-General, Habitat III*

As I described briefly in the introduction, in October 2016 the United Nations held its third Habitat conference, Habitat III (otherwise known as the "United Nations Conference on Housing and Sustainable Urban Development"). Begun in 1976, and focusing initially on rural development issues, the conference ran again in 1996 ("Habitat II") with a focus on sustainable development, and again in 2016 ("Habitat III"), with a focus on rapid urbanization, environmental deterioration, and the challenge of providing quality of life for urban residents.

In a sense, Habitat III asks challenging questions about the role of professionals (especially environmental designers) in meeting human challenges and promoting quality of life. How can they do so by using the evidence of what has succeeded and what has not? How can the work of the sciences inform this task, and provide a more effective response? How should governments support, empower and, if necessary, compel the work that is needed to ensure human well-being in the future?

This comes at a time when the world is urbanizing at a rate never before seen in history. Indeed, at current rates, the area of new urbanization created over the next five decades may exceed the area created through all of human history to the present.

This is a staggering fact, not least because of the disturbingly low quality of much of the present urbanization. This urbanization falls into two main categories. On the one hand, formerly rural immigrants are populating new "informal settlements" with poor sanitation, limited access to urban opportunity, criminal predation, and other serious environmental deficiencies. On the other hand, new "market-rate" development is often sprawling, fragmented, automobile-

Opposite: *Delegates entering a Habitat III conference venue in Quito, Ecuador.*

dependent, and extremely resource-inefficient. As my own research has shown, the implications for greenhouse gas emissions as well as other impacts on critical resources are nothing short of catastrophic, for the well-being of the species in future generations (if not sooner).

This urbanization is not only wasteful. The evidence suggests that it is deficient in the very qualities that urbanism offers to its residents, namely, opportunities for contact, creative exchange, and human development. These opportunities are particularly important for women and disadvantaged populations. Instead of promoting greater quality of life for larger numbers of people with lower impacts on resources, it seems that modern cities have somehow managed to give us the worst of both worlds: limited and inequitable human development, with a catastrophic cost for the environmental resources on which human well-being and even survival ultimately depend.

This is the urgent backdrop of the "New Urban Agenda." It seems that something has gone terribly wrong with our "modern" structuring of cities and towns, down to its very conception of what a city is — and this has happened at just the historic moment when we need to engage cities and urbanization to achieve their very best.

It is here that the question of professional responsibility arises most clearly. Certainly there are questions for economic systems, for governance, and for technological efficiency. But at another level, there are disturbing questions for the role of architects and urban designers — or more accurately, the role they have willfully abdicated. They can respond, and thus they are responsible.

The New Urban Agenda calls on architects and urban designers (among others) to support the creation of "well-designed networks" of "safe, inclusive, accessible, green, quality" public space systems, including streets, thereby providing access to "sustainable cities and human settlements for all". It calls for "appropriate compactness and density, polycentrism and mixed uses," in order to "prevent urban sprawl, reduce mobility challenges and needs and service delivery costs per capita and harness density and economies of scale and agglomeration" for human development and well-being. It also calls for "measures that allow for the best possible commercial use of street-level floors, fostering both formal and informal local markets and commerce, as well as not-for-profit community initiatives, bringing people into public spaces and promoting walkability and cycling with the goal of improving health and well-being."

This is, in other words, the same agenda outlined by Jacobs and Alexander — the model of cities as fully walkable, diverse, human-scale places, in which buildings line streets and other important public spaces, providing active edges and dynamic networks of interaction. Nowhere is to be seen the "loose sprawls" of functional segregation criticized by Jane Jacobs, or the "project land oozings" of Le Corbusier's "Towers in the Park". Nowhere are the privatized shopping malls of Victor Gruen. Nowhere are the supercampuses and superblocks, or the segregation of pedestrians from vehicles, or other hallmarks of CIAM modernist planning. Nowhere is the static conception of cities as modernist artistic creations, glorifying the industrialization of the human environment. Instead, the city is an evolutionary co-creation of myriad people, a dynamic network of human interaction and placemaking.

The New Urban Agenda also calls for the re-incorporation of "cultural heritage, both tangible and intangible, in cities and human settlements" as well as "traditional knowledge and the arts." It demands implementation "tapping into all available traditional and innovative sources at the global, regional, national, subnational and local levels."

There are crucial economic dimensions as well. As Jane Jacobs long argued, and as I explored in the first section of this book, cities have the capacity to promote enormous human development and wealth in all its forms. But to do so, they must be properly structured to foster diverse interactions over a continuous urban network, in what Jacobs referred to as "thoroughgoing city mobility and fluidity of use."

We saw in Section I how this city network must reside primarily in the structure of public spaces, including streets and other pathways. Of course many connections do occur in private and semi-public places, like office meeting rooms, conference venues, shop floors, restaurants and other gathering places. Many more occur over communications networks, including email and phone. But all of them have their "spine" as it were, in the public space system of the city, the ultimate connector between diverse people. As the sociologist Robert Putnam has pointed out, social networks can be "multi-stranded" with many layers of connection, but all of them have to have a physical and public component at their root.

Accordingly, the New Urban Agenda places notable emphasis on public space, recognizing the fundamental role of streets and other public spaces as "drivers of social and economic development," "enhancing safety and security, favoring social and inter-generational interaction and the appreciation of diversity" as well as "promoting walkability and cycling towards improving health and well-being." As Habitat III Secretary-General Joan Clos observed, a city without public spaces is not really a city at all.

And yet we continue to build just such non-cities, sprawling across the globe in chaotic bursts of fragmented development. Sometimes they are informal settlements for the poor, lacking in adequate, safe and inclusive public spaces. Sometimes they are more expensive developments for the middle and upper classes, featuring privatized shopping malls, gated neighborhoods, and vast stretches of automobile-dominated, resource-intensive sprawl. Although these new developments do carry some positive benefits, especially the alleviation of the problems of poverty, evidence demonstrates that their negative impacts on social, ecological and economic sustainability will be profound.

On this last point, recent history ought to be instructive. In the 2008 global financial crisis, it was little noted that the beginning of the crisis — its "Ground Zero" was in fact the sprawling, car-dependent suburbs of the United States. This was the first major "hangover" from the "crack cocaine" of economic development that is sprawl, as I have argued previously.

The pattern of foreclosure maps from US cities at the time is telling. In city after city, strong clusters can be seen along an outer ring of "drive 'til you qualify" suburbs — cheaper far-out subdivisions with easy-terms mortgages, located far from most jobs and services. Inside these donut rings, higher-density urban areas had far fewer foreclosures. It was not a coincidence that these inner areas were more compact, walkable, transit served — that is, lower-carbon, and less sensitive to the rising energy costs that pushed many homeowners over the edge, triggering a wave of cascading mortgage defaults.

Figures IV.1.1 and IV.1.2: Foreclosure maps in the USA, precipitating the global financial crisis of 2008. The foreclosure rates were far higher in the exurban "drive 'til you qualify" suburbs. Left, Denver. Right, Houston. (Sources: Denver Post, Houston Chronicle.)

Indeed, this Ground Zero precipitated the worldwide financial crisis of 2008, and the "great recession" that ensued. The rise in energy prices, a cyclical recession, and the re-adjustment of artificially cheap mortgages, all converged into a "perfect storm" of economic distress. But this was no mere freak event. It was very likely a harbinger of more and worse to come, if we don't get to the core problems that created it: interlocking failures of finance, regulation, energy use, planning and design.

We knew that these cookie-cutter suburbs were overly dependent on cheap fossil fuels, and profligate with other resources. Research shows that their carbon footprint alone, taken as a planetary model, would quickly swamp all other efforts to get a handle on greenhouse gas emissions. In fact this is uncomfortably close to the model still in too much of the US, and in too many other parts of the world.

But what was truly breathtaking was how soon the scheme collapsed financially, with such global economic devastation. We might have been forgiven for thinking we had a few more decades of this cheap ride on unsustainable resource use. On the contrary, we saw that what was ecological had already become economic — or more precisely, what was unecological had become uneconomic.

So for this and the other reasons already mentioned — public health, social interaction, ecological benefits — the New Urban Agenda ought to be welcome news indeed for those who are concerned about the proliferation of sprawl, and the need for a return to the principles advocated by Jacobs and Alexander. Indeed, the Agenda is a hard-won achievement for the many people who participated in its development.

But of course, there remains an enormous challenge of implementation. While it is gratifying to have a "new urbanism" (by any other name) on the agenda, this is only the start of the work ahead. Now the challenge is to find the levers of change, and to alter what we may think of as the "operating system of growth" to generate a more benign kind of urbanism and architecture. And in this work, it will be critical to employ an evidence-based approach, rooted in the rigorous methods of science, and the knowledge of what works and does not work.

Particularly important will be the role of planning and design professionals, as Jacobs and Alexander long argued. As I will discuss in the next chapter, that reform process is well under way — and its continuing controversies help us to see the nature of the work remaining.

2. OLD URBANISM, NEW URBANISM?*

The global destruction of cities and countryside, of human cultures and of nature itself, can only be reversed by a global philosophical, technical, cultural, moral and economic project: by an ecological project. The city is not the unavoidable result of a society's activities. It can only be built and maintained when it represents the goal of individuals, of a society and its institutions. A city is not an economic accident but a moral project. Forms of production ought no longer to dictate the form of the city; but the form of the city, its organic nature and moral order, must qualify and shape the forms of production and exchange.

— *Léon Krier*

Of all the urban movements of the early 21st Century, New Urbanism may be the most explicit in acknowledging a foundational influence from Alexander and, especially, Jacobs. New Urbanism is certainly one of the most prominent movements within the urban planning and design professions, and a force that must be reckoned with. It may also be one of the most controversial, for a mix of reasons that are worth examining carefully.

Perhaps the simplest and most accurate way of describing New Urbanism, and its nominal membership body, the Congress for the New Urbanism (CNU), is that both are modeled after the enormously influential CIAM (Congrès International d'Architecture Moderne), the early 20th Century movement that set the blueprint for modernist city design. Like the founders of the CIAM, CNU founders believed that conscious design by professionals must play a role in the establishment of humane and enduring (or as we would term it today, "sustainable") cities.

However, the CNU was not conceived as an extension of the CIAM, but as the agent of its overthrow. The founders of the CNU placed much of the blame for the unsustainability of modern cities — their profligate resource use, fragmented social relationships, declining inner neighborhoods, and sprawling suburbs — at the feet of the CIAM

---

* *Portions of this essay were also published in the book Sustainable Urban Forms: Theory, Design and Application, edited by Bashir Kazimee, published by Cognella, 2016.*

Opposite: *The walkable mixed-use and transit-oriented suburban community of Orenco Station, on the Portland light rail line, where the author served as project manager.*

leadership, and what are now characterized as their catastrophic mistakes. At the same time, the CNU was only too eager to exploit the successful strategies of the CIAM to create a new reformation.

As part of its strategy, the CIAM created a "charter" that embodied its core concepts of city-making. The Athens Charter was formally published in 1943 by Le Corbusier. In an exhaustive series of 95 points (echoing Martin Luther's Ninety-Five Theses that launched the Protestant Reformation), the book documented the key concepts that had already emerged from a series of CIAM conferences, culminating in a plenary meeting in 1933. The meeting had taken place aboard a cruise ship, the SS Patris, traveling from Marseilles to Athens — the latter city giving the document its name.

Key elements of the Athens Charter can be summarized as follows:

- **Function-based zoning.** Work, home, recreation and transport were to be segregated into zones carefully planned according to a rational scheme of spatial allocation. Further separations were to be made between office, industrial and other commercial uses. These zones were to be organized into large functional units, including pedestrian-only "superblocks".

- **Functionally restricted streets.** The use of streets as mixed public and pedestrian spaces was to be banished (expressed in Le Corbusier's famous pronouncement, "we must kill the street"). Instead, pedestrians were to be removed to their own circulation network (typically within superblocks, or in grade-separated crossings). Streets, now for vehicles only, were to be widened and spaced farther apart, with fewer intersections and access points. A functional classification system was to be introduced to allocate separate lanes and roads based on vehicle speed.

- **Segregation of buildings.** Buildings were no longer to line or enclose streets to form continuous urban fabric; rather, each building was to be set far back from streets, and set away from other buildings in a clear functional layout. Residents were to have access to fresh air and light afforded by tall buildings and grade-separated pedestrian paths.

- **Demolition of historic fabric and pattern.** Apart from a few exceptional cultural relics, historic buildings and neighborhoods were to be torn down to make way for more hygienic and functionally efficient architecture that was more appropriate to the age of machinery and industrial production. Under no circumstances must any stylistic features from the past be re-used in the new architecture, as it would amount to "mingling the false with the genuine."

- **The city as a technical creation by specialists**. Cities were to be rationally planned through a top-down process, with speed, efficiency, and economies of scale and standardization as overriding goals. Technical specialists armed with statistical information must control the design and management of the form of cities, through a centralized control process. The rights of private individuals must be subordinated to collective need, as defined and enforced by these specialists.

- **The city as a designed end state rather than an open, evolutionary, form-creating process.** The goal of design was to create a static solution, rather than a dynamic process. On the contrary, cities were seen as too chaotic, too messy, and there was not enough clarity of order.

In all these respects, architecture (through urban design) would provide the guiding expertise for city-making. The new model — rational, mechanical, industrial, with the car at its center — would be a powerful new force for economic development. This development would not oppress human beings, but on the contrary, liberate them, by providing a new kind of mobility within a productive, rationally ordered world.

We can note two facts about the car-based CIAM vision. One is that it was extraordinarily successful: what was built was remarkably faithful to the CIAM outlines, and it did indeed fuel stupendous economic growth, notably in the United States. Indeed, much of the sprawling suburbia of the United States, though often stylistically different from Le Corbusier's pristine modernism, closely followed the blueprint of the Radiant City: wide streets, spread across a functionally classified hierarchy, segregated land uses, and large districts of monocultural building types (tract houses, strip centers, industrial superblocks, and corporate office towers in green park-like settings).

The other fact is that the success of the CIAM vision has left us with an enormous challenge for the Twenty-First Century: how to manage rapid depletion of resources, destruction of ecosystems, toxic pollution, and, more recently, the ominous threat of climate change. To this unsustainability of natural resource impacts, we can add the apparent unsustainability of social and economic systems.

During the 1960s and 1970s, growing numbers of citizens began to decry the perceived failures of CIAM-inspired post-war projects, and a number of articulate critics also rose up to rally the opposition. They included Paul Goodman, whose 1971 book *After the Planners* galvanized many local citizen groups; Oscar Newman, whose 1973 book *Defensible Space* critiqued the amorphous pedestrian realms of CIAM plans; Léon Krier, whose writings and drawings were highly influential (and whose quote begins this chapter); and Peter Blake, whose 1977 book *Form Follows Fiasco* savaged the very notion of functionalism at the heart of the CIAM.

But the most influential critics of all were, of course, Jane Jacobs and Christopher Alexander, whose ideas we have already examined as powerful critiques of the elements of the CIAM model.

Jacobs, Alexander and the others inspired a generation of architects and urban designers to embrace a new approach to urbanism: more diverse, more contextual, and more respectful of the existing patterns of nature, history and human activity. Along with "Postmodernist" critics in architecture, who argued for a revival of pre-Modernist building types, they argued for the return of traditional street and neighborhood types.

Flash forward to 1975, when California Governor Jerry Brown appointed the Berkeley architect Sim Van der Ryn as State Architect, responsible for planning the government's facilities in Sacramento. Van der Ryn, a friend and colleague of Christopher Alexander, enlisted his fellow Berkeley architect Peter Calthorpe to help in completing a series of innovate "green building" projects for the State. But the two quickly realized that buildings alone were not enough, and it was important to deal with urban form — and especially, alternatives to CIAM-style automobile-based planning. For Calthorpe, the concept of "transit-oriented development" came to be at the heart of his thinking: we need development patterns that allow people to get out of their cars, and walk, bike or ride transit to close-by destinations. This can only be done if we integrate public transit with all the other modes of travel.

Around the same time, ecologists Mike and Judy Corbett decided to build a prototype community to serve as a demonstration alternative to the auto-dominated sprawl they saw all around them. In addition to his training in ecology, Mike Corbett was also an architect. Like Calthorpe, he too became persuaded that green buildings in isolation were not enough" and that the unecological, land-consuming patterns of American sprawl had to be changed. Their project, Village Homes, featured skinny pedestrian-friendly and bike-friendly streets, diverse home types, ecological water runoff facilities, and "green" homes, in a compact street-fronting layout.

On the other side of the continent, architecture students Andrés Duany and Elizabeth Plater-Zyberk were studying at Yale University, and living in an old Victorian neighborhood near campus. After studying Jacobs, Alexander and other reformers, they went home to observe the marvelous successes of their own neighborhood firsthand. Thanks in part to encouragement from their professor, Vincent Scully, and influence from the Luxembourg architect Léon Krier, they came to believe that they too could build a new town that was a radical departure from the sprawling, homogenized model of CIAM-inspired development. In 1981 their clients, Robert and Daryl Davis, commissioned the planning of Seaside, Florida, which also featured a dense network of skinny, pedestrian-friendly streets, mixed uses, native vegetation and other features. The buildings were also more ecologically designed, with smaller footprints, natural ventilation, and climate-appropriate regional and vernacular construction.

Calthorpe, Duany and the Corbetts were certainly not the only ones experimenting with a "new urbanism." Calthorpe's Berkeley colleague Dan Solomon worked with Alexander and others on innovative new urban design projects based on "pattern languages" of traditional urban form. In the suburban towns of Los Angeles, Stefanos Polyzoides and Elizabeth Moule were also developing new projects that built on historical urban patterns.

The USA was also not the only place that was experiencing a new generation of so-called "neo-traditional" urban developments. In France, François Spoerry, impressed with the power of traditional urban cores, developed new urban settlements such as Port Grimaud, near Marseilles, as early as the 1960s. Spoerry overtly rejected the principles of CIAM, including its prohibition of traditional and vernacular forms. Léon Krier, whose effect on Duany and Plater-Zyberk was, by their own description, profound, was also involved in a series of European projects, as was his brother Rob. Other architects had been defying the CIAM urban agenda for many years, including Maurice Culot (Belgium) and Quinlan Terry (UK).

In 1979, Judy Corbett was hired by California Governor Jerry Brown to direct the Local Government Commission, an agency created to facilitate "innovation in local environmental sustainability, economic prosperity and social equity." After Brown's term ended, the LGC was re-formed as a private non-profit, remaining under Corbett's leadership. In 1991, the LGC organized a conference on sustainable urban development, inviting Calthorpe, Duany, Moule, Plater-Zyberk, Polyzoides and Solomon. At Yosemite National Park's splendid Ahwahnee Hotel, the group (which also included Corbett's husband Mike) presented a list of principles to about one hundred government officials. The Ahwahnee Principles upended many of the principles of the Athens Charter, and prefigured the later Charter of the New Urbanism.

Buoyed by the reception, in 1992, Calthorpe, Duany, Moule, Plater-Zyberk, Polyzoides, and Solomon had a series of discussions about founding a more permanent organization. Duany, relating the advice of Léon Krier, recommended a structure that very closely paralleled the CIAM's structure. After all, Duany said, "CIAM was the last organization that effectively and comprehensively changed the way we design the world." Now, nothing less would be required to meet the challenges of modern development.

The next year the group founded the "Congress for the New Urbanism," along with their new director, Peter Katz. The first Congress was in Alexandria, Virginia, and featured relatively intimate discussions of organizational issues. By 1996 the organization had a fully articulated Charter, similar to the Ahwahnee Principles but with more comprehensive detail. It was ratified at a much larger Congress that year in Charleston, South Carolina, and signed by Secretary of Housing and Urban Development Henry Cisneros, along with several hundred other attendees. The CNU was already showing its deep influence at the highest levels of US government.

The CNU's Charter is grouped into three sections, following the scale of urbanism: the region, the neighborhood and the building. Each section includes nine points, for a total of twenty-seven. In addition, a preamble sets out the broad goals of the movement, which are then articulated in each section.

The Charter of the New Urbanism's key points almost exactly oppose the key points of the CIAM's Athens Charter:

- **Mixed use instead of function-based zoning.** Work, home, recreation and transport are to be integrated within mixed-use neighborhoods, and sometimes, within individual mixed-use buildings.

- **Mixed streets instead of functionally restricted streets.** The design of streets aims to promote multi-modal transportation centered on the pedestrian. Streets are critical public spaces, and, within neighborhoods, should be narrow to calm traffic and de-emphasize the automobile. Furthermore, they require a dense connective network to function well as pedestrian travel pathways. While the car and other vehicles must be accommodated, mobility must not be acquired at the expense of access.

- **Integration instead of segregation of buildings.** In the words of the Charter, "a primary task of all urban architecture and landscape design is the physical definition of streets and public spaces as places of shared use." Urban design must create coherent public spaces with the edges of buildings, and avoid what Jane Jacobs derisively called the "project land oozes" of CIAM-based planning. This is critical to achieve a successful, active pedestrian and public realm, and balance automobile use with other modes of travel.

- **Adaptive re-use, not demolition, of historic fabric and pattern.** "Preservation and renewal of historic buildings, districts, and landscapes affirm the continuity and evolution of urban society." Nor is historical pattern banished in new buildings: "Architecture and landscape design should grow from local climate, topography, history, and building practice." Furthermore, "Individual architectural projects should be seamlessly linked to their surroundings. This issue transcends style." That is, style is not to be specified, but may follow whatever criteria constitute a contextual response that is also supportive of other criteria of urbanism.

- **The city is co-created by all citizens, and is not merely a technical creation by specialists**. The Charter's preamble proclaims the collaboration of "a broad-based citizenry, composed of public and private sector leaders, community activists, and multidisciplinary professionals. We are committed to reestablishing the relationship between the art of building and the making of community, through citizen-based participatory planning and design."

- **The city is not a "tree" (as Alexander noted) but a place of "organized complexity" (as Jacobs noted)** wherein many people, businesses, nonprofits, government agencies and other entities generate parts of the city, within a long-term co-evolutionary process.

As a movement, New Urbanism suffers from an interesting kind of schizophrenia. As my colleague Emily Talen has written, there are at least four subcultures within the movement, with varied and often conflicting agendas. Criticism between practitioners can at times be fierce, and debates rage over architectural languages, ecological practices, measures to safeguard affordability and equity, and other controversies.

Even more vociferous is some of the criticism from outside of the New Urbanism community. Some of the best-placed criticism points to the uneven, sometimes unacceptable quality of projects, the flaws in the development process, and the failure to provide for the natural and contextual dynamics of place. (Indeed, this has been a criticism of Christopher Alexander himself.) Other criticisms have pointed to the failure to respond to human movement patterns and the "movement economy" — a point that Jacobs herself made.

A broader category of criticism focuses on the role that New Urbanism has played in providing upper middle class development, which critics claim has fueled gentrification. To be fair, New Urbanists have been involved in many affordable and low-cost housing projects as well. However, the point that housing affordability is a challenge not yet met, by New Urbanists or by many others, is a fair one.

Another category of critique is, for me, particularly important in the context of the New Urban Agenda. New Urbanism as a movement has remained too bounded by its particular set of problem-solving issues — too USA-specific, too specific to wealthy democracies and upwardly mobile, well-educated communities — and has not yet taken up the broader challenges of human settlement in our age, including the daunting challenges of poverty, unemployment, exclusion, informal settlements, the dynamics of global capital and real estate investment, and the influence of the USA as a model, for better or worse. Indeed, it is precisely because the USA is a model for much of the rest of the world — often a regrettable one — that the

New Urbanists' failure to embrace a more thoroughgoing global urban agenda represents a lost opportunity to be more effective in the trans-national reforms that are needed.

Put differently, one could say that the New Urbanism as a movement has not yet sufficiently implemented the mantra, "think globally, act locally." For these issues are indeed globally interconnected, just as markets and communications and design movements are increasingly globally interconnected — again, for better or worse.

This is an orthodox opinion that has wide currency within the culture today. We mustn't be "old-fashioned" because "that was then and this is now" — the "modern" age where we expect everything to have a certain different look, and to express a certain modern artistic sensibility.

This is also an opinion that has received scant critical review in the light of the new revelations of the sciences, and the evidence of what works best for people and for cities. It is also an opinion that, as the next chapter discusses, poses a significant barrier to the implementation of the New Urban Agenda, and the quality and success of cities in the future.

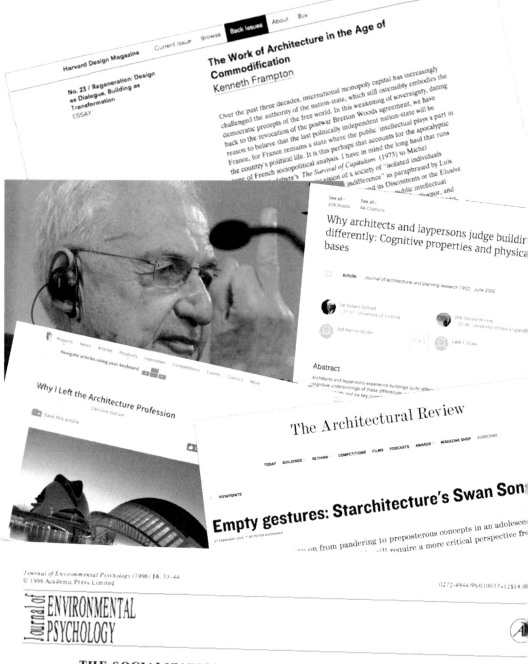

Harvard Design Magazine — No. 23 / Regeneration: Design as Dialogue, Building as Transformation — ESSAY

The Work of Architecture in the Age of Commodification
Kenneth Frampton

Over the past three decades, international monopoly capital has increasingly challenged the authority of the nation-state, which still ostensibly embodies the democratic precepts of the free world. In this weakening of sovereignty, dating back to the revocation of the postwar Bretton Woods agreement, we have reason to believe that the last politically independent nation-state will be France, for France remains a state where the public intellectual plays a part in the country's political life. It is this perhaps that accounts for the apocalyptic ... of French sociopolitical analysis. I have in mind the long haul that runs ... Lefebvre's *The Survival of Capitalism* (1973) to Michel ... vision of a society of "isolated individuals ... indifference" as paraphrased by Luis ... and its Discontents or the Elusive ... public intellectual

Why architects and laypersons judge buildin... differently: Cognitive properties and physica... bases

Article   Journal of architectural and planning research 19(2) June 2002

1st Robert Gifford   2nd Donald W Hine   3rd Werner Muller   Last J Shaw

Abstract

Architects and laypersons experience buildings quite diffe... cognitive underpinnings of these difference... and six key com...

Projects News Articles Products Interviews Competitions Events Classics More
Navigate articles using your keyboard

Why I Left the Architecture Profession
Christine Outram

Save this article

The Architectural Review
TODAY BUILDINGS RETHINK COMPETITIONS FILMS PODCASTS AWARDS MAGAZINE SHOP SUBSCRIBE

VIEWPOINTS

Empty gestures: Starchitecture's Swan Son...
27 FEBRUARY 2015 • BY PETER BUCHANAN

... on from pandering to preposterous concepts in an adolesce... ...ill require a more critical perspective fr...

Journal of Environmental Psychology (1996) 16, 33–44
© 1996 Academic Press Limited

0272-4944/96/010033+12$18.00

Journal of ENVIRONMENTAL PSYCHOLOGY

THE SOCIALIZATION OF ARCHITECTURAL PREFERENCE

MARGARET A. WILSON

Department of Psychology, University of Liverpool, P.O. Box 147, Liverpool, L69 3BX, U.K.

Abstract

The apparent difference in the appreciation of architecture between architects and 'lay' people has been the focus of much research. If architects truly have different standards of appreciation from nonarchitects, it is then most likely that these standards of judgement are acquired within the schools of architecture during the period of architectural education. The paper describes a cross-sectional study of the architectural preferences of students at two schools of architecture at five different stages of their education. Smallest Space Analysis (SSA) of the students' evaluations of 26 examples of contemporary architecture suggests a process of socializ-ation within the schools of architecture whereby students develop standards of j...

3. "ARTISTIC SPRAWL" AND THE BARRIER OF ARCHITECTURE

"It is not always clear whether we are using our position to engage in an intellectual discourse or an incredible ego free-for-all. Unfortunately, we have not been able to provide any dignity to the profession due to our complete technical inability to conquer market pressures and our willingness to be totally manipulated... The work we do is no longer mutually reinforcing, but I would say that any accumulation is counterproductive, to the point that each new addition reduces the sum's value."

— *Rem Koolhaas, leading architect, quoted in* ArchitectureWeek, *8/1/2007*

Among the sprawling landscapes of the United States, Silicon Valley may be one of the clearest antitheses of the New Urban Agenda on display today. Here can be seen vast stretches of car-dependent urbanism with tree-like organization of parts, functionally segregated, created only by technocrats, with little historic fabric or pattern, lacking diversity (of income, or other varieties), and featuring gigantic supercampuses with inward-turning buildings, set back far from any walkable streets.

But this is hardly the low end of the development market, professionally speaking. Indeed, the great architects of the day have been designing these buildings, to the glee of their credulous clients. The late Steve Jobs, speaking about Apple's new Norman Foster-designed supercampus, told the Cupertino City Council, "I really do think that architecture students will come here to see this, I think it could be that good." The building takes the form of a giant donut.

Other supercampuses designed by famous architects or "starchitects" include the Facebook campus by Frank Gehry, with a new addition by Rem Koolhaas' firm OMA, and the Google campus by Bjarke Ingels's practice, BIG.

These and other designs are certainly arresting, exotic, dramatic. They may or may not be great art. (I rather think not, but I will leave that judgment to others, as that is not the issue in any case.) What

Opposite: A slew of recent soul-searching articles and research papers showing the architecture profession struggling to be relevant to current challenges. The Guardian newspaper documented a recent angry exchange between architect Frank Gehry and a critic, photographed here by J L Cereijido.

they clearly are not is urbanism, of the kind identified by Jacobs, Alexander, or the New Urban Agenda. Indeed they are textbook species of physical sprawl, masked by "artistic sprawl" — the alluring avant-garde dissonance — of today's professional leadership in architecture. The actual structure is very far from Jacobs' "organized complexity" or Alexander's "city that is not a tree," and much closer to the kind of urbanism that both Alexander and Jacobs excoriated. The only real change is in the distractingly exotic artistic decoration.

Koolhaas may be the most articulate of today's more introspective architects, and he often endeavors to lay out a clear (and often incisively self-critical) rationale for contemporary practice. Like Alexander (whom he has stated he admires), Koolhaas is frank about the failures of the profession and its discordant results, as for example in his comment "the work we do is no longer mutually reinforcing." He seems to agree with Alexander that our systems as currently configured are failing to produce wholeness.

Koolhas' criticism of CIAM-era modernism has been equally trenchant. Here again is the passage, shown previously, from his well-known 1996 essay "Whatever happened to urbanism?" (in *S,M,L,XL*):

> Modernism's alchemistic promise — to transform quantity into quality through abstraction and repetition — has been a failure, a hoax; magic that didn't work. Its ideas, aesthetics, strategies are finished. Together, all attempts to make a new beginning have only discredited the idea of a new beginning. A collective shame in the wake of this fiasco has left a massive crater in our understanding of modernity and modernization.

The reference to the failed attempt to transform quantity into quality echoes Alexander's call for a return to a qualitative approach, replacing abstract replication with wholeness-extending transformations. In effect, Koolhaas is agreeing with Alexander that the "alchemistic promise" of abstraction and repetition has been a kind of architectural "dry hole."

Unlike Alexander, however, Koolhaas does not acknowledge a clear responsibility for architects to reform this state of affairs — for the simple reason that, as he sees it, the situation is now beyond any possible control or, therefore, responsibility. Indeed, later in the same essay, Koolhaas seemed to relish the architect/artist's resulting liberation from responsibility:

The seeming failure of the urban offers an exceptional opportunity, a pretext for Nietzchean frivolity. We have to imagine 1,001 other concepts of city; we have to take insane risks; we have to dare to be utterly uncritical; we have to swallow deeply and bestow forgiveness left and right. The certainty of failure has to be our laughing gas/oxygen; modernization our most potent drug. Since we are not responsible, we have to become irresponsible.

This narrative would seem to offer a blank check to architects as artists, and as such, a serious conundrum for the implementation of the New Urban Agenda. If we are not responsible, then we can ignore the call to responsible professionalism, and the other reforms identified in the New Urban Agenda.

As the previous discussion should have made clear, Jacobs would also have very little patience for this abdication of professional responsibility. Her first book was a self-described "attack" on the ill-considered outcomes of professional actions, and all of her books were in a sense descriptions of the responsive, and responsible, pathways to effective actions to deal with "the kind of problem a city is."

Nor is Koolhaas alone in arguing for the primacy of artistic novelty over evidence-based problem-solving. Indeed, for those who (like myself) have taught architecture, and visited architecture schools in a number of different countries, it is not too much to say that the primary aim of architectural design today is, very simply, not to find the best possible solution for human environments, but rather, to create adventurous new sculptural works of art on a gigantic scale.

Along the way, various functional and technical goals must be dealt with, of course, and these are supposed to address human need, hopefully in an elegant way. But we are still bound to the realm of abstraction and repetition, now only liberated to express any artistic gesture we please. In effect, we are still stranded at the bottom of Koolhaas' "crater of modernity and modernization." Only now we are free to play with the bits of rubble, recombining them into endlessly varied and novel assemblies.

From the perspective of Jacobs and Alexander, however, this over-dependence on novelty is a problem, and a serious one. For if we were truly concerned with the human quality of life, beyond the momentary pleasures of artists and connoisseurs, then the first consideration would focus on whatever evidence indicated the best solution, from whatever source. We would not confine ourselves to a particular historically bounded industrial form language, re-assembled into dramatic and novel shapes. Indeed, we would not take that approach at all, but something much more radical.

Jacobs echoed this idea when she declared that the city is not and must not be thought of as primarily a work of art. It is a place of life, and the art must support the life — not vice versa. Art is indeed a vital dimension of human experience, but it is not all of human experience, and must not hijack the other aspects of life. Indeed, it has a duty to support the other aspects of life, and to illuminate their meanings. As she said in *Death and Life*:

> We need art, in the arrangements of cities as well as in the other realms of life, to help explain life to us, to show us meanings, to illuminate the relationship between the life that each of us embodies and the life outside us. We need art most, perhaps, to reassure us of our own humanity. However, although art and life are interwoven, they are not the same things. Confusion between them is, in part, why efforts at city design are so disappointing.... [This] is to make the mistake of attempting to substitute art for life.

Jacobs was harsh in her criticism of artist-architects who fail to grasp this distinction, and the consequences for cities and their inhabitants:

> The results of such profound confusion between art and life are neither life nor art. They are taxidermy.... Like all attempts at art which get far away from the truth and which lose respect for what they deal with, this craft of city taxidermy becomes, in the hands of its master practitioners, continually more picky and precious. This is the only form of advance possible to it.

Alexander was even more harsh about the irresponsibility of artist-architects. For him the problem was rooted in the failures of 20th Century industrial technology, as I have already explored. The problem for artist-architects was that they allowed themselves — and still do, he argued — to be co-opted uncritically by agents of environmental industrialization, and to allow their architecture to become distorted in a very serious way. Here he is in a 2002 interview that he gave me for the web journal *Katarxis3.com*:

> **Christopher Alexander:** I'd say that the biggest problem with 20th century architecture was that architects became involved in a huge lie. Essentially what happened at the beginning of the 20th century was really a legacy of the 19th. New forms of production began to be vis-

ible. And in some fashion, artists and architects were invited to become front men for this very serious economic and industrial transformation.

I don't think they knew what was happening. That is, I don't think in most cases there was anything cynical about this. But they were actually in effect bought out. So that the heroes of, let's say, the first half of the 20th century — Le Corbusier, Mies Van Der Rohe, Gropius even (very nice man, by the way) — were brought on board in effect to say, OK, here's all this stuff happening, what can you do with it? Let's prove that it's really a wonderful world we're going towards. And instead of reflecting on questions about, well, what was it that was going to be wonderful about this world — from the very beginning, the architects became visual spokesmen, in a way to try to prove that everything was really OK. Not only that it was really OK, but somehow magic.

You know, there was this phrase, *elan vital,* which was bandied about a lot in the middle years of the century, and in the early years of the century as well — of, there's something incredible happening here, we're part of it, we're reaching forward. But all of this was really image-factory stuff. And what they didn't know about the late 20th century was only known to a few visionaries like Orwell and others who could actually see really what was going on.

I don't think this is a very flattering view, and I suppose architects would reject it, angrily. But I do think it's true.

Michael Mehaffy: It's essentially a program of apology for industrialism?

Christopher Alexander: Glorification, of something that is inherently not glorifiable. And it's really very very similar to the ads we see on TV every day now, except this was being done with architectural imagery, and with buildings. And the architects are busy, right to this day, still trying to perpetuate that process that they successfully did in the 20th Century.

As both Alexander and Jacobs repeatedly stressed, art has a vital place in human affairs. Yet the place of art in contemporary architecture has become, in a sense, pathological — a creature of marketing, a cog in the malfunctioning machinery of industry and capital.

This is not an insight unique to Jacobs or Alexander — indeed, one can find whole journal issues on "commodification and spectacle in architecture" (the name of a 2005 edition of *Harvard Design Magazine,* with a foreword by the eminent critic Kenneth Frampton), or scathing essays by other critics like *Architectural Review's* Peter Buchanan. What is perhaps unique to both Jacobs and Alexander is that they proposed substantial remedies — what amount to proposed pathways out of Koolhaas' "crater of modernity and modernization."

For example, Jacobs also pointed to the dangerous and sometimes hidden influence of money in generating urban ills. Here is a passage in *Death and Life*, talking about slum investments — but she could just as easily be talking about other distorting influences of what she termed "money floods":

> Cynics — or at least the cynics I talk to — think that pickings are made so easy nowadays for exploitative money in cities because the investment shadow world represents powerful interests, with a big say somewhere behind the legislative and administrative scenes. I have no way of knowing whether this is true. However, I should think that apathy on the part of the rest of us has something to do with the situation.

But unlike Koolhaas, Jacobs was no urban nihilist. For her the problems of money were not "in some dark and foreboding way, irrational" (as she said in the last chapter, quoting Warren Weaver). We had the means and the ability to respond — and hence the *respons*ibility — for example, through changes in tax policy (part of a larger topic that I will explore in the last section). Like the problems of organized complexity, these problems *could* be understood, and managed:

> The forms in which money is used for city building — or withheld from use — are powerful instruments of city decline today. The forms in which money is used must be converted to instruments of regeneration — from instruments buying violent cataclysms to instruments buying continual, gradual, complex and gentler change.

As Jacobs argued later — notably in her book *The Nature of Economies* — there is a close analogue in the way that biological systems operate to evolve complex forms of order. This was an analogue that Alexander also repeatedly explored, as we have seen. As we have also seen, Alexander went much farther than Jacobs into detailed questions of the natural and especially biological processes of form-generation, and the lessons for human designers.

In this biological comparison, art, we may say, is not unlike the expressive signaling of creatures, when they wish to express signs that convey meaning: *I am a strong and healthy mate,* or *I am ag-*

gressive and powerful, or *I carry a deadly toxin.* Of course the expressive characteristics of human art are vastly richer and more complex. Their powers of abstraction and inter-connection are vastly greater. But as the linguist Noam Chomsky has long argued (with a notable influence on Alexander), the "deep grammar" of human language, and ultimately of human art, draws from the same source of deep structural meaning.

This implies, however, that there is a natural balance between the expressive functions and the deeper structural functions by which human needs are satisfied. The expressive functions may soar into the realm of abstraction and complex cultural ideas; but they are not wholly invented from a blank slate. They have their roots in the natural and biological world.

This balance has profound implications for aesthetics, a topic that Alexander later explored. In a sense, the patterns that we find beautiful are natural outgrowths of the patterns of biological and natural order that we also find quite beautiful. This insight is one of the fundamental ideas behind the topic of biophilia, and there is intriguing evidence of its importance to human well-being.

Another, more controversial idea — but one that is overdue for a proper examination on the evidence, free of stylistic ideologies — is that many of the patterns of traditional art and architecture are universal expressions that are rooted in biological and physical realities. We cannot wholly ignore them, and we should certainly recognize that they imply a balance with deeper patterns of human experience and need, quite apart from specific (often highly abstracted) artistic expressions.

One could say, then, that the historical shift to an over-emphasis on the expressive functions of architecture has hobbled its capacity to meet human needs — rather like the heavy plumage of certain species of bird of paradise hobbles their ability to fly. Worse, in our case we have in effect condemned ourselves to creating a new plumage with every flight, ever heavier and more cumbersome.

Indeed, it is even worse than that: now the wings must be redesigned too, in some clever inventive way. Perhaps they need some dramatic new swoop at the back, some curlicue at the ends? Whatever we do, we must not do the same old boring Bernoulli shape. Perhaps we will use the same old feathers and bones, but they must take on some radical new form.

Another instructive analogy is with the dorsal fin of a porpoise. Suppose the porpoise said to itself, whatever I do, I must not repeat that old tired shark dorsal fin from 300 million years ago. That is not of my time, and I need something exciting and original. I know that the complex ocean environment has not really changed — the complexities of turbidity and laminar flow. I know that the shark's dorsal fin is an exquisite solution. But I am forbidden to use it!

As this little comparison suggests, the consequences for our evolutionary capacity to generate successful environmental structures are profound. We can no longer rely on the most robust forms of adaptive problem-solving embodied in our own genetic repository, regardless of how successful they have been in the past. We have trapped ourselves in an ever more escalating, ever more desperate pursuit of novelty — and it is motivated by a corrupting idea of consumption, brought about by the distortions of a faulty industrial age.

Here is the critic Kenneth Frampton, speaking (in the aforementioned issue of *Harvard Design Magazine*) of the early modernist architect Peter Behrens, also considered the "father of corporate branding":

> … When [Behrens] became the architect to the AEG corporation in 1908, he would have hardly understood the demagogic ephemeral nature of branding in today's terms. At the turn of the century, Behrens could still entertain the illusion that he was determining the overall quality of a new industrial civilization, whereas today's brand designers are not only dedicated to the gratification of consumer taste but also to the stimulation of desire, knowing full well that everything depends on the sublimating eroticism of consumption as opposed to the intrinsic quality of the thing consumed.

Peter Buchanan, critic for *Architectural Review*, has been even more scathing about the outcome of contemporary consumer-oriented design culture (in "Empty Gestures: Starchitecture's Swan Song," 2015):

> Future architects will look back at our times astounded by our confusions, gullibility and inability to exercise critical judgement... The flaws in all this stuff, and its utter irrelevance to the urgent problems of our times, are so obvious future generations will be aghast it was ever taken seriously, let alone mistaken for heralds of the future.

In this unreformed view of architecture, no longer can we build on context. No longer are we free to use whatever is the best possible solution from a human point of view, from whatever source in time and space. No longer can we carefully evolve adaptive solutions that grow in complexity and coherence. On the contrary, as Koolhaas has pointed out, "the work we do is no longer mutually reinforcing." It is chaotic, noisy, disordered.

It is of course unfair to blame the architecture profession solely for all the complex malfunctions of cities, and of our other complex forms of unsustainable disorder. As Jacobs, Alexander and others described, it is necessary to understand other areas of malfunction, including the development process, the distorted processes of economic feedback, broader misconceptions of the city, and other failures.

At the same time, neither is it reasonable for architects to suppose that they can go on with business as usual, cloaking ever more conceptually exotic guises on the same disastrous industrialization of the built environment. Neither is it reasonable for architects to hide behind their artistic rationales, and evade professional responsibility for the quality of the human environment. The times demand a more radical, thoroughgoing set of reforms, for architecture no less than for urbanism.

As Buchanan argues, the status quo is, at best, irrelevant to the urgent problems of our times. At worst it is a major impediment to the successful implementation of the New Urban Agenda, and its ability to respond to those problems. As I will explore in the next chapter, perhaps no problem is more urgent than the urban response to climate change.

4. THE REVEALING PROBLEM OF CLIMATE CHANGE*

"In wretched outcomes, the devil is in the details."

— *Jane Jacobs*

Arguably no problem facing the human species today is more daunting — and at the same time, more pressing — than the reduction of greenhouse gas emissions to mitigate the increasingly grave threat of climate change. While the science is still unclear about the range of alternative pathways to mitigation and adaptation, there is now an unequivocal consensus within atmospheric science and related disciplines that the phenomenon is occurring, and that it is already beginning to bring — and without remedy is likely to bring with increasing severity — a series of human catastrophes.

Yet it is also surely true that greenhouse gas emissions are only one aspect of an even wider human problem of unsustainable resource depletion and degradation. Both topics raise deeper issues still about the ability of humans to respond effectively in the face of inherently uncertain scientific knowledge about critical future events, and the often-associated (and increasingly problematic) consequences of political controversy and inaction.

It is encouraging to observe, however, that we humans have acted effectively on occasion to manage just such future events, under just such conditions. Perhaps the most relevant example is the so-called Montreal Protocol in 1987, an international treaty to control emissions of substances that deplete the planet's critical ozone layer. The treaty, together with a series of follow-on actions, has been widely hailed as a positive example of global environmental management (UNEP, 2014).

However, when it comes to the reduction of emissions of greenhouse gases (hereafter termed GHGs) the problem appears much more daunting. First, it is evident that there are many more econom-

---

* *Portions of this chapter were included my doctoral dissertation, Urban Form and Greenhouse Gas Emissions: Findings, Strategies, and Design Decision Support Technologies, published by Delft University of Technology, School of Architecture and the Built Environment.*

Opposite: *New Orleans in the wake of Hurricane Katrina. Photo by Jocelyn Augustino for FEMA.*

ic and political disincentives against taking strong action, shared by many more interests — notably including developing countries, who often see such action as a serious threat to their own pressing economic and human development goals.

More deeply, there is a high degree of uncertainty arising from the sheer complexity of the systems that shape consumption and emissions — most notably, the urban systems in which we move, consume, waste, and otherwise generate most of the ultimate demand for resources and emissions. It is safe to say that the dynamics of these systems — that is, the systems that comprise cities, suburbs and towns, together with their hinterlands — are among the most complex of any we know. They include myriad variables, many of them obscure, together with their myriad interactions. The situation is even more complex because urban systems are affected by perhaps the most notoriously difficult variables of all, those of human behavior.

Yet precisely because urban systems act as concentrated sources of GHG emissions, they present an especially attractive target for management. The wide variations in per-capita emissions between cities with different forms — for example, the high GHG emissions associated with sprawling suburban forms, relative to more compact urban forms — does suggest this is an important area for investigation and development.

Furthermore, precisely because urban systems are complex, progress in understanding their dynamics in the formation of GHG emissions may well produce other insights about the dynamics of urban systems and related phenomena, with potential applications beyond the specific problem of GHG emissions mitigation. In this sense, the problem of urban dynamics and GHG emissions may well be a kind of "lens" issue, whose examination may help to bring into focus other so far intractable challenges in our time.

My own involvement in research on urban form and greenhouse gas emissions (the subject of my doctoral dissertation completed in 2015) was motivated by my own recognition of a significant lacuna in the research on emissions from urban systems. In 2009 I was invited to participate in the IARU Scientific Conference on Climate Change in Copenhagen, a lead-up to the unsuccessful climate treaty negotiations of that year. I was asked (by a colleague and session organizer who was a member of the Intergovernmental Panel on Climate

Change) to present some survey research on the role of urban form that I had previously conducted. My recognition of the immature status of the research at the conference, and the failure of the subsequent treaty negotiations, convinced me that important research work remained to be done to support and to inform policy and practice in the future. Only with a more solid evidence-based foundation could we make progress in an otherwise lethargic world of policy and practice.

Specifically, I found that there is a relatively mature body of research on building systems, their emissions sources, and potentially effective strategies for management. At another, larger scale, there is also a relatively mature body of research on the emissions generated by transportation systems, notably automobiles and other vehicles. These two components do account for a significant percentage of urban-generated emissions, and indeed all emissions generated from consumption activities — perhaps as much as half, depending on the methodology used to measure emissions generation.

However, I found that an important part of the picture is incomplete. It was readily apparent that these two components do not cover the full set of urban factors that affect emissions, and there is a range of significant if smaller urban factors between them that are much less well understood. They include infrastructure systems (including streets) and their patterns of scale and connectivity, infrastructure operating energies and transmission losses, patterns of sun and wind, patterns of distribution of uses and activities, and patterns of consumption, among others — in short, the many factors that constitute and are shaped by urban form beyond the individual building scale, but short of the scale of transportation systems per se. Crucially, this intermediate zone also connects building systems to the systems of transportation, and helps to explain how they are interrelated through urban form. Thus, it is a key part of a complete picture of the role of urban form.

The urban factors in this intermediate zone — the factors of urban morphology — are also the factors that were of such interest to Jane Jacobs and Christopher Alexander throughout their careers. It soon became apparent to me that a contribution of research to address this lacuna could be useful to my own work, and to the further investigation of their ideas.

There was a second crucial piece of that agenda. I recognized that to be useful in practice, my research project must do more than identify a set of findings, which were likely to remain abstract. It must provide tools to actually guide design in practice — or at least, provide the basis for them, allowing further development and improvement by others — in the form of decision support and scenario-modelling tools. I will not describe here the prototypical "scenario-modeling" tool that I developed — it is beyond the scope of this book, and covered in another book — other than to say that one can readily see the influence of both Christopher Alexander and Jane Jacobs in the result. I can also add that this is just an early version of the kind of tool that is needed, and as I concluded, more work on this and other tools is urgently needed.

This topic is particularly urgent because, as my earlier research suggested, alternative models of practice and supporting policy could achieve significant emissions reductions from current baselines. By contrast, "business as usual" development models are likely to result in dramatic increases of rates of emissions. This is because these inefficient models are now guiding development in many emerging economies around the world — a condition that is likely to further accelerate dangerous levels of emissions in the decades ahead.

Yet as noted previously, progress in reversing these trends has been stymied by geopolitical problems, inherent scientific uncertainties, and incentives against action — as the 2009 Copenhagen treaty negotiations demonstrated. In North America, which has become a model emulated by other regions, there is relatively poor comprehensive guidance for policy and design, and a low level of action in response. Project methodologies abound (for example, ratings systems like LEED-ND) but, as I discussed in my dissertation, they have been criticized for their lack of basis in evidence

This means that there is an urgent need for concrete advancements in effective mitigation science, translated into effective practice and policy. Specifically, there is a need for effective modelling of the dynamics of emissions from urban form, and the results of specific urban design and policy choices available. Only then can actions be tied to outcomes, including new incentives and new drivers of effective changes to policy and practice. This research must be inter-disciplinary in nature, combining climate science, urban morphology, urban design, behavioral economics, software engineering technology and other disciplines. That was the broad context of my own specific research, and the research framework on which it was developed.

While I was deeply concerned by what I learned initially about the magnitude of the problem, I was also equally impressed by preliminary evidence I found for the magnitude of the potential opportunity. My initial research showed a striking correlation between urban form and rates of emissions per capita in cities around the world — correlations that were not readily accounted for by other evident factors, such as climate, demographics, cultural norms or other expected variables. Of course, correlation is not cause, and the work remained to tease out the factors and show how they are causative, as part of a coherent explanatory model.

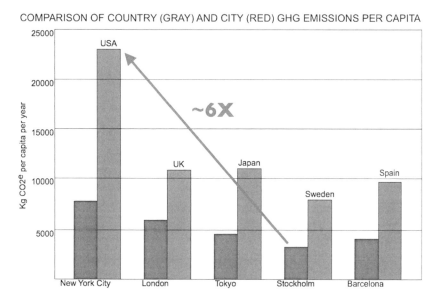

Figure IV.4.1. Comparison of country (gray) and city (red) GHG emissions per capita. Data is from 2005-2007 national inventories gathered under UNFCC standards. Source: World Bank (2011)

The initial evidence I found played a major role in motivating, and later formulating, my core research hypothesis. Figure IV.4.1 is a typical example. It shows a striking divergence in emissions per capita between five cities and the countries in which those cities are located (using data from national inventories in 2007-2009). The emissions for those countries as a whole include other cities, of course, as well as suburban and rural populations. As can be readily seen, there is a major delta — on the order of 200% to 300% be tween dense, mixed, multi-modal cities like New York, London, Tokyo, Stockholm and Barcelona, and the United States, the UK, Japan, Sweden and Spain as a whole.

The comparison between countries is even more revealing. For example, the per-capita emissions for the United States as a whole are on the order of 300% higher than those of Sweden. This delta cannot easily be explained away by obvious factors such as economic prosperity, since Sweden has a higher per-capita income than the USA. Nor is climate an obvious factor, since Sweden's winter climate is harsher on average. There are indeed other factors that might account for some of the delta, such as contributions of non-emitting energy sources and the like. But it became apparent to me that none of these factors could readily account for the magnitude of the delta. The one consistent variable was a great divergence of urban form, from dense, mixed, multi-modal cities to much lower density, dispersed, mode-dependent settlements.

Perhaps the most sobering delta of all was that between the USA as a whole and the city of Stockholm — an astonishing 600% increase in per-capita emissions. I pondered the meaning of this divergence. Was the average citizen of the USA six times more prosperous, healthy or happy in their life choices? There was certainly no available evidence to suggest that. Or, as seemed much more likely, were US citizens simply squandering over 80% of their GHG-emitting energy resources, without receiving any real benefits? Was part of this profligate waste coming from the influence of urban forms? If so, how could this be documented, and what could be done to reverse it — particularly in view of the rapid urbanization now taking place in many parts of the world?

I drew three key conclusions from this research. First, the effect of urban form on greenhouse gas emissions is far higher than currently acknowledged. Especially important, sprawling, disordered, and especially car-dependent places, offering "drive-through" lifestyles, have very high rates of per-capita emissions in comparison to more compact, walkable, transit-served places.

Second, the baseline of "business as usual" development continues to generate high-emissions forms of urbanism around the world. The implications for continued increases in greenhouse gas emissions, and increasingly catastrophic effects of climate change, are profound. They call for urgent global action, as a matter of priority.

Figure IV.4.2. Typical car-dependent development around new McDonald's sites, built in the last ten years, in (clockwise from upper left) China, India, Romania and Brazil. In spite of the UN's "New Urban Agenda" and similar reforms, this high-resource consumption pattern is still "business as usual" for urban development around the world today. Images: Flickr.

Third, the issues of greenhouse gas emissions are inseparable from those of resource depletion, ecological impacts, and environmental contamination (including pollution and invasive species). All of them are inseparably linked to the kinds of cities and towns we build. When we build more integrated, compact, mixed-use cities with healthy public space systems, of just the kind called for in the New Urban Agenda, all of these joined-up problems are mitigated. When we build sprawling, disordered, high-consumption cities, with disordered or diminished public space systems, all of these problems are exacerbated.

It seems we have a fundamental choice. We cannot leave these problems to fix themselves — they surely will not — but neither can we treat them in isolation from one another, and from the larger "kind of problem a city is." To do so would be to play "Whack-a-Mole" with our problems, and to see the proliferation of more unintended consequences. We can only treat cities, and the other matters under our care, as "joined-up problems," requiring joined-up responses.

This is indeed what Jacobs and Alexander urged us to do.

5. BEWARE OF "VOODOO URBANISM"

"I got wrong that the creative class could magically restore our cities, become a new middle class like my father's and [we all] were going to live happily forever after. I could not have anticipated among all this urban growth and revival there was a dark side to the urban creative revolution, a very deep dark side."

— *Richard Florida, Professor, University of Toronto*

Over the last half-decade or so, a distressingly similar story has been heard from many cities around the world. Newly popular city cores are drawing more people, pushing up prices, and driving out small businesses and lower-income residents. City leaders, alarmed at the trends, try to build their way out of the problems, on the theory that more supply will better match demand, and result in lower rents and home prices. But the efforts don't seem to work — and even seem to exacerbate the problems.

That's because, as we've seen, cities aren't simple machines, in which we can plug in one thing (say, a higher quantity of housing units) and automatically get out something else (say, lower housing costs). Instead, cities are "dynamical systems," prone to unintended consequences and unexpected feedback effects. By building more units, we might create "induced demand," meaning that more people are attracted to move to our city from other places — and housing prices don't go down, they go up.

Unfortunately, we have been treating cities too much like machines, and for an obvious reason. In an industrial age, that has been a profitable approach for those at the top, and in past decades, it seemed to fuel the middle class too. More recently, the results have been destructive, creating cities of winners and losers, and large areas of urban (and rural) decline. Even government programs meant to address the problems have seemed at times like a game of "whack-a-mole" — build some social housing here, see more affordability problems pop up over there.

In the years after World War II, and especially in the United States, the largest areas of decline were often in the inner cities, leaving the "losers" of the economy behind, while the "winners" (often

Opposite: Rapid development in the core of Portland, Oregon. Photo: M.O. Stevens, Wikimedia Commons.

wealthier whites) fled to the suburbs. But more recently it has been the cores of large cities that have become newly prosperous, attracting the winners of the "knowledge economy".

Meanwhile, the inner-tier suburban belts and the smaller industrial cities have suffered marked decline, with a predictable political backlash from the "white working class". Lower-income and minority populations have been relegated to even more peripheral locations, with limited opportunities for economic development. This gap in opportunity means a gap in the lower-end "rungs of the ladder" that are so essential for immigrants and others to advance.

This more recent pattern of core gentrification and geographic inequality has also been an unintended result of conscious policies. This time we aimed to achieve not suburban expansion, but the urban benefits of knowledge-economy cities, and their capacities as creative engines of economic development. In the USA, authors like Ed Glaeser and Richard Florida have come to prominence by promoting the economic power of city cores. Florida's "creative class" ranks alongside concepts like "innovation districts" to promote a critical mass of talent and interaction. Glaeser's "triumph of the city" points to the environmental efficiencies of compact living, as well as the economic benefits.

These and other authors have cited as inspiration the urban economics of Jane Jacobs, who did indeed champion the capacities of cities as creative engines of human development. But Jacobs warned against the kind of "silver bullet" thinking that imagines an innovation district or a downtown creative class is going to generate benefits that will automatically trickle down to the rest of the city. On the contrary, she pointed to the dangers of *any* form of "monoculture" — including the monoculture of an innovation district or of a creative class.

Instead, Jacobs argued for a more diverse kind of city — diverse in population, diverse in kinds of activities, and diverse in geographic distribution too. Hers was a "polycentric" city, with lots of affordable pockets full of old buildings and opportunities waiting to be targeted.

This is a point that Ed Glaeser, Richard Florida and the other fans of "innovation districts" might not yet comprehend. Glaeser for one has been harsh in criticizing Jacobs' defense of old buildings — for example, in Greenwich Village — which he sees as a sentimental preservation instinct that only feeds gentrification. His formula has been to demolish and build new high rises.

But Glaeser and other critics seem to miss Jacobs' point. For Jacobs, the answer to gentrification and affordability is not an over-concentration of new (often even more expensive) houses in the core. Rather, we need to diversify geographically as well as in other ways. If Greenwich Village is over-gentrifying, it's probably time to re-focus on Brooklyn, and provide more jobs and opportunities for its more depressed neighborhoods. If those start to over-heat, it's time to focus on the Bronx, or Queens. Or Cleveland, Detroit, Baltimore, New Orleans...

There is no end of good urban fabric, in the US and in other countries, that is ready for some positive gentrification, the kind that increases diversity and opportunities for human development. (As we also offer targeted protections for existing residents.) It is not wise to over-concentrate on the existing cores, in the belief that this "voodoo urbanism" will magically benefit all of the city's residents.

A second, related issue is the scale of urban plots or lots. Here too we need diversity at the smaller scales, just as we need geographic diversity at the largest scales of the city. Just as old buildings tend to be more affordable, accommodating smaller businesses and start-ups, so too, small plots and lots tend to be more affordable for those same users.

But as the cores experience hypertrophic growth, often the pressure to build very large buildings on very large sites also becomes irresistible. A mix of small and large plots can help to tamp down this tendency. At the same time, other tools can manage overheating of the core, and steer growth into new locations. For example, as Jacobs recommended, new public projects in new locations can serve as catalytic "chess pieces" to redirect growth into more benign forms.

These are examples of Jacobs' "toolkit" approach — one that is badly needed today to cope with the dynamic challenges of rapid city growth around the world.

What are the tools available? In a recent conference on urbanization, affordability and displacement in Los Angeles, speakers brought up the following tools and approaches:

1. ***Taxation, including land value tax.*** Patrick Condon, professor at the University of British Columbia in Vancouver, described

the "Vienna Model" — new projects are taxed heavily, which depresses land cost without raising costs for market-rate housing. The taxes go to affordable projects, and to buying more land — which is then less expensive. Other cities tax the land value directly, using so-called "Georgist" tax policies. Similar tools can help to conserve resources (like land) and reward good development. As I will discuss in the last section, such policies can help to "monetize externality costs" (like sprawl).

2. Financial tools to damp down speculative real estate bubbles. Housing is a human need, not an interchangeable investor commodity — yet current policy is rewarding a dangerous new wave of speculation. The last time this happened, 2008, the world found itself in a global financial crisis. We need better tools, including local regulations, that control excessive speculation. We need less childlike faith in the magic of unfettered markets.

3. Better tools to unlock under-utilized sites. There are enormous reserves of wasted land, empty lots, parking lots and other suitable sites in many cities — but there is a shortage of imagination and tools to access them. In the USA, the National Trust for Historic Preservation recently cited a 2014 survey that found that in just a part of New York City, nearly 2,500 vacant lots and more than 3,500 empty buildings had enough capacity to house 200,000 people.

4. Tools for "gentle densification". These include accessory dwellings, duplexes or rental conversions, pocket neighborhoods, "tiny houses," and other innovative forms of compatible, human-scale housing, as alternatives to "jamming it in."

5. "Beauty In My Back Yard". Many cities are full of beautiful, neighborhood-compatible typologies, including rich traditions of human-scaled apartments. Where sites are available, such positive alternatives should be developed through "win-win" consultations with residents.

6. Targeted protections for existing renters and owners, and aggressive help for the homeless. There can be no excuse for letting people suffer, particularly when proven alternatives have been demonstrated by other cities. Salt Lake City in the USA, for example, has demonstrated one positive approach to ending chronic homelessness; there are others. Some cities have developed policies that legally disincentivize increases in rents above inflation (including property tax re-assessments based on higher incomes).

Above all... **Stop scapegoating NIMBYs** (that is, those who respond to projects with "not in my back yard"). It is popular today to blame NIMBYs for everything from gentrification to loss of affordable housing. Nonsense. These are complex phenomena, and they are no more amenable to stripping the rights of NIMBYs than they are to other simplistic "silver bullet" solutions. Furthermore, most people agree that those who live in a community should have the right to participate in land use planning that affects their public realm, with a voice in decision-making. As Jane Jacobs said, sometimes NIMBYs are right: although a project type may be needed, "things should be done differently."

Of course, residents need to participate in a pro-active problem-solving approach, and not simply be in opposition to all projects. That assumes, however, that such an approach is being offered by the City and other entities — but often this is not the case, and in those situations, NIMBYism may be the only approach available to residents.

The political environment in many countries is ugly enough without fomenting more needless divisions within communities that have been allies in the past, including the historic preservation community, and the community of neighborhood activists who are best placed to help improve their own neighborhoods. There is more than enough blame to go around, and more to the point, there is more than enough opportunity for citizens to work together on better "win-win" approaches that address the broader needs of cities.

As Jacobs reminds us, we need to become wiser stewards of urban diversity, in both scale and location, so that we can counteract the effects of overheated urban growth. By doing so, we can support a more even and equitable growth of smaller businesses, and viable employment for lower and middle classes. Out of that creative exchange, we will continue to get unimaginable marvels of innovation, and we might also get the next new world-famous startup. But we will also get many thousands of other healthy and creative businesses, forming the real backbone of great cities.

And instead of monocultures of the rich, and of society's winners, we will get the economic diversity on which the continued growth and vitality of cities actually depends.

SECTION V:

KEY LESSONS AND HOPEFUL EXAMPLES

1. CONNECTIVITY:

Cities need a continuous fabric of walkable, multi-modal streets and public spaces — and structures that support it.[*]

"Whatever city neighborhoods may be, or may not be, and whatever usefulness they may have, or be coaxed into having, their qualities cannot work at cross-purposes to thoroughgoing city mobility and fluidity of use, without economically weakening the city of which they are a part."

— Jane Jacobs, The Death and Life of Great American Cities

Both Jacobs and Alexander saw the city as a kind of tissue of human activity and interaction. That spatial structure was in part generated by that activity, and in part shaped and limited the activity itself.

Both of them recognized that the physical arrangements themselves were not enough — neither Jacobs nor Alexander was an "environmental determinist" — but both also recognized that bad physical arrangements could disrupt the critical relationships between the parts of the city, with devastating knock-on effects.

In particular, as Jacobs noted, a formerly viable urban area, fragmented by intrusive structures like freeways or superblocks, could find its economic and social vitality devastated. Freeways are an all too common example, and Jacobs recounted the sad history of New York City. However, parks and other large single uses can also be equally damaging to the urban fabric at their edges. As Jacobs pointed out, the trouble arises when these areas are bisected or fragmented by the borders of these uses, leaving weak fragments. The borders of these uses create what she termed "border vacuums" — something very destructive to viable neighborhoods.

To counter this kind of urban damage, the goal she advocates is to maintain a continuous walkable urban fabric, as a key ingredient along with other ingredients. If the fabric is walkable, the streets are

---

* *Portions of this essay were delivered as part of the annual Sir David Anderson Lecture at the University of Strathclyde in 2011. I am indebted to my hosts Sergio Porta and Ombretta Romice for the invitation, and for their kind assistance in securing the Sir David Anderson fellowship that year.*

Opposite: *The remarkably well-connected street grid of central Portland, Oregon.*

more likely to be populated with pedestrians, and the neighborhood has a chance at sparking some real life. This wasn't just theory: this is what she observed in the successful regenerating neighborhoods.

Alexander too wrote about the continuous spatial network of the city, so different from the neatly segregated parts of a "tree" diagram — as is so visible in many suburban street patterns. He pointed to many patterns for pedestrian-focused networks, including "Web of Shopping," "Pedestrian Braid," "Paths and Goals" and others.

We can think of urban land, Jacobs said, as being of two types. One type is what she called "general land" — the land on which people can move freely on foot. It includes streets, small parks, even building passages.

The other type, which she called "special land," is all those uses that are not commonly used as thoroughfares by pedestrians. This includes most buildings, such as housing, office, retail, schools, civic and so on.

She argued that there needs to be a well-balanced spatial distribution of these two kinds of land, with a level of permeability for the "general" land, the land for pedestrians. Clearly it was a bad thing if these areas were fragmented by, say, freeways, into small fragments that are no longer functionally viable. And this was what happened to many older neighborhoods that were cut up by motorways.

But another key point was that even the beneficial uses of special land, things like housing and schools, could actually cause a problem if they simply got too big. They would fragment the general land at the borders, and create again the problem she termed "border vacuums." The dead ends that result would cause a die-off of human activity.

For those who know the work on Space Syntax, Jacobs' is a very similar kind of analysis — if streets lose connectivity say, because a motorway blocks off local streets, then the network connectivity is affected in a much wider area surrounding this fragmented element.

Again, the space itself has a structural effect on what can happen within it. (As the saying goes, if you don't believe that, try walking through a wall!) We can readily appreciate the structural consequences of greater distances, say — we will have to walk or drive farther, and we will have to use more resources. But since we are dealing with a complex system of connections, the properties of interconnections, as well as the distances, are also important. "Connectivity" becomes an important property in and of itself, along with scale.

But this suggests that any large single use — any superblock scheme that tends to remove itself from the surrounding fabric — can be problematic. That probably goes for the superblock schemes of so-called Neighborhood Units, like the famous 1929 Clarence Perry scheme. Jacobs was very critical of this kind of unitized scheme, in large part because of its lack of connectivity to the surrounding fabric, and the resulting damage that she observed.

But what about situations where you have no alternative — say, large parks, or rivers, or other uses? Here she quotes the great urbanist Kevin Lynch, who argued that such border vacuums can be converted into "seams," if they were given depth on either side of them. She gave the example of Central Park and some of the uses that penetrate on both sides of its edges — for example, the Metropolitan Museum of Art extending in, Roosevelt Park extending out, and so on. The same thing happens at the edge of the East River — the South Front Seaport extends into the water and helps to knit the edge back into the city. Bridges of course do the same thing.

My own home town of Portland, Oregon also did the same thing quite successfully. We took down our Harbor Freeway, which fragmented the city, and put up a linear park, and then we added uses along it, so that it does not remain a "border vacuum." And there are quite a few bridges across the river too, so many that one of Portland's nicknames is "Bridge City" — but they do help to knit the city together across what would otherwise be a very fragmenting border.

And of course, when taking down such a freeway, we always have to ask if we've compromised the mobility that a city needs. And I'm happy to say that Portland has had very good mobility — certainly on a par with other cities that have built more freeways. In fact, Portland has freeways that run right into the city — and of course that's another kind of structure that can cause great fragmentation and damage to urban fabric. Portland however has a very noteworthy feature: significant parts of the freeways through the center of town are actually submerged, and the walkable street grid continues above it, with pedestrian sidewalks, light rail and other modes of travel.

Again, this follows Lynch's formula for stitching together a seam across what would otherwise be a border and a barrier, and thereby activating the areas around it.

Portland also demonstrates some other surprising examples of otherwise large uses that would typically create "border vacuums" that are in fact integrated into the walkable urban fabric to a surprising degree. The campus of Portland State University is not in fact segregated in a typical isolated superblock campus setting, but instead is integrated right into the walkable urban grid of the downtown area. The same is true of many of Portland's inner-city industrial districts, also integrated into walkable urban fabric. These are quite appealing, walkable neighborhoods, and they support significant mixed use, including high tech and office. An example is the well-known Pearl District, also a former industrial district that still has industrial and office users (including Microsoft and Google), and it remains very walkable and appealing.

What about shopping malls, "big boxes" and so on? In the very center of Portland is a shopping mall called Pioneer Place, and it is one of the most popular in the region. It spans over four blocks — but instead of taking out streets, it preserves the street grid and uses tunnels and bridges to spread into a larger complex, right over the walkable urban fabric, including the light rail line.

What about hospitals? Portland has a major hospital complex called Good Samaritan, again spanning over a number of blocks, and using bridges and tunnels to do so. Again the surrounding urbanism is very beautiful and walkable. These are successful examples from a "modern" city with a successful economy.

Indeed, Portland has managed to keep a kind of continuous carpet of walkable urbanism, right across the city. It maintains these walkable connections within a network of principal through streets that's about 1/4 mile, or 400 meters. That number seems to be closely related to the optimum balance between pedestrian mobility and vehicular mobility, or the scale at which pedestrian-dominated areas give way to vehicle-dominated areas. It is not that these larger through streets are not pedestrian-friendly — indeed they can be, and must be — but that this is the point where pedestrian-dominated streets (such as narrow lanes, "woonerfs" and the like) give way to longer, straighter avenues and boulevards where vehicles have more free movement.

Our colleagues Sergio Porta and Ombretta Romice in the Urban Design Studies Unit of the University of Strathclyde, working with their students, have shown that this 400 meter number seems to be surprisingly invariant across many cities. We can see for example in Bologna, where the major through streets average about 400 meters on center (see illustrations below). In Oslo, we can see again the same pattern. Or in Paris, once again we find same thing. We note how Paris, like Portland, has grade-depressed railways and motorways, and the urbanism continues very beautifully overhead. In fact London does the same thing — a typical example is Oseney Crescent in Camden Town. This is part of the essential railway service to London. Notice again that the street level still offers a very walkable, attractive streetscape without "border vacuums".

So we can see that it's possible to build cities this way, and to maintain this walkable urban carpet, even in a thriving modern urban economy like London or Portland. It's not necessary to chop them up in the name of mobility, as we did in the United States, very much to our regret. In fact, if we've learned anything, it's that the more we try to build for mobility, the more we tend to lose it — the paradox of "induced demand."

Another implication is that it's not necessary to push arterial highways out to the perimeters either, where they too often become generators of sprawling "out of town" facilities. As we have seen in the United States, this kind of planning only serves to trigger the growth of even more low-density, low-connectivity, car-dependent urbanism. Instead we can take these important arterials, and all their movement and all their people, right into the heart of cities, as Portland shows, so long as we keep them grade-depressed, like railways. (Tunnels are also an option, though more expensive still.)

But one may ask, is vehicular mobility still accommodated at the finer scales? Yes, indeed, there is a remarkably effective permeable network, graduated in a progression from the local streets to the walkable avenues, like Portland's Hawthorne Boulevard. At the next level are multi-way boulevards, like this example in the Willamette District, just outside Portland — with slip lanes and accommodation transit. Notice also the significant on-street parking that is provided, with four lanes during peak periods, and additional on-street parking during other times. This avoids the urbanism-killing big parking lots of American urbanism. In this kind of boulevard layout, the travel lanes could be up to six or more lanes, as it is in Paris and other cities, and remain pedestrian-friendly with an additional median. And as these examples show, the pedestrian realm here still has some generous features.

Going up the scale of street sizes and the vehicular mobility they provide, we finally arrive at the fastest kind of throughway, the grade-depressed freeway system that we discussed before. The result of this mobility, along with other factors, is that Portland's inner core areas are remarkable success stories of regeneration over the last few decades.

I am pleased to report that on carbon metrics, Portland is also doing well relatively speaking, although there is much more to do. By a recent per-recession assessment, Portland was 14 percent below its 1990-level target, which as far as I know, has not been duplicated by any other US city. We all have a long way to go, but this is an encouraging indicator.

Portland has also come a long way from its declining urban core of the 1960's, and I think we can begin to see the importance of taking down the elevated motorway and re-establishing these other links. I think we're seeing confirmation of what Jane Jacobs observed, confirmed by other research — that when urban areas are fragmented by freeways and other barriers, it creates other kinds of damage to the urban tissue around them for some distance. People become isolated. Businesses shutter their doors. A whole series of spiraling negative conditions kick in.

Jacobs also suggests that it's possible to reverse-engineer these phenomena, and "unslum" the damaged places, by reconnecting them to the wider urban fabric. That connectivity to the wider city and its diverse economy helps to diversify the neighborhood itself, and bring more opportunity. That's a very hopeful prospect.

PHOTO ESSAY FOR CHAPTER V.1:

A typical day living in Portland's continuously well-connected, walkable urban fabric

Figure V.1.1. Walking, biking, transit and car are all viable choices for travel in Portland's well-connected urban grid. This intersection, next to the celebrated Powell's Books, includes streetcar, bikes, walking, cars, bus, and a light rail connection three blocks to the south.

Portland is a case in point of the renaissance of which I speak. It is a modern American city with a prosperous economy, and yet it also demonstrates quite well the urban structure that Jacobs and Alexander championed. It thereby demonstrates that sustainable urban development is not antithetical to a prosperous economy with ample opportunity for employment. Indeed, as this book argues, these things are increasingly tied together.

In the 1960s and 70s, Portland was a fairly dreary town, not so different from Pittsburgh or Chattanooga in those days. But as in those other cities (and countless more), city leaders here were inspired to change things. Jacobs and Alexander are often mentioned as inspirations in part for these changes, and Jacobs herself came here occasionally to comment on and encourage the work. Alexander's "pattern language" methodology was also used to develop much of the planning for the city in those years (as well as the better-known University of Oregon, recounted in his book *The Oregon Experiment*).

Figure V.1.2. Downtown Portland in the 1960s, full of freeways and parking lots. The riverfront freeway to the left was later removed to create the much-loved Tom McCall Waterfront Park. Photo: Oregon Historical Society.

Figure V.1.3. Pioneer Square, often described as the city's "living room," occupies the site of a former parking lot. It now has two light rail lines passing by it as well as a streetcar line nearby.

Luckily, the city had great urban bones — its small walkable blocks, streetcar grid and diverse mixed-use fabric. The city's remarkable renaissance was begun with some added public spaces (Pioneer Square, Ankeny Square etc.), appropriate contextual infill (Pioneer Place, RiverPlace, etc.), adaptive reuse of existing buildings (EcoTrust's Vollum Center, University of Oregon Graduate Center, etc.), and a mix of light rail, streetcar, bikeways and better bus service.

FIGURE V.1.4. Portland's remarkably well-connected walkable grid, stretching continuously across the river, freeways and other obstructions. Principal through streets are spaced at roughly ¼ mile, or 400 meters, which is a common pattern in walkable cities. The author's apartment building is at the circled dot on West Burnside, to the center left of the map. Image: Google Maps.

To give a flavor of the urban renaissance that happened here (and can happen elsewhere), I will offer a personal report on life in one particularly livable part of town, where I have my own home and office.

Figure V.1.5 Portland's walkable grid stretches right across the 405 freeway in West Portland (at bottom of photo), with light rail, streetcar and bus lines, as well as bike pathways and wide walkable sidewalks. At right is the Northwest neighborhood, and at left is Goose Hollow. The author's apartment is at center top. Image: Google Maps.

I live and work in an area that adjoins Portland's well-known "Northwest" neighborhood, also called the Alphabet District or Nob Hill. I actually live just across the borderline, in an area called Goose Hollow. Geographically, However, Goose Hollow and Northwest are part of a continuous urban area bounded by the West Hills on the west and south, the river on the north, and Downtown and the more famous Pearl District on the east.

Figure V.1.6. Farmer's Market in Portland's Northwest neighborhood, a beautiful and functional place to live for the author and many others.

This is a remarkable place — close to a textbook example of well-connected, mixed, walkable, multi-modal urbanism. It's economically diverse, with people of very modest incomes as well as wealthy people and those in between. It's also very beautiful and livable. I live in a historic 1911 "courtyard apartment" — very typical for the area — with a balcony overlooking the neighborhood. It's one of 45 units on a 10,000 square foot lot, or about 930 square meters. For planning geeks, that's a net density of 196 units per acre, or 480 to the hectare — unusually high by the standards of most American cities. The gross density of the neighborhood is above 20 units to the acre — about 24 or so depending on how it's measured — which is one of the highest in Oregon. (Yet the neighborhood has very few tall buildings — a point that fans of tall buildings should note, along with other cautionary evidence. My very livable yet high net density apartment is 6 stories.)

Figure V.1.7. The author's 1911 courtyard apartment building, typical for the neighborhood, with a net density of 196 units to the acre (about 480 to the hectare). The author's apartment is on the far side, with a balcony overlooking the neighborhood.

I live and work in a small one-bedroom unit with quite reasonable rent by US West Coast standards, about $1.55 USD per square foot per month, or about $17 per square meter. That includes heat, water and sanitation. It should be noted however that rents have been soaring here in recent years, a result of the phenomenon I have called "voodoo urbanism" (see chapter IV.5). I also pay about $25 per month in electric bills, using the local utility's renewable "green" energy option. I don't own a car, and I bike or take transit to most locations, and use car-share for others I can't get to. The location itself is a major factor in affordable (as well as very pleasurable) living.

Figure V.1.8. Although Northwest Portland is one of the densest neighborhoods in Oregon, its diverse mix of housing, including single-family detached, duplexes, rowhouses and apartments, makes it remarkably livable and attractive.

On a typical day here I wake up, shower and get dressed, make some coffee, answer some emails, then walk or bike to a nearby deli to read the paper, say hello to friends and acquaintances, and eat a bagel or some huevos rancheros. Then it's back to the office (in my apartment) to make some calls, do some work, or prepare for a meeting. On some days I teach an on-line course from my home at a university where I am an adjunct. Frequently I'll head off to a meeting, most often on my bike, which is often faster than driving or transit would be. On the rare occasion that I need to drive to a meeting, I check out a ZipCar from just around the block, or I carpool with colleagues.

Figure V.1.9. Elephant's Deli, where the author often walks to have breakfast, read the newspaper and visit friends.

For shopping I can bike to three different grocery stores within about 4 blocks of here. One of them is a high-end specialty store, another is a warehouse-type organic store, and another is a more generic and affordable grocery store. My bank, dentist, laundry, print shop and other routine services are also in the same area. I can also bike easily to the famous Powell's Books (see Figure V.1.1), or other downtown department stores and specialty stores, for office supplies, clothes, or household goods.

Figure V.1.10. The Portland Streetcar passes in front of Good Samaritan Hospital and a row of shops offering neighborhood services.

I do have to drive to visit my two daughters and five grandkids (or they have to drive to visit me) a few times a month. Both live in smaller nearby towns close to their workplaces. One family lives in a beautiful small town up in the Columbia Gorge called White Salmon, and another in an exurban town called Wilsonville, farther south in the Willamette Valley. For those visits I check out a ZipCar, since neither family is on a reliable transit connections to here. (This is a significant problem for the suburbs here, although the city itself has quite good transit.) For most trips, including regular business meetings, I am able to bike or take transit. When I head to the airport for a business trip, I use the light rail line, which has a station a few blocks away from here.

It's true that this neighborhood is not as practical for families with more than one or two children. When my wife and I were raising our three daughters, we briefly considered living here. However, we opted to live in a nearby suburban town, and we did own cars — although the neighborhood was also walkable and bikeable, with well-connected mixed-use streets and reasonably good transit. (The core of Portland and other cities is not the only kind of place that is experiencing a renaissance of urbanism.)

Figure V.1.11 A number of former residences have been converted to retail uses at the ground floor along Portland's NW 23rd Avenue forming a complex and spatially attractive streetscape.

To be clear, Portland is far from perfect: it has its share (or more) of problems with over-gentrification, loss of affordability, displacement, inequality, homelessness, traffic congestion, poor-quality over-development, loss of livability and heritage, and other common urban ills in the USA. But it has those problems in spite of, not because of, the near-perfect urban form in its core. Bigger problems occur in the sprawling suburbs, where over two-thirds of the region lives, and where car dependence, traffic congestion, poor transit service, and other related ills occur, as they do in so many other cities, new and old. However, another more recent kind of problem is also occurring in the core of the city — a destructive kind of hypertrophic growth, resulting from ill-conceived policies that amount to "killing the city with kindness." This is the phenomenon I referred to as "voodoo urbanism", discussed in more detail in Chapter IV.5.

Typical suburban "drive-to" shopping mall

Portland's downtown Pioneer Place mall

Typical suburban hospital "supercampus"

Portland's Good Samaritan Hospital

Typical suburban university "supercampus"

Portland State University

Typical industrial "supercampus"

Portland's Eastside Industrial Area

Figure V.1.12. Comparison of Portland's connected, walkable urban form to 20th Century models criticized by both Jacobs and Alexander. Top left: typical isolated "drive-to" shopping mall surrounded by parking. Top right: Pioneer Place, a multi-block complex connected by tunnels and bridges, and allowing the walkable street grid to continue at grade, and serving pedestrians, bikes, cars, and two light rail lines. Upper left: A typical suburban hospital "supercampus", and upper right, Portland's Good Samaritan Hospital, again a multi-block complex connected by tunnels and bridges, allowing the street grid to continue at grade, serving pedestrians, bikes, cars, and a streetcar. Lower left, a typical isolated university campus, and lower right, Portland State University, once again a multi-block complex with a continuous walkable street grid throughout, connected also by bridges and tunnels, and featuring a streetcar. Bottom left, a typical suburban industrial supercampus, and bottom right, Portland's Inner Eastside industrial area, including a light rail line. Photos: Google Maps.

205

2. DIVERSE OPPORTUNITY:
*"Cities for all" are necessary not only for justice — they are necessary to how well a city actually performs.**

"Cities have the capability of providing something for everybody, only because, and only when, they are created by everybody."

— Jane Jacobs, The Death and Life of Great American Cities

Just now we are fortunate to have a global framework agreement on the "New Urban Agenda" as a basis for shared response to our growing urban challenges. In December 2016, all of the nations of the United Nations General Assembly adopted this outcome document of the Habitat III conference by consensus, and that is a remarkable achievement. At the same time, much work remains to be done to translate the aspirations into actual implementation actions.

Like a lot of us I'm sure, I have been thinking very much about how we are going to implement the agenda in the context of the rapid urbanization of our age. It is sobering to think that, by some projections, we may well create more urban fabric in the next fifty years than we have in all of human history. That is why this question of the New Urban Agenda is such an urgent one.

No less equally, we need to be thinking about a joined-up approach to the Paris climate accords, and to the Sustainable Development Goals — without which, we will simply not be able to meet this set of challenges facing humanity just now. We are all well aware of the forces that all too eagerly act in their own self-interests, and manifest the "tragedy of the commons." We need to counteract these destructive forces.

But as part of the process, we need to answer the question, "what's in it for everyone?" How does the New Urban Agenda offer us a positive future, while its alternative is a dark and undesirable one?

* This essay is based on a talk given at Habitat Norway in Oslo, February 2017. I am indebted to Kjersti Grut of Habitat Norway for the invitation. I am also grateful to Elizabeth Razzi, Editor-in-Chief of Urban Land magazine, for the commissioning the research and development of the article on Medellín, Colombia, discussed herein.

Opposite: Street vendors in an increasingly prosperous former slum area of Medellín, Colombia.

One of the central conclusions of the New Urban Agenda is that we must ensure that we have cities for all." But what does it mean to say that we need "cities for all"? Why is that important, and why should we work on it as a focus of our efforts?

As Alexander and, especially, Jacobs, argued, this is not only a matter of justice or fairness or political equity — as significant as those goals are. (And yet, as controversial as they are for some self-interested parties.) In fact it is a core requirement for cities to do well what they actually *can* do for all of us — to provide human development in the fullest sense of the word, including economic and social development. As we have discussed, they must also do so in a sustainable way, without producing the kind of catastrophe that does indeed seem to loom ahead, by all the evidence.

To put the point bluntly, *a city that is not for all cannot be a sustainable city, period.* But the corollary is that an open, interconnected, accessible city, that offers diversity and opportunity for all, and that offers the "rungs of the ladder" for human development for all, *is also good for everyone's bottom line.*

That's the "headline" if you will, but let me talk about some more specifics that will be useful for our work in implementation of the New Urban Agenda. To do that I want to talk about the remarkably useful conceptual framework that Jacobs has given us to work with these challenges.

Earlier in the book — and again in the last chapter — I discussed Jacobs' arguments on how important it is to have a continuous, connected, diverse, fine-grained urban structure, down to the scale of human beings, particularly as they interact within public spaces. Many people understand that, or at least they understand her four key recommendations — mixed-use diversity, walkable street networks around small blocks, diversity of building conditions and ages, and concentration of people and activities. What perhaps isn't as well recognized is Jacobs' later work as an economist — someone who has connected these elements of urban structure to the economic performance of a city, or a nation or a globe.

We now understand, in large part thanks to Jacobs, that cities generate economic growth through networks of proximity, casual encounters and what are called "economic spillovers." The phenomenal creativity and prosperity of cities is now understood as a dynamic interaction between web-like networks of individuals who exchange knowledge and information about creative ideas and opportunities. As we have discussed earlier in the book, many of these interactions are casual, and occur in networks of public and semi-public spaces— the urban web of sidewalks, plazas, parks and so on. More formal and electronic connections supplement, but do not replace, this primary network of spatial exchange.

Just as important, cities perform best economically, and environmentally, when they feature pervasive human-scale connectivity. Like any network, cities benefit geometrically from their number of functional interconnections. To the extent that some urban populations are excluded or isolated, a city will under-perform economically and environmentally. This is key to the economic importance of "cities for all" and "right to the city," and it's key to motivating the implementation of that aspect of the New Urban Agenda.

By the same logic, to the extent that the city's urban fabric is fragmented, privatized, sprawling, car-dependent or otherwise restrictive of diverse, open encounters and spillovers, that city will under-perform — or, as we see in too many cities today, that city will require an unsustainable injection of resources to compensate.

One of the most hopeful and instructive examples of the results of this approach is in the Colombian city of Medellín. Among the dangerous cities of the world, few have equaled the troubled reputation of that city. At its peak, the former base of narcoterrorist Pablo Escobar recorded over 3,000 murders per year, and many more robberies and assaults. For decades many of the city's public spaces were desolate and unsafe. Slum areas, swelling with refugees from political violence in the countryside, were overtaken by equally violent gangs.

But by almost all accounts, Medellín has seen one of the most remarkable urban turnarounds in modern history. Crime is markedly lower, and the city is graced with well-attended new civic spaces, libraries and art galleries. Business is good — indeed, the envy of many other cities across the globe. What's more remarkable is the unconventional path the City has taken to this recovery.

Part of the turnaround certainly began when Escobar was killed in 1993, the climax of a storied manhunt. A more general police crackdown followed, and the murder rate was cut by more than half. Even so, for years afterward the city languished as urban quality of life indicators remained stubbornly low. Many attribute the real transformation to a shift in urban policy that brought about a revitalization of the poorest parts of the city. That in turn has brought remarkable benefits for the rest of the city too.

Some of the biggest changes were managed by Medellín's charismatic former mayor, Sergio Fajardo, who is now governor of the province in which Medellín sits, Antioquía. A Ph.D. in mathematics, Fajardo is also an architecture fan — his father was a noted Medellín architect — and he has long had a fascination with the capacity of architectural and urban interventions to catalyze wider benefits. As mayor, Fajardo inaugurated a remarkably ambitious plan of "integral urban projects," as they are known locally.

Such projects are typically not in the wealthiest areas of town — on the contrary, they are in the poorest slums. "We are going to go to the spaces of the city where we know we have the most need, and we are going to come up with architecture as a social program," Fajardo told *Newsweek* magazine in 2010. "Some people say, 'Well, it's just a building.' It's not just a building. It's a public space, and the dignity of the space means the whole society has invested there. The whole society is present there."

Nor are the projects simply alluring examples of international "starchitecture" — rather, they are buildings by local firms that provide educational and recreational opportunities, like libraries, parks and schools. One notable example is the Parque Biblioteca España, a striking group of rustic black cubes set in a verdant hilltop of the once-notorious Santo Domingo neighborhood. Designed by Bogotá architect Giancarlo Mazzanti, the project is representative of Fajardo's "architecture as a social program."

There are five such projects, and Fajardo sees them as key catalysts for the improvement of the city. These are, he says, a major example of his strategy for the city: "public space of the highest quality, at the site where the libraries belong, at the heart of the community," and where each community is thereby "enriched by the library, where all citizens have access to books, technology, entrepreneurship centers, all the tools needed for full development."

Another project, the renovation of the popular Jardín Botánico and Orquideorama, features a distinctive pavilion of geometric wooden hexagons and helixes by local Medellín architects Plan:B Arquitectos and JPRCR Arquitectos. Other projects include schools and community centers, also with striking architecture. Fajardo has made education a major priority, but has used architecture as a tool in that process. "People who say that a beautiful building doesn't improve education don't understand something critical," he told *Newsweek*. "The first step toward quality education is the quality of the space. When the poorest kid in Medellín arrives in the best classroom in the city, there is a powerful message of social inclusion."

Fajardo, along with his former Director of Urban Projects, Alejandro Echeverri, initiated not just building projects but also an innovative series of micro-lending and community-led investment programs. Some of the biggest investments were in transportation and public space infrastructure. For example, Fajardo's administration completed the Metrocable system — a series of aerial trams up into the steep hillsides — begun by the previous administration, and added new extensions.

One of the most dramatic, now a big tourist draw, takes visitors to the stunning Parque Arvi, an ecological park whose new wooden buildings complement the natural setting. Tourists ride the aerial tram alongside local slum residents, some of whom might be enjoying the park from their nearby neighborhood. Visitors can canoe along creeks, ride a zip line through the tree canopy, or go horseback-riding through the forest.

One of the most attention-getting projects was surely the outdoor escalator system introduced into one of the poorest and most dangerous favelas, Comuna 13. The escalators, stretching a quarter mile up a steep hillside, were requested by the residents themselves through a citizen-led appropriation process, and cost about $6.7 million US dollars. Extensive media coverage brought out the skeptics — how could such an unconventional, expensive system help to improve such a notorious slum? — but today, few can deny the remarkable changes that have come to the area since the escalators were installed.

Where once residents trudged up a dangerous sewage-laden path — a hike the equivalent of scaling a 28-story building — now they pass uniformed attendants as they step onto covered escalators, taking them up a steep, visually stunning axis through the neighborhood. Between and around the six escalator segments is a series of new small public plazas extending outward with steps and walkways. Around these plazas, new home-grown businesses have sprung up, and many nearby homes have been beautifully improved. A new series of concrete pathways has been extended from these spaces too, with more new businesses, remodeled homes and well-tended landscaping.

Visitors frequently marvel at the livable appeal of the public spaces. Where once it might have been unthinkable, lush plants and public art remain undamaged. Graffiti is there, but largely confined to key walls, where its colorful patterns seem to actually animate the public spaces. The stunning setting, overlooking the valley below, brings a steady stream of visitors who come to take in the sights.

Fajardo likens such integral urban projects to what he calls "urban acupuncture" — a term popularized by former Curitiba, Brazil mayor Jaime Lerner. Under Lerner's administration, Curitiba became famous for a series of innovations that greatly improved urban quality of life. For example, a Bus Rapid Transit system made it easier to get around inexpensively, and a garbage-for-groceries exchange program solved the problem of waste disposal in the slums. Lerner was also an architect who was unsatisfied with architecture as a mere visual amenity; like Fajardo, he sought to use architectural and urban projects to catalyze wider improvements.

In the introduction to his 2003 book titled *Urban Acupuncture*, Lerner explained the idea this way: "As with the medicine needed in the interaction between doctor and patient, in urban planning it is also necessary to make the city react; to poke an area in such a way that it is able to help heal, improve, and create positive chain reactions." The goal, Lerner says, is to create "revitalizing interventions to make the organism work in a different way."

Lerner, Fajardo and others are quick to distinguish this approach from the "silver bullet" solutions that some urban planners promote — for example, recruiting an international "starchitect" to create an attention-getting building as a tourist destination. The goal is what has come to be called the "Bilbao Effect," named after the celebrated Guggenheim museum in Bilbao, Spain, designed by American architect Frank Gehry. But as Hispanic-American urban planner Andrés Duany points out, such a new element is supposed to bring wonderful results for the city all by itself, without building on the surrounding urban fabric — a phenomenon Duany decries as an example of "magical thinking."

Duany points out that most subsequent "Bilbaos" have not lived up to their reputation. "Their effects on their cities is roughly equivalent to the effects of ancient cave paintings of antelopes on the next day's hunt," he says. By contrast, he notes, "wherever planning has succeeded, it has relied upon the patient re-weaving of the urban fabric into whole cloth, socially, physically and economically." Medellín's success, he thinks, has come from its successful repair and reconnection of the most damaged parts of the city's urban fabric. Handsome architecture is only a tool in that process — a signal that the surrounding neighborhood and its people have value, and are worthy of development opportunities.

As Fajardo points out, this is not simply a matter of physical changes. The residents themselves have become involved in these projects — in their planning and operation, and in the other surrounding activities they have generated. This means a different relationship between the planning bureaucracy and the residents. Fajardo is known for the "civic pacts" he made with different constituencies, not merely "giving them a say," but giving them "co-responsibility" — that is, transparent responsibility for success or failure. Letting constituents take full credit for success was, Fajardo found, a powerful incentive for cooperation.

Fajardo's skill at making things happen in spite of the bureaucracy has become legendary, and his popularity rating on leaving office was at a historic high near ninety percent. While in office he seemed to combine a mathematician's mastery of game theory — the art of understanding and managing rules, incentives and likely outcomes — with a humanist's sense of open collaboration and trust. That winning formula has earned him admirers far beyond Medellín. Although he was focused on improving the well-being of the least well-off citizens, he earned the trust of the local business establishment too, demonstrating that his strategy offered strong wins for rich and poor alike.

Fajardo is quick to point out that the successes were not his alone. He came to office with an alliance of leaders with expertise in a broad range of relevant fields including finance, education and urban development — the so-called "Group of 50," which later grew to about 200, becoming Fajardo's "brain trust." The group created a series of intensive workgroups to tackle specific problems within the city and develop effective strategies and tactics.

Fajardo's team replaced the old crony reward system with an emphasis on more transparent metrics. That immediately shifted the dynamic of rewards, says Federico Restrepo, Fajardo's director for planning. As he told researchers from Princeton University's Institute for Successful Societies in 2010, "discussion became objective and perfectly justifiable in terms of numbers and data. The level of subjectivity, which is usually associated with political negotiations, went down drastically."

Fajardo has been active in the International Association for Educating Cities, a network of cities begun in 1990 that fosters collaboration "on projects and activities for improving the quality of life of their inhabitants on the basis of their active involvement in the use and evolution of the city itself," as the Association's website puts it. This is clearly very close to Fajardo's thinking.

"A city is an educator," Fajardo told the Association in 2007. "Education in a broad sense, as a tool of social transformation that makes its citizens of the world and makes them equivalent in knowledge and development opportunities." Fajardo, the former university professor, came to see "the educated city" as the unifying theme of all his work. "Whatever we did, we explained it around this narrative about education understood in the broad sense," he told the Association. That means giving people lifelong learning opportunities from hands-on involvement with improvement projects in their own neighborhoods.

"We must close the gap between the public administration and the citizen," Fajardo explained. This is not a nebulous goal, but a concrete plan of action. "For us it is basic to recognize and encourage new leadership; use our person to person interventions directly to reach the communities; share the processes of transformation step by step; generate working groups on projects; encourage and respect the work of the citizens groups; emphasize clarity in the processes; and hand over to the community the responsibility for caring for everything that has been achieved."

Duany invokes the principle of "subsidiarity" — the capability to work on neighborhood-scale projects, retained by the neighborhoods themselves, but with the capacity-building assistance and collaboration of the city as a whole. Duany and his colleagues offered a similar strategy for the recovery planning of New Orleans, using "neighborhood resource centers" to bring tools and resources for building to neighborhoods across the city. Similar trends are under way in other cities, variously known as Tactical Urbanism, Pragmatic

Urbanism and Peer-to-Peer Urbanism. In this global movement for urban innovation, Medellín's successes are gaining fame.

It is not just livable public space that is a goal, Fajardo says, but also the reduction of violent crime — the ultimate threat to well-being and to urban vitality. In that essential goal, the conventional tools must be supplemented by the new tools of urban intervention. "You need the police, the justice system, the military, and all these things" he told magazine. "And we have done those in Colombia. But we have to close that entrance door [to a life of crime]. It's a door that is very wide open in Medellín."

Integrated urban projects can open an alternative door, he thinks, by creating urban environments that offer opportunity and real participation. "We have to dedicate quite an effort to building hope," he told *Newsweek*. "Everyone, eventually, should see the possibility for success for themselves here. That means quality education, full public education—in science, technology, innovation, entrepreneurship, and culture." And, he says, it means a sense of responsibility for one's own home and neighborhood.

Over a decade after Fajardo's term began, not all is rosy in Medellín, certainly. After Fajardo's term ended, crime has risen again and remains stubbornly high — in 2012, for example, there were still over 1,000 murders, though that's less than half of the 1990s peak. The new crimes are also those now common across much of Latin America, largely exchanges between small gangs of narcotraffickers. By most accounts, the city does feel much safer and more appealing. Tourists are coming in surging numbers, and once-desolate public spaces are now thriving with night life. But Fajardo and others recognize that there is much more to do.

Nor are all the urban interventions popular with everyone. Some comuna residents criticize the metrocables, arguing that they are much more expensive than the buses they replaced. Others feel that Fajardo should have spent more time ending corruption in the police force. Observers also caution against giving too much credit to the urban interventions for reducing crime: Fajardo's term happened to coincide with a truce negotiated by the national government and the city's violent paramilitary gangs.

But Fajardo is a strong advocate for the benefits of the participatory principles used in the city's urban interventions. "This formula, apparently simple but with a very deep sense of what participating democracy should be like, functions in Medellín, and anywhere in the world for that matter, because it rescues the true sense of politics," he told the International Association of Educating Cities.

How does he define this "true sense of politics?" It is, he says, "nothing more than working with people for people, where the general interest always prevails over private interest, where everyone is invited to get involved in the changes, where no favors are negotiated for bureaucratic office or contracts, and dignity and differences are respected."

For Fajardo, this is not just an equitable policy, it is an economic development strategy. In a region of the world where the population of such informal settlements is exploding — as it is in much of the developing world — there is a lot at stake, Fajardo believes. Cities with greater opportunity for all will be more competitive, and will be more successful in protecting and enhancing their natural resources, their economies and their quality of life.

Indeed, he says, he believes "this is the only way to achieve the social transformations being demanded in the 21st century."

PHOTO ESSAY FOR CHAPTER V.2

Medellín's remarkable renaissance

Figure V.2.1. A steward on the new escalator system of Medellín's Comuna 13 chats with a young resident.

I spoke to Sergio Fajardo, former Mayor of Medellín and later governor of its province, Antioquía, about the strategy to connect all parts of the city. Key to that strategy has been to place important civic institutions (like libraries and museums) in formerly isolated neighborhoods that are also now connected by the overhead metrocable system, and other more convenient forms of transit.

Michael Mehaffy: You are known for using construction projects in the slums as a catalyst for further improvements. Why, as you see it, is this strategy effective?

Sergio Fajardo: As a government, we must always ask what problems we have to solve. This self-examination, for our city, brought the recognition that we live in a society with deep social inequalities, and we have accumulated a great social debt. In addition, the violence generated by drug trafficking has left deep roots and a feeling of "no future", most evident in our poor neighborhoods where opportunities have been few, and where the absence of the state has allowed violent people to occupy the spaces. Recognizing, then, all our problems, and considering that we decided to participate in politics to bring hope and to transform our society, we opted for policies that will help the development of communities by implementing a range of development tools simultaneously.

Figure V.2.2. Left, a typical pathway in Comuna 13, which is steep, dangerous and unsanitary. Right, the residents opted, through the City's participatory budgeting program, to build an escalator system that is patrolled by unarmed community stewards.

SF: In the poorest communities, where violence had its deepest roots, we intervened with what we called "Integral Urban Projects" — covering physical, social and institutional dimensions. That integral program allowed us to implement projects on three levels: what we call *estructurantes, detonantes y articuladores* (structural changes, catalytic triggers, and tactical connectors). These all operate under one simple principle, but one that summarizes our approach: *the most beautiful to the most humble.*

Figure V.2.3. New sidewalks, stairs, planters and small public spaces along the new escalator line give residents new house frontages to improve and occupy. Some have opened stores and other businesses.

MM: What are the major issues that have to be taken into account to ensure success in this work?

SF: This program sought to allow access to decent housing by the most vulnerable citizens; to protect the ecosystem and to promote environmental sustainability; to promote citizen participation in the development of the territory; to raise standards of public space for regional balance; to generate equity and social development; to upgrade informal settlements; to eradicate extreme poverty; and to promote actions that would encourage urban dynamics to foster peace and coexistence.

Figure V.2.4. Residents relax in a new public space next to a store along the new escalator line. The store's name is "The Penny Less Shop."

SF: Our social intervention promotes community involvement. Participatory planning legitimizes the actions in the territory and creates spaces for discussion, dialogue, exchange and dissemination. This constitutes the foundation of coexistence, solidarity, and stronger deterrence of violent behavior.

We institutionally intervene under a concept of integration that involves, among other things, knowledge of the territory, a close relationship with the community, the responsible management of money, and careful planning and management of the transfer of functions, when handed over to the entities responsible for their continuation.

Figure V.2.5. Residents walk past street vendors on a narrow, pedestrian-friendly neighborhood street as the Metrocable passes overhead.

MM: Some have referred to this strategy as "urban acupuncture" [a concept related to Jane Jacobs' strategic use of public projects as "chess pieces"]. I think you have said so as well, isn't that right? How do you define this term?

SF: Undoubtedly the urban acupuncture strategy was implemented in our case. Our physical interventions had to reach the areas that were most vulnerable, the spaces that were associated with violence or that were fear-producing, but we could not stop there. We had a goal of moving from fear to hope, and the instrument was social planning. Perhaps it's an evolution of urban acupuncture, because it allows the integration of all development tools in complete balance between the physical, social, and institutional.

Figure V.2.6 The view from Medellín's new Metrocable as it approaches a new library, the Biblioteca España, in the neighborhood of Santo Domingo. Photo: Savio Albeiror, Wikimedia Commons.

SF: For us each project implementation was done by type and sector. The Santo Domingo neighborhood has a new library and park located there [see photo above], and in the adjacent neighborhood, Granizal, is a sports pitch, and those facilities triggered the development of each sector. In that way, we achieved a social transfer between the communities in those neighborhoods that had previously been isolated within their borders and suffered as a result. So as a fundamental part of the transformation, we thereby restored a sense of shared citizenship to people.

Figure V.2.7. The Metro light rail line now connects to formerly isolated, low-income parts of the city.

MM: How is this a different approach from the "Bilbao effect" — the creation of a building by an architect of international fame as a "silver bullet" — for example, to attract wealthy tourists?

SF: I really did not intend to generate a tourism effect, not immediately. Our proposition was "the most beautiful to the most humble" and we called on the Colombian architecture community to create urban references as the highest expression of the redefinition of the spaces and public buildings in poor neighborhoods. Over time, we wanted to restore confidence in the territories and their institutions, creating a community maturation process, with emphasis on education and culture. This would allow us all to host our own neighbors, and so understand ourselves as part of a larger society. That is to say, we began to organize our affairs, unraveling ourselves of the social debt that we had with these communities, so as to be also hosts to the national and the international communities.

Figure V.2.8. In addition to the Metrocable and light rail line, bus, bike, walking, motorbike and car are viable transportation choices in Medellín's well-connected transportation system. The city also offers a bike-sharing system, being used here by the bicyclist at center left.

MM: I know that you put a great emphasis on resident participation and transparent processes. Why do you think this is important?

SF: The management of social policies should be grounded in reality and should take into account variations in different social conditions, matched to the plans and programs as developed. For this reason, the participation of the people plays a very important role, in forming organizational spaces, social relations and institutional linkages. We need a set of targeted actions to promote development opportunities, build skills, and add synergies. This public participation facilitates the regulation of political, social and economic patterns, and the needed relationships between public policy actors.

Figure V.2.9. A biker rides along a new walking and biking path built into the hillside, which has allowed new stores and seating areas to spring up.

SF: It is up to different sectors to recognize the existence of other actors, i.e. the public sector should provide security, social cohesion and governance, and promote decentralization through the transfer of responsibilities. The exercise of responsibility between state and society is a way of honoring the public.

In simpler words, one can say that when the community is involved — when the community is taken into account from the beginning in all urban transformation processes — the highest social impact is achieved. When the projects are completed, they will not be seen as simple infrastructure. The people are going to feel themselves a part of those projects, and that's why they will always care.

Figure V.2.10. New stairs and landscaped public spaces in the Comuna 13 neighborhood provide safe and attractive connections to the rest of the city.

3. ADAPTATION:

We need to harness the power of evolution and adaptive morphogenesis, using it to generate forms that can more successfully accommodate human needs, activities and experiences.

"An environment or community will not come to life unless each place, each building, each street, each room, becomes unique, as a result of careful and piecemeal processes of adaptation."

— *Christopher Alexander,* The Battle for the Life and Beauty of the Earth

As both Jane Jacobs and Christopher Alexander asserted throughout their careers, much of what has gone wrong with cities has come from failures to understand or respond in a direct, adaptive way to real human activities or needs, or the real and complex cities and towns in which they exist. Instead, say Jacobs and Alexander, planners, architects and city officials have responded to abstract *ideas* of what human beings might need — or even more remotely, what the systems might require that we have instituted to serve human needs as we have understood them. This approach has produced widespread failures, and an increasingly unsustainable condition.

Confirming that insight, a considerable body of research shows a remarkable divergence between what professionals believe is a good solution, and what is often seen as a good solution from the point of view of the people whose lives are in question. If that is true, it represents a major barrier to our ability to achieve a sustainable, healthy basis for the future of settlements — and it is a barrier that must be overcome, if we are to actually implement the New Urban Agenda.

An insight about this state of affairs comes from social psychology, and the topic known as "construal level theory." In essence, the theory helps to explain how people make "construals" about the nature of the world around them, including, in the case of professionals, the nature of the problems to be solved. The more psychological distance there is between a person and the actual concrete set of issues to be treated, the more people — including professionals — must

Opposite: The entry area of Christopher Alexander's Eishin School near Tokyo, Japan.

substitute their own abstract "construals" for the more concrete issues of an actual place.

The result of this greater abstraction can be a failure to understand what actually matters to the people who live in that place on a daily basis. If we are planners, we might substitute our own construals of orderly arrangements of the parts (as we saw with Christopher Alexander's "A City is Not a Tree"). If we are transportation engineers, we might substitute our construals of efficient movement for the qualities that make a place actually worthy of travel in the first place. If we are architects, we might substitute our construals of what a great sculptural building might be, when consciously regarded by connoisseurs like ourselves — not what ordinary people actually experience and actually need. (I discussed this problem at length in Chapter IV.3.)

It follows that one straightforward requirement for understanding what human beings need from their environments is to ensure that we are indeed in close touch with those same human beings — that we involve them in the processes of design, and that we empower their capacity to make many small and large choices and adjustments to meet their own needs. While we will necessarily make some decisions about the structures of their environments, a great deal of the art of our work is in giving them as much capacity to enrich their own lives as possible. We are not so much providing them with something that we think will enrich their lives (for example, what we judge to be a great work of art) but rather, we are providing an environment that offers to them the *capacity* to live their own rich life.

As Christopher Alexander says in the opening pages of his book *The Battle for the Life and Beauty of the Earth*:

> The purpose of all architecture, the purpose of its spatial-geometric organization, is to provide the opportunity for life-giving situations.... When this purpose is forgotten or abandoned, then indeed, there is no architecture to speak of.

This definition of architecture is fundamentally different from the dominant one shared by many architects, which is to create great works of art, in the manner of gigantic sculptures. Whether or not these are worthy works of art, the problem is that this represents a construal of our *own* values as artists, or artistic connoisseurs, in place of the values of those who actually live in a place.

Alexander's definition, however, in no way diminishes the artistic dimension of architecture. It does not demand that we forsake all of art for a cold functionalism, or a dull vernacular. Rather, as Jane Jacobs discussed, it only points out *how* the artistic aspect of architecture should relate to its human and quotidian aspects. It should serve to illuminate and celebrate the *actual* life of the city, not supplant it with a wholly foreign (and abstractly construed) series of gigantic sculptures. The result, as discussed earlier, becomes "no longer mutually reinforcing" — in Alexander's term, it lacks *wholeness.* It becomes disordered, noisy, malfunctioning — and unsustainable. In Jacobs' memorable words, the result is no longer art at all, nor life — it is "taxidermy."

In this context, a close involvement with the people for whom the designs are made is not only a matter of promoting democracy and public involvement in civic affairs — which is a valid aim in itself, to be sure. However, for one thing, many of the people who will live in a given place will not arrive there until long after a given design process has completed. Rather, the involvement is actually necessary to ensure the *quality* of what gets built, from a human point of view. That is true both for the creation of new structures, and for the ongoing modification of existing ones — which may or may not be done with the assistance of design professionals.

This form of involvement is not a tokenistic "consultation." Rather, it requires a different conception of design, less about providing a static "finished" state, and more about providing the capacity for users to modify, and sometimes co-create, different parts of their own environment. It aims to develop something close to the idea of "affordances" as developed by the psychologist James J. Gibson, namely, providing to the users themselves "the possibility of an action on an object or environment."

This kind of creation and modification already goes on at many scales of space and time, although we often ignore it. In the most immediate scales, I can open a door, close a window, draw a blind so that the sun is just so, or move my chair to see the passersby outside — or move to a more private place farther back in my home. In the larger scales of time and space, I might remodel my home, or build a new one, or move to an entirely new location. My neighborhood might join in the planning of a new sidewalk design or a new transit stop.

The evolution of cities and towns is made up by changes like this, small and large, over a day or over a century. Some of them are provided as finished states by specialists and "experts", but many more are created by a wide variety of actors and agents, including ordinary people. As the city changes, patterns form and re-form. What worked before can be (and often is) copied by another owner, or later in time.

In this way, we pass on to one another "genetic" information — that is, knowledge about how to make a nicer door, a nicer building, a nicer neighborhood. These processes were extremely common in older cities and towns. (Indeed, this was close to Alexander's idea of a "pattern" that is shared by members of a community in a "language.") But they still occur today — perhaps more than we realize, with greater importance than we realize.

As we saw in the last section, for Alexander, "adaptive morphogenesis" is the process by which the form of the environment gradually grows in its complexity and its capacity to meet needs — much as biological systems evolve through adaptation to become more complex, more differentiated, and more effective in achieving results that are beneficial to the organism. In *The Nature of Order*, Alexander spent considerable time examining these lessons from biological systems.

Alexander's analysis implied a broad critique of "modern" design and construction systems. They are too rigid, too tree-like, too reliant on experts producing static "finished" products, and not sufficiently evolutionary, nor sufficiently adaptive. This was often because the scale was inappropriate — too big, or too repetitive, or too standardized. The economies of scale and standardization needed to be replaced by an economy of place and differentiation.

As I have discussed previously, the most conspicuous influence of Alexander's ideas in the technology world has been in the world of software, first in the development of pattern languages of programming (also known as design patterns), then in wiki, and then in the development of Agile, Scrum, and Extreme Programming. All of these topics deal with the egregious failures of too-rigid technological approaches, and constitute more "agile" alternatives that have a better capacity to evolve a better adaptive fit for the problem at hand.

In the built environment, the implication is two-fold. One, our goal as designers should be to provide more of exactly this kind of "affordance" — that is, greater capacity by users to modify and evolve their own environments, at a range of scales of space and time, including small ones.

This principle can take many forms — for example, the moveable chairs that William H. Whyte recommended for public spaces, or the ability of restaurants to colonize the adjacent sidewalks in a relatively ad hoc way (now a ubiquitous pattern in many cities), or the preservation of smaller lots or plots, to allow more fine-grained development by a more diverse range of owners and users.

The second implication is more radical, and probably more controversial among today's architects, especially stylistically ideological ones. It is that <u>users should be free to employ any pattern that is most adaptive and successful, from any source.</u>

By definition, some of the best solutions are already well known and established, for the simple reason that they have clearly worked before, and that knowledge has become common, or is available in a recognizable pattern, often understood as a "traditional design". These include not only some solutions that worked a decade ago but also a century ago, or even a millennium ago.

Looked at from the broader perspective of evolutionary theory, this is not so surprising. The needs of human animals include universal ones of thermal comfort, shelter, food, spatial security, ability to move about, ability to interact with one's fellows in a way that maximizes opportunity and minimizes threat — in short, all the things that cities give us. In a real sense, cities are evolutionary structures that represent good adaptive solutions to the problems of living well in large groups of people.

Cities can accommodate many other aspects of human need, of course, including psychological needs, and many of these also have deeper roots in human evolution than we have realized. As I discussed in the last section, this is one of the revelations of the topic of "biophilia" — our innate preference for certain kinds of environmental structures, especially those associated with living systems.

There is an even more radical implication, according to Alexander. As we saw in previous sections, natural processes give rise to certain natural morphological properties, which are fantastically varied but also remarkably simple in their essence. They include properties like centers, boundaries, gradients, local symmetries, alternating repetition, and other characteristics (which he catalogues within "fifteen properties").

Because these properties are rooted in our deep evolutionary experience, and even the deep order of things, it is not surprising that we find them repeatedly in works of art and architecture over thousands of years and many different cultures and contexts. Indeed, many of the most powerful patterns, the ones that move us deeply, have exactly the properties that Alexander described — say, the interlocking harmonies and dramatic contrasts of a Bach fugue, or the local symmetries and levels of scale of a graceful temple. Even though we are not (or no longer) part of the cultures in which these works were made, they have a universal power.

It is this universal power that, Alexander argued, is encoded into patterns, and shared by means of languages. Functionally they take the form of the kinds of patterns seen in his book *A Pattern Language* — Entrance Rooms, Light on Two Sides and so on. But aesthetically they are also coded, into motifs, ornamental patterns, "orders" and other elements of traditional design languages.

These coded bits of knowledge are surprisingly sophisticated and powerful, and we are beginning to recognize that our own supposed "modern" practice of sweeping away all traces of "historicism" is, from an evolutionary perspective, actually quite primitive and foolhardy. A more sophisticated, nuanced and complex approach would open us up again to the vast repositories of history and nature. While generally would generally not literally reproduce an exact structure form the past, it would certainly feel free to re-generate new structures with unique properties, from the generative grammar of ancient and universal patterns. This is indeed how most of the rich, complex, well-loved architecture of the past was generated.

These and other patterns of experience and knowledge represent a kind of "repository" of useful solutions to ongoing and often recurrent design problems. That was one of the key goals of Alexander's work on patterns, and indeed, one of the things that the software designers found most useful. They encode important adaptive solutions that help us to re-generate successful forms, with at least the essential aspects resolved.

As we saw in the earlier discussion of pattern languages, these adaptive solutions often express simple common configurations of things in the human environment, irrespective of period, style, political expression, or ideological intents. For example, pitched roofs tend to shed water and snow better than flat ones; roughly rectangular doors of about a meter wide and two meters high tend to work better than sizes that are much different; flat floors and perpendicular walls of roughly square shape tend to work better than other shapes. These common designs are rooted in the most common geometries of human beings (usually a little more than a meter and a half tall and a half meter wide), their movements on foot, and the common configurations of their needs (social interaction with others, etc).

It must be stressed (for this point is often misunderstood) that this is not a rigid template-based approach. (As "traditional" architecture can be, when produced with defective "modern" approaches — resulting in what has been called "modernism in drag".) As long as the essential adaptive form-creation or "morphogenesis" is completed, the artist is entirely free to embellish, accentuate, articulate, express, combine, echo, interconnect, in all manner of profound new ways. But this artistic aspect takes its place within the fundamental architecture of human and urban order, and within its wholeness. At every stage, the goal is to transform the order and wholeness, and to make it something living and new. The goal is not to *supplant* this existing order with a willful contrivance of artistic novelty.

There are many kinds of evolved design patterns that are available as generative kernels within this process of adaptive morphogenesis. They represent well-adapted solutions within a broad human context, not necessarily universal to all of humanity but certainly broadly applicable to a local context, and broadly useful for the human needs there.

These patterns often get recycled within the evolution of a society, creating a kind of fugue between the pattern and its new expression, with new elements added. This new expression amounts to a kind of "revival," not a literal copying but a new expression of the older patterns. For example, it is easy to see that the Romans revived much of Greek architecture, and the Romanesque and later Renaissance architecture revived much of both the Roman and Greek architecture. Jefferson revived Palladio, who in turn had revived Vitruvius — and so on and so on.

We now understand that these kinds of revivals or recapitulations go on all the time in many different societies — not only the Western Classical tradition — and they are responsible for some of the most spectacular architecture ever known to humanity. The places they have produced — Rome, Paris, London, and many more

— are among the most enduring, well-loved, sustainable (because they have sustained) urban precedents known to humanity. It seems beyond ludicrous to suppose that we must never, ever make anything like them again.

Alexander's hopeful message is that the patterns of a more healing kind of growth are already all around us. We can find them in the structures of nature, and the processes that produce them. We can find them in the collective intelligence of traditional structures and traditional knowledge, ready to be re-opened, revived and regenerated, as part of the living tissue of our globe. The writer Jorge Luis Borges put it best, "that between the traditional and the new, or between order and adventure, there is no real opposition; and what we call tradition today is a knitwork of centuries of adventure."

Let us only resume that knitwork, and discover the renaissance that nature and history offer us.

PHOTO ESSAY FOR CHAPTER V.3

Signs of a renaissance in urban architecture

New projects that rival the human qualities of the best ones of history.

For this section I wanted to show some examples of the renaissance of more adaptive urban architecture of the sort suggested herein. There are thousands of examples that I could show of this young architectural renaissance — perhaps millions — from many parts of the world. They include work by recognized architects and designers as well as innumerable projects by non-professionals. To give just a small but tangible sampling of this work, I have included here some of the work by Christopher Alexander and his associates, including this author.

Christopher Alexander himself has completed a number of projects that demonstrate his ideas for a more humane architecture based on adaptive morphogenesis, wholeness, and "life-giving comfort and profound satisfaction," as he put it. Perhaps his best-known example is the project he and his associates (notably his colleague HansJoachim Neis) completed for the Eishin School near Tokyo, Japan.

Figure V.3.1. A gateway in the Eishin School, by Christopher Alexander and associates.

This project was the case study for his last book, *The Battle for the Life and Beauty of the Earth*. The buildings clearly exhibit a generative result that shows the effects of the "DNA" of Japanese architectural form languages. Yet they are also more eclectic, more differentiated, and more unique in their own way — exactly as Alexander advocates.

Figure V.3.2. Judo Hall at the Eishin School near Tokyo, by Christopher Alexander and associates.

Figure V.3.3. Christopher Alexander's interest in the geometry of carpets led him to a commission to design the Carpet Museum interior in San Francisco, California.

Christopher Alexander also advised the Prince of Wales, who developed an urban extension of the town of Dorchester, in the UK, called

Poundbury. The development is often mocked by modernist architects, who fail to note its remarkable progressive urban achievements.

Figure V.3.4. A public space in the new urban neighborhood of Poundbury, UK. The project's urban and architectural form fits in with the regional character, unlike the vast majority of new suburban development.

Figure V.3.5. A grocery store in one of the neighborhood centers of Poundbury.

Figure V.3.6. Houses in Poundbury follow the vernacular pattern of the area.

Figure V.3.7. a new public square nears completion in Poundbury. Good-quality public space is often a casualty of "modern" suburban development.

The community demonstrates a number of sustainability innovations, including "green" buildings, local materials, energy produced from an "anaerobic digester," and especially, reduction of car-dependence. As Clive Aslet wrote in *The Times of London*, in an article titled "Charles has silenced the 'toy-town' sneering":

> [Poundbury] was planned so that people could walk from their homes to the shops, to the school, to their jobs. Social housing was — to use the jargon — pepperpotted among posher homes; 35 per cent of property is affordable. By providing a mix of property sizes the Duchy of Cornwall, which owns the town, enabled people of different ages and income levels to live in one sustainable community. And to work there too, in spaces that have been provided near homes.

Figure V.3.8. A house designed and built by the author in 1984, after studying and working with Christopher Alexander. It featured passive solar design, native vegetation, permeable paving, and other "green" technologies — unusual for the time.

Figure V.3.9. More photos of the house designed by the author.

Figure V.3.10. Another house built by the author following his studies with Christopher Alexander. It featured simple low-cost construction systems and recycled materials.

Figure V.3.11. The author was project manager and co-designer for a walkable mixed use project with major new transit connections (sometimes called a "transit-oriented development") on Portland's suburban light rail line, known as Orenco Station. Its urban and architectural form was generated very much in adaptation to the local history and urban pattern.

Figure V.3.12. Some architects are fond of criticizing the so-called "historicist" architecture that is sometimes used in "New Urbanist" projects, like Rosemary Beach, Florida, shown here. As this book has argued, the logic behind this criticism is defective. The real question is, does a place have life, and is it therefore successful from a user's (not an architect's) point of view? Is it using the best available solutions to meet human needs, from whatever time or place?

4. ENVIRONMENTAL SUSTAINABILITY:
Cities offer us very powerful ecological and resource benefits — but we need to understand and empower their network dynamics.

"What is required is a new definition of the city as a contact system, as a set of interactions and flows that define the kinds of network that enable creativity and innovation to thrive and grow."

— Mike Batty and Peter Ferguson

Both Jacobs and Alexander pointed to the capacities of cities to promote a more sustainable way of life, with greater resource efficiency and much lower ecological damage. Both of them also linked these benefits to other benefits of cities, including quality of life for human beings, and opportunities for human and economic development.

However, neither Jacobs nor Alexander examined in detail the actual structural characteristics of cities that lead to these benefits. There are certainly strong hints in their discussion of cities as networks of overlapping and diverse interaction, and in Jacobs' idea of a "spillover" — which I will discuss below. However, in the years since Jacobs and Alexander first expressed their insights, research has continued into the ecological characteristics of cities — with some surprising findings.

For those who do research in the sustainability of cities, one tantalizing puzzle looms large. On a number of metrics, higher-density cities are measurably "greener" than other places — that is, in many respects their residents have a much smaller ecological footprint. But in our current models, we can explain only about half of that difference, perhaps even less. Like the "dark matter" problem of physics, this "dark greenness" is both somewhat embarrassing, and very intriguing.

To be sure, some of the greenness of cities is not so hard to explain. For example, people drive less in bigger cities, because it's

---

* *Portions of this chapter were drawn from an article that appeared on The Atlantic's CityLab website in 2012.*

Opposite: *A tram passes by a bicyclist and pedestrians in the beautifully livable town of Freiburg, Germany.*

harder to drive, and because it's easier to get around without a car. (In fact, driving per person has actually gone down in recent years, even before the economic decline — and evidence suggests it's because more people are living in compact, walkable cities and suburban neighborhoods.)

Other factors are small in themselves, but do add up: the closer spacing of buildings results in lower transmission losses and pumping energy; there is less embodied energy in roads and other infrastructure, and less operating and maintenance energy; urban residences tend to be more compact and energy-efficient; and more rural and natural areas are preserved, which provide important "ecosystem services."

But the most intriguing reason may be the one we understand the least: people in cities actually interact and use resources in a more efficient kind of pattern — specifically, a network pattern. When we look at individual factors in isolation, we miss the synergetic effects of this network pattern, which may well explain why we can't account for the observed magnitude of efficiency.

But there are other models that might help us — especially those that explain the dynamics of networks. In particular, there is a phenomenon in economics that's known as a "Knowledge Spillover" (also known as a "Jacobs Spillover," reflecting work on this idea by Jane Jacobs). It's one of the reasons that cities are such powerful economic engines — and very likely one of the reasons we make cities at all. Simply put, it's the idea that within a city, if you are making x, and I am making y, then our combined knowledge might allow us to make z together — but only if we are physically close enough that our knowledge can "spill over" from one sort of enterprise to another.

In practice, many such "spillovers" gradually connect and reinforce each other, creating a kind of virtuous circle of economic activity, and over time, spawning whole new industries. (Think of the automotive industry centered in Detroit, or the personal computer industry centered around Palo Alto.) This pattern is a classic kind of "interactive network," familiar to many other disciplines.

The Jacobs Spillover is one form of an "externality" — an effect of an economic transaction that is not agreed to by the parties of that transaction, or factored into the accounting of such an economic transaction, but does have a consequence for one or more of the parties, whether positive or negative. An example of a large-scale negative externality is the depletion of resources like oil, or the accumulation of greenhouse gases that cause climate change. These phenomena will eventually impose a real cost, whether or not it is factored into the transactions. (Thus, one promising line of research is in ways to "monetize" these externalities, so that they can provide more direct economic benefits or penalties, and thus work to incentivize the sustainable use of resources.)

But the key observation of interest to us is that the spillover is an output of one system, which becomes an input into another — and this "virtuous circle" has a synergetic effect, increasing the economic efficiency of the city. This seems to be the case particularly when multiple variables are involved, and the synergies can compound through a kind of network effect. For Glaeser et al. (1992, 2009), this synergy from spatial proximity represents a core advantage of cities, and may even explain why cities are economically attractive places at all. This was also a theme of Jacobs' own book The Economy of Cities (1969).

Nor is the Jacobs Spillover the only such externality that seems to be operating in cities. We may also consider the physical proximity of the consumption of resources, which may account for similar kinds of urban synergies. For example, Stockholm and other cities use "combined heat and power" to utilize the waste heat from power generation to heat homes. Many businesses use the waste output of one process as the input of another — for example, wood manufacturing businesses may use waste wood chips as a fuel source.

Such resource "spillovers" seem to operate in other realms too. If my daily activities are grouped close together, I may use the same trip by streetcar to stop along the way to meet another need that I might otherwise accomplish with a separate trip. These "transit spillovers" might account for a significant part of transit reduction in urban areas, beyond simply reduced distances between destinations.

It seems likely that all of these spillovers might in fact have additional interactive spillover characteristics — that I might, for example, also find a new job near my home on the way to another destination, and then share a creative bit of knowledge with a colleague, and then perhaps purchase some wood pellets at the local furniture store, and so on. That is, such spillovers might in fact form a kind of "spillover network" that has additional synergies. As this network grows within the city, its capacity to generate additional unforeseen spillovers also grows exponentially with its number of nodes, following the compounding power of networks.

A spillover is also an example of a process in which the output of one system becomes the input of another system, which is then able to transform it in some important way. A close analogy is the "metabolic pathways" of biological systems. Such processes typically do not operate in isolation, but as part of complex "metabolic networks." This allows a complex interactive sequence of processing, with the efficient assembly of very complex outputs as a result.

In ecological systems, we can see a corollary when the excess chemical output or "waste" of one system becomes the input or resource of another. When these processes are part of a larger ecological network, the productivity of the system in biological terms can be greatly accelerated, while the "waste" of the system — the outputs that are not re-used — can be greatly reduced, or even brought to essentially zero. This network of "spillovers" — that is, of outputs becoming inputs — therefore represents a dramatic increase in the "efficiency" of the system — its ability to achieve high states of order with low waste.

Is a similar kind of process perhaps going on in cities? Can we use this model to understand and perhaps enhance the puzzling but remarkable resource efficiency of cities? Can we use it to confront the daunting problem of climate change, and, as suggested by the empirical observations, dramatically reduce the emissions of people within cities? This problem takes on special relevance as we see new patterns of urbanization around the globe, and the indications are that these new urban areas will follow the US model of very high consumption of resources with high levels of waste, and very high emissions per capita — a disturbing implication for the prospects of catastrophic climate change.

This concept seems to present a number of fruitful lines of investigation.

One revolves around the subject of urban density, or persons per unit of land — a controversial and problematic topic to be sure. Is urban density the only identifiable factor that affects this externality, or can we measure and model other factors? What about certain patterns of spatial distribution — for example, of uses, or of street networks, or of transit modes? What about Jacobs' own hypothesis that walkable street-based urbanism, with its close stitching of private and public realms, was a critical mode of human connection, not reproduced in other forms of transportation?

What, too, is the role of human experience and choice, within the environment of a neighborhood or a city? As I discussed in the previous section on climate change, does the "choice architecture" of a neighborhood substantially affect the consumption patterns of people who live there? It seems perfectly plausible: if the walking paths within my neighborhood are unattractive, or conceptually unavailable to me when I am choosing to travel, I am less likely to choose to walk there. On the other hand, once I am in a car, if the neighborhood environment makes it easier for me to drive through, consume fast food, use disposable packaging, eat meat and so on, then I am more likely to make those choices — as indeed people do, on the evidence.

This structure of the neighborhood and its "choice architecture" seems to extend down to the scale of the sidewalk and its "intricate ballet," in Jacobs' memorable phrase. The networks of movement, interaction, experience and choice also include the smaller-scale structures of building fronts, entries, yards, forecourts, sidewalk seating areas, gates, gardens, and other myriad structures in the critical transition realm between public and private. This system of "place networks," as I call it, is an overlooked but, I think, critical realm of urbanism, deeply connected to all of the other issues we have been discussing. (I will have more to say about what I am calling "place network theory" in a forthcoming volume.)

There is another interesting question to explore. Why is it that some suburban areas seem to have comparable levels of economic activity from spillovers, without the close proximity of people in cities? Why do they also have high emissions rates, which might suggest here is no correlation with economic spillovers as we suggest here? We hypothesize that this is because they are reproducing the conditions of proximity that facilitate spillover within cities, but doing so artificially, through relatively high-resource consuming activities — particularly, they are driving many trips of long distances in single-occupant automobiles. They are also performing other high-consumption, low-efficiency activities — living in isolated large homes, consuming poor-durability goods, living a "drive-through" lifestyle. They are able to maintain the economic spillovers after a fashion, using automobiles, cell phone contact, email, and other more artificial forms of contact — but only with a lifestyle that requires prodigious (and very likely unsustainable, it appears) consumption of resources. (This is the model that I previously referred to as the "crack cocaine" of economic development. It is highly effective in producing a quick economic "high" — but only at the expense of a planetary-scale hangover.)

If this phenomenon can be substantiated, how would a useful model be developed? What would be the metrics, variables, dynamic elements?

Another, more distant but ultimately most important line of inquiry is to explore strategies to exploit this phenomenon, assuming it can be substantiated. Can planners use strategies of "self-organization" to catalyze the spontaneous growth of such urban "metabolic networks"? Can they be facilitated with economic tools, such as pricing signals and other mechanisms? What is the role of "top-down" planning, such as the placement of initial elements of infrastructure and the like? My hunch is that a mix of all these strategies could be powerful and effective.

This, I suggest, indicates a promising research agenda for further investigation. The tangible goal might be to develop a "spillover network" or "metabolic network" model that might explain some of the more significant synergies and metabolic network-like aspects of urban systems, with the capacity to make differential comparisons based upon morphology. Such a model would ideally be capable of making useful predictions about choices in urban and infrastructure design, and urban and economic policy. Such a model might also facilitate the ability to monetize the currently unpaid costs of unsustainable urban development, and the long-term economic benefits of more sustainable development.

PHOTO ESSAY FOR CHAPTER V.4

The remarkable example of Freiburg, Germany

Impressive achievements on sustainability metrics using urban form in combination with other technologies.

Figure V.4.1. The small German city of Freiburg. Photo: Thomas Maier, Wikimedia Commons.

Freiburg is a remarkable case of a relatively small town (220,000) that, like Portland and other cities, has experienced an urban renaissance in the last several decades. In the case of Freiburg, the city has retrofitted its historic neighborhoods with convenient forms of transit and energy-saving technologies, and it has built new urban extensions to accommodate population growth. These new neighborhoods feature a number of impressive innovations, including shared ownership, affordable housing, community gardening, convenient multi-modal transit, renewable energy, and other efficient, low-cost resource systems.

Within the city, the public transit system has been upgraded to offer convenient transportation by tram, rail, bus, walking, biking, or driving. Cars are accommodated in "traffic-calmed" areas, including so-called "shared space" areas that are safe for pedestrians.

Figure V.4.2. Bikes, pedestrians and rail users mix freely in the livable core of Freiburg. The tram offers an easy ride to the city's new urban extensions.

As in Portland, regional planning has focused development within the city boundaries, limiting sprawl. Strict ecological standards protect the area's natural ecology as well as its vineyards, orchards and farms, which provide a significant export economy as well as goods for the city itself.

Figure V.4.3. In the city's center, beautiful historic buildings are retrofitted with renewable energy and conservation technologies, providing the sustainability benefits of both.

Figure V.4.4. Vendors prepare for a busy market day in the city's central square, offering produce and other goods from the region. The market operates every day, and provides an important outlet for area farmers and producers — and healthy food for the city's residents.

Most of the historic buildings in the city center were destroyed by Allied bombing during World War II. The city decided to rebuild on the original medieval pattern, not reproducing the previous buildings exactly, but producing new buildings in the same architectural form language. In this way the city really did experience a kind of renaissance, of livable and human-scaled architecture.

Figure V.4.5. Konviktstrasse, an infill development area completed in the 1980s.

Figure V.4.6. New apartment homes line community gardens and playgrounds in the new urban extension of Vauban. Roofs are made from solar panels. Photo: Arnold Plesse, Wikimedia Commons.

The city prepared twelve guiding principles for its "Charter of Sustainable Urbanism" to be used in shaping its new development. The twelve principles are grouped under three headings: Spatial, Content, and Process.

Figure V.4.7. The new urban extension of Rieselfeld includes a walkable grid of streets, gardens, playgrounds, public buildings, and homes in a compact, ecologically efficient form. None of the buildings are over six stories, and many of them feature balconies and terraces overlooking adjacent gardens and playgrounds. Photo: Volatus, Wikimedia Commons.

Principles of the City of Freiburg's "Charter of Sustainable Urbanism":

- **Spatial:** I Diversity, Safety & Tolerance; II City of Neighborhoods; III City of Short Distances; IV Public Transport & Density. (Continued below.)

- **Content:** V Education, Science & Culture; VI Industry & Jobs; VII Nature & Environment; VIII Design Quality.
- **Process:** IX Long-Term Vision; X Communication & Participation; XI Reliability, Obligation, Fairness; XII Co-operation & Partnership.

Figure V.4.8. Paving stones from the city's recently re-paved center, using natural stones from the area in traditional patterns.

In the development of the city's new urban extension, Reiselfeld, the plan followed seven crucial principles:

- **Human Scale:** In its architecture, and urban space design, the new neighborhood should be built to a human scale. There should be a clear differentiation between public, semipublic and private spaces. Public spaces should be defined by continuous urban fabric shop/houses or terraced houses along the street to a maximum of five or six stories.
- **Identity:** Since the social stability of a district depends on residents identifying with their neighborhood, the neighborhood must have a good image, with its own unique and consistent character.
- **Social structure:** From the beginning the neighborhood must have a balanced social structure. This means that while social housing is an important element, it must be balanced by market rate housing.

- **Infrastructure:** For the neighborhood to have its own identity it must contain all the essential infrastructure. Shops, schools, kindergarten, health care and senior services, work places, restaurants, churches, sports and other facilities must all be included.

- **Transportation:** It is of the highest priority to encourage use of public transportation; the new district must be connected to the city center and other parts of Freiburg by tramway and bus.

- **Ecology:** Ecological principles must influence architectural design and urban design. Buildings should make use of passive solar energy, solar collectors and photovoltaics.

- **Community participation:** It is important to develop a process of community participation in the planning and building designs for the new neighborhood.

5. SYSTEMS REFORM:

If we want better cities and towns, we need to change the "operating system for growth."

We must find ways to transform, throughout society, our processes, our ways of thinking and doing, in every field that touches the built environment.

— *Christopher Alexander,* The Nature or Order

Both Jacobs and Alexander argued throughout their careers that reforms were needed in order to build better cities and towns. In each case, they gradually delved deeper into the systems that would need change: into planning models, architectural practices, attitudes towards existing places and their lessons, regulations and codes, laws, economic incentives and disincentives, and other topics. All of these things might be thought of as elements of a kind of "operating system" that governs urban growth. Like a computer operating system, the urban "operating system" allow some "programs" to run, while others cannot; some tasks can be done, while others cannot; and some outcomes can be achieved and others cannot.

To explain the profound importance of this subject — so important that I believe it's a proper concluding topic for the entire book — I will give a case study of the recovery planning after Hurricane Katrina. What follows is a personal account of my own involvement, and what I came to see as both the failure of our current "operating system for growth," and the hopeful story of the good things that happened, and can still happen, under a different kind of operating system.

By the time I got to New Orleans for the first of several Hurricane Katrina recovery planning projects, the first lesson that struck home was how ill-prepared we were to accomplish the simple task that the residents most urgently asked us to do, over and over again. "Please help us to rebuild our homes." A smaller number also asked for help rebuilding their small businesses, which were often within or near their homes. But these were not the wealthy and powerful we were dealing with.

Opposite: Residents of New Orleans mingle with tourists in the city's iconic Jackson Square.

We dealt with renters too, and their landlords — but in New Orleans, a remarkable number of people, including many very low-income families, owned their own homes. Of course they needed financial help—but more than that, they needed help navigating through a blizzard of bureaucracy, much of it private. They often found themselves in an absurdist nightmare, required to produce mortgages and insurance papers and other documents for homes that had washed away, along with all their records.

Nor were they prepared to navigate the bewildering complexities of contracting, financing, design, permitting — in effect, overnight to become residential homebuilders, a field in which they typically had zero experience (and zero time to perform, let alone learn). Nor did they have experience with the design of homes, or the correct restoration of historic properties, or the best way to respond to the neighborhood character and quality, or any of innumerable other demands. For almost all that I spoke to, it was an overwhelming ordeal.

In this context, the promise of endlessly delayed relief funding was doubly cruel. It had the effect of putting lives in limbo, shutting off alternative local solutions, and making the rebuilding, when it did finally come, all the more difficult. Worse, the money was often mismatched to the actual local need. If an insurance adjuster offered, say, $10,000 for a lost roof, but the lowest available contractor price was $20,000, the fed-up homeowner—who was very unlikely to have another $10,000 lying around in the bank — might as well decide to pocket the $10,000 and move to Baton Rouge. Such a shortfall was all too common.

And this was no way to rebuild a city.

Our response was to propose immediate, locally based "neighborhood rebuilding centers," offering knowledge, expertise, access to resources, pattern languages — and above all, peer-to-peer sharing of information through a neighborhood wiki. These centers would be, in effect, small neighborhood research libraries, where residents could come and get solutions to their many detailed problems. Above all, they could help each other to learn the issues and solutions for their own neighborhood and situation.

Who were the best contractors, and when were they available? How do you talk to an insurance adjuster, and present your case? How can a plan be prepared for permitting and construction? How can we figure out any of the ten thousand things we have to know that are specific to this neighborhood — its base flood elevation, the history of its houses, the zoning requirements, and so on?

In the world of utilities, there is a well-known challenge called "the last mile problem." It turns out that, rather than the many miles that lead up to it, this last gap is the most difficult to bridge. In this last-mile gap is where many small and detailed connections and extensions have to be made, and it can't be done wholesale, top-down. It has to be done bottom-up, one house at a time.

Something similar was going on with the redevelopment after Katrina. We were focusing on everything except the last-mile problem — lots of talk about big solutions, big pots of money, massive rebuilding projects by movie stars and big national charities. But that wasn't where the real challenge was. It was in the last mile, in the humble case-by-case self-organization at the level of the house and the neighborhood.

Our solution was to propose resources targeted to the last mile — not only top-down ones, like expert technical knowledge and funding, but bottom up ones, like peer-to-peer knowledge sharing. We proposed a neighborhood wiki system that would allow sharing of tips, ideas, and how-to knowledge. It would be a tool of local empowerment and self-organization.

We also proposed a pattern language format — following Alexander's lead, a locally customizable system of design elements to assist with homes and neighborhoods. We brought our friend Ward Cunningham, the inventor of Wiki, onto the team to help to develop the software. We brought Alexander himself onto the team.

To their credit, the Louisiana Recovery Authority (LRA) strongly supported the proposal, even offering to fund a pilot project — until their lawyers got their hands on it. "There is a data protection issue," officials were told. "The government could be held liable if information were used by one party to damage another." Curiously, that kind of liability seems to have been no problem for the likes of Facebook, Twitter, and other peer-to-peer social media — and, for that matter, Wikipedia itself.

But the government was risk-averse, and in this there was a kind of paralysis. A lack of certain action meant no action. More than that, the LRA seemed to be unsure even whether this kind of rebuilding effort was really the right priority after all. In frank discussions with Andy Kopplin, the director of the LRA, he candidly told me that "perhaps the best strategy is just to rebuild in Baton Rouge." I found myself wondering whether this was a recovery program, or a program of retreat.

To be sure, the rebuilding of a great city like New Orleans is a daunting challenge. It simply cannot be done top-down, and I understand if Kopplin felt as though he'd hit a brick wall. But I think the lessons do show that a city like New Orleans can be rebuilt bottom-up, with top-down support. The challenge is daunting but not insurmountable. Indeed, that's how a great city like New Orleans grew up in the first place.

New Orleans is a marvel of informal order. Its older neighborhoods are loose jazzy improvisations of buildings and details and quirky outdoor spaces, all exquisitely human scale and aimed at pedestrian delight. A walk down one of its streets reveals the layers of human activity and change that have grown up there, re-organizing, and transforming neighborhoods bit by bit. It is also a marvel of durable livability.

But this self-organizing growth is hardly random. New Orleans displays a complex cultural language of patterns and elements that were borrowed, adapted and applied — some of them French, some Spanish, some purely local — and in many cases, a kind of creole fusion of them all, into something new and remarkably coherent.

There were also top-down patterns that supported bottom-up growth. For example, the historic French farm tracts had property lines that extended perpendicular to the river, in a complex pattern that fans out and back as the river wends its way. Along these property lines, major streets would later be built, giving the city's street pattern its distinctive radial form.

So it goes: bottom-up, top-down, bottom-up again, forming a fugue, a weave, an urban fabric. People interacting, creating businesses, building houses, shaping gardens and details, layering on top. Applying carefully refined patterns, with careful evaluation and skill. It is neither all top-down nor all bottom-up, but a catalytic weave of the two.

And how the two weave together and support one another is everything.

The gardening analogy is apt. You cannot command plants to grow in the form you specify. But you can take steps to assure that they do grow, bottom-up, with your supportive top-down actions. You can plant the right seeds — good genetic material. You can build trellises that will support the growth of the plants. You can fertilize, and water, and prune where necessary. You can shape the growth in the way you need and want.

Just so with cities: you can plant genetic seeds as design patterns and types, you can build "trellises" in the infrastructure and streets, and you can fertilize with incentives, and prune with regulations and disincentives. You can empower local people to grow and diversify into something infinitely richer and more complex than you could have ever specified as an act of top-down design.

You can develop genetic material, the "DNA of place," through a rich repository of design ideas — and where better to do so than from the several thousand years of human experience building successful settlements? So Greece passes its genetic material on to Rome, Rome on to Spain, Spain on to the West Indies, and finally it arrives in New Orleans in a delightful, well-adapted mix (along with English, French, and other sources) creating an exquisitely local, high-performing architecture.

Contrast that with another strategy, which is to empower individual heroic top-down designers, the modern architects. They come to New Orleans with the best intentions, intent on creating something "fresh," "innovative," "exciting and new." It is a kind of novelty act — and the lessons of history show that this top-down approach is doomed to fail. But no one learns these lessons.

No one wants to believe them, because everyone has the best of intentions. Take, for example, the Make It Right Foundation, Brad Pitt's project to build exciting new "designer" homes in the Lower 9th Ward. Celebrities have come to raise money. Star architects have come to offer their designs. In ten years, over 90 homes have been built.

But over 300,000 homes were destroyed by Katrina, almost 100,000 of them in New Orleans. At the current rate, Make It Right would fully rebuild New Orleans in a little over 1,000 years.

More troubling is the precedent the Make It Right homes have set. Let us not learn from the successes and delights of New Orleans itself, they suggest. Let us not empower local people with local solutions. Instead, let us bring international architects to craft novelty inventions, and bestow them upon these lucky denizens. If these novelties happen to perform poorly — if they rot quickly, or have other problems — well, who knew?

New Orleans knew, if we wanted to look at the lessons of time and climate and locality. (Indeed, the Make It Right Foundation's Wikipedia entry notes that "the foundation has been under fire in recent months after over two dozen of the green homes built started exhibiting severe signs of rotting.") New Orleans has the embodied knowledge of how to make an exquisite street, a delightful house, a durable and enduring piece of the city. But we are in the bad habit of ignoring it.

The heroic top-down model is failing us, whether employed by architects, movie stars, or government agencies, because it cannot solve the last-mile problem. It cannot tap into the genetic repository of solutions and small adaptive actions that form the self-organization of a great city.

But just as wise top-down actions can support the bottom-up evolution of a great city, so unwise top-down actions can thwart it, and even destroy it. New Orleans, like many great American cities, was already in deep trouble well before Hurricane Katrina. It was in trouble because it failed to recognize that an equitable urbanism — an equitable geography — is not only more just, it is good for the bottom line.

During the first half of the 20th century, New Orleans offered a growing employment base around shipping, and thousands of people — many of them African-Americans — migrated to the city to work on the docks. At its peak, the city population was over 600,000. But by the 1960s, containerization had put an end to many of those jobs, and the population shrank for the first time.

Around that same time, suburban "white flight" — aided and abetted by government policy — accelerated the population decline, so that by the time of Hurricane Katrina, the city population was well below 500,000. Many of the remaining residents were poor and African-American. To the legacy of racial discrimination they could now add crumbling infrastructure and lack of access to viable urban resources and opportunities.

This is what, in New Orleans, we came to call "the hurricane before the hurricane" — the slow disaster that is 20th century urban planning, as it existed in New Orleans. This is what has happened to so many U.S. cities like Detroit, Baltimore, Cleveland — and so many other suburbs. This phenomenon is sometimes termed "shrinking cities" — but that is a misnomer. The New Orleans metro area is over 1.1 million, almost double the city's population at its peak. The city has not shrunk, but rather, has turned into a kind of demographic donut — emptying at the core, and thickening at the edges.

The same pattern exists in Detroit, the poster child of "shrinking cities" — and so many other American cities that have devastated cores. These conditions were not overtly planned, but the actions that brought them about certainly were: GI mortgages, the Interstate Freeway System, mortgage redlining, functional zoning, bad transportation planning, and a host of other policies, incentives, and disincentives.

The fact is, in focusing simple-mindedly on the physical plan, we have taken our eye off the real ball: the larger system of incentives, disincentives, laws, rules, codes, standards, and models that constitute our urban operating system for growth. And we have failed to recognize that the operating system that produced New Orleans' urban disaster — the hurricane before the hurricane — is still with us.

As Jacobs and Alexander have both pointed out, that system is built on an old, mechanical, top-down idea of the city. It sees the city as a collection of parts that need to be rationally segregated and then recombined to work properly — just as the parts of an engine are rationally segregated by function. If there is something wrong in one of these segregated compartments, the way to fix it is to target that spot with some additional top-down resources. If poor people lack housing, build some new housing for them. If a street is too congested with traffic, build a wider road or even a freeway.

As we've seen, Jacobs offered a powerful rebuttal to that system. In place of rationally segregated compartments, sorted out by use and type and population, she was a champion of diversity and connectivity right across the city. She noted that cities are indeed self-organizing systems, and they thrive on the kind of pervasive connectivity that can be seen in a city like Manhattan, with its highly interconnected grid of streets and sidewalks.

There was an important economic dimension to Jacobs's ideas too. As we noted in earlier chapters, it was not a coincidence that a city like New York could take penniless immigrants from Russia and Italy and Ireland, and convert them in due course into middle-class shop owners and executives and creative people of all types. The city functioned as a connective human-development system, allowing them to connect to ideas, knowledge, and opportunity and benefit from a kind of metabolic process.

The best way to get a city working well, she said, is to get all its parts connected and interacting in balance, neither letting some areas get over-concentrated with growth and wealth, nor others depleted of activity and left in poverty. For the poorest areas, the best thing that can happen is "unslumming" — allowing residents to contribute more to the overall economy, instead of creating a burden on it. Increasing wealth, if it increases diversity, is a good thing. A monoculture of poverty is not a good thing.

Similarly, for wealthier areas, gentrification past a certain point also becomes unhealthy, if it means the loss of diversity and a monoculture of wealth. It then becomes important to decant some growth to other areas of the city where it can be more beneficial. It is a bad thing for the entire city to allow these wealthier areas to continue hypertrophic growth — just as it is to allow poorer areas to remain mired in poverty.

To these strategic approaches we need to add other reforms of the "operating system for growth." We need new kinds of codes, more context-sensitive, more focused on form than on use. We need new kinds of regulations that are simpler and more effective. We need to manage "money floods" as much as "money droughts", making sure that the flow of money responds to the context and to the necessary feedback. We need changes to the models of neighborhoods and buildings, learning from precedent, and incorporating the genius of a diverse past.

In time Jacobs's ideas have come to be taken up by many others, including prominent economists and complexity scientists. She was right, they agree, that cities are complex adaptive systems that self-organize, and our challenge is to understand this "kind of problem a city is" as she put it, and to manage its "organized complexity." If we fail to understand or to manage cities in this way, we are likely to make all kinds of mistakes that are devastating to the people who live in them.

And so we have. We have continued to mistreat cities, and to allow them to under-perform. We get hyper-performance not from the natural dynamics of cities but from artificial (and unsustainable) injections of resources, into artificial urban environments. Since World

War II, we have built an enormous new world of sprawl, requiring massive (and massively profitable) consumption of fossil fuels and other finite resources. We have used this resource Ponzi Scheme to prop ourselves up — and now it is a global process. The institutions that are "too big to fail" grow ever bigger, until now they are entire nations: China, the United States...

So there is much more at stake than whether New Orleans re-builds — or whether the other devastated areas of the Gulf Coast re-build. There is more at stake than any one disaster, be it Sandy, Rita, Fukushima, or any of a thousand other calamities. What is at stake is whether we can understand and support the vitality of cities, their capacity to promote resilience, ecological performance, and sustainable prosperity. New Orleans is not just one place, but an exemplar of what is happening to us as a species and the question of whether we will develop the models and tools to change our "operating system for growth," as we surely must to avert disaster.

New Orleans, perhaps as much as any city on the planet, has what it takes to create an urban renaissance — and the tenuous signs of growth are already there. The only question is, will we learn to support them, and turn this young and vulnerable renaissance into a mature one?

PHOTO ESSAY FOR CHAPTER V.5

The slow renaissance of New Orleans

A painful struggle to overcome the current defective "operating system for growth"

Figure V.5.1. New Orleans' Marigny neighborhood features this typically eclectic but delightful mixed-use café/bar with rooms above, successfully repaired and re-opened shortly after Hurricane Katrina.

Figure V.5.2. A typical postwar strip mall outside of New Orleans, heavily damaged by the hurricane. These areas were rebuilt much more quickly than other, older parts of the city and region. The "operating system for growth" favored their reconstruction: old zoning regulations, bank lending rules, transportation engineering standards, financial protocols, economies of scale, and other "generative" elements.

Figure V.5.3. A house in New Orleans' Lower 9th Ward (top), flooded and also heavily damaged by a fallen tree, was rebuilt by the Preservation Resource Center with the author acting as a consultant for strategy and design. The blow to the side of the house was commemorated in a new notch with a porch, creating a more livable kitchen nook. The lower image shows how the house looks in 2017. Image: Google Maps.

Figure V.5.4. A group of small infill houses designed and built by architect Andrés Duany in the Bywater neighborhood of New Orleans, building on the form and character of the existing neighborhood. Image: Google Maps.

Figure V.5.5. Houses by actor Brad Pitt's Make It Right Foundation in the Lower 9th Ward, designed by famous architects to stand out, and not to fit in, to the neighborhood fabric. Image: Google Maps.

Figure V.5.6. Houses in Musician's Village built by Habitat for Humanity. Perhaps too repetitive and standardized? Photo: Google Maps.

Figure V.5.7. Left, plans for a new mixed-use square in the Gentilly neighborhood, developed by the DPZ planning team that included the author, during the city's recovery planning. Right, how the sprawling site still looks today. The site is still typical of most postwar suburban car-dominated developments, with very large and under-utilized streets and parking areas.

Figure V.5.8. The author and a number of colleagues proposed "Neighborhood Renaissance Centers" to provide technical resources and peer-to-peer exchange of information as well as community planning processes. The centers proposed to use pattern language as well as wiki-based planning resources, working with both Christopher Alexander (pattern language creator) and Ward Cunningham (Wiki inventor). The display at right is a mockup of the community planning wiki tool.

Figure V.5.9. Urban evolution in two New Orleans houses that were identical when first built. Over time the different owners made significant changes that differentiated the two houses significantly, yet they still maintain a visible harmony. Buildings like these were the subject of author Stewart Brand's book How Buildings Learn. Brand has stated that he was deeply influenced by both Jacobs and Alexander.

CONCLUSION: TWO URBAN FUTURES*

There is no new world that you make without the old world.

— Jane Jacobs

As I said in the introduction to this book, it is easy to focus on the problems of cities, and the ways they currently exacerbate the broader challenges that humanity faces. This book has focused instead on the powerful capacities that cities (and towns) already offer us, to help us to respond to those same challenges — and the hopeful signs all around us that we are beginning to learn these lessons, and to produce fruitful results. That is the young urban renaissance that is under way today.

It is also easy to attack the demagogic claims that have come to dominate our political environment in the last few years — for example the manifestly implausible idea that somehow building walls and excluding people will restore jobs and economic might. But I suggest it is more important to see the popularity of these claims in some quarters as the frustrated reaction to an equally deluded way of looking at urban economics, which supposes that growth comes solely from centralized stimulus and control. Hence if one group is not getting the goods from this centralized entity (be it big business, big government, or a complex of both) then it must be because another group is, and the only remedy is political revenge.

Both the action and the reaction are rooted in an older, more primitive industrial conception of the world — one that is now dangerously obsolete.

As we have explored, that is a carefully articulated message from the careers of both Jacobs and Alexander. Both of them have pointed to the intricate structural details of a more regenerative kind of city and its technologies, more rooted in the organized complexity of nature and the wholeness of natural systems, and more capable of achieving the kind of urban renaissance we need.

Jacobs reminds us that we must turn our attention away from silver bullets and magic formulas from afar or from above, and instead

---

* *Portions of this essay were published on the CNU* Public Square *blog in 2017.*

Opposite: *Residents of Hanoi, Vietnam enjoy car-free weekends in the area around the beautiful central lake of the city.*

look within — to our own capacities and the capacities of our own neighborhoods and cities, to generate new growth and new wealth. We must refrain from expecting large quantities to be delivered up by large centralized entities, and start to work toward more polycentric economies, and more polycentric governance systems.

We have previously (in chapter I.2) discussed another very important implication, and it bears repeating here. Of course it is possible, up to a point, to replace the diversified, continuous public realm of urbanism, and the healthy catalytic growth it produces, with a system of segregated, machine-like capsules: automobiles, isolated offices and campuses, suburban housing monocultures, and the like. It is possible, in other words, to trade away a "natural human-capital city," for an artificial kind of city that is nonetheless economically productive, at least in a historically limited and short-term sense. Indeed, we can see many examples of this kind of city around the world today.

However, this economic development can only be sustained with massive injections of resources — notably fossil fuels — whose limitations and negative impacts are only too obvious. Much of the economic growth that such a city produces is ultimately illusory, because it is consuming the basis of its own future growth. It is a kind of Ponzi scheme, the economic equivalent of "eating the seed corn."

At the same time, we can certainly recognize that people in developing countries face a very difficult situation. We can understand and support the urgent need to alleviate poverty and improve health and quality of life — for children, for women, for vulnerable populations, and for humanity as a whole. As we have discussed, urbanization is indeed a powerful way of reducing disease and hunger, improving longevity, reducing population growth, increasing efficiency, and expanding opportunities for human development in myriad ways.

But it is a central conclusion of this book that not all urbanization is the same, and not all urbanism is the same. In the last century, we have made a kind of devil's bargain with a quantitative approach that has failed to sufficiently account for the qualitative in urbanism. We have exploited economies of scale and standardization with great viral and metastatic power, but we have ignored economies of place and differentiation, to our great long-term detriment. As Jane Jacobs memorably put it, "we have left out feedback" — left out the proper accounting of externalities. As Christopher Alexander put it, we have failed to be sufficiently adaptive in our city-making — to human beings, to the qualitative aspects of life, and to the natural world on which we all ultimately depend.

The result of this maladaptive growth is a deep form of disorder, constituting a growing threat to the quality of our cities, and to our ultimate ability to sustain and prosper. The visible byproduct of this pathology is overall ugliness, with isolated elements of titillating beauty cloaked on here and there — like so much colorful product packaging, over a toxic industrial product.

This is not a trivial outcome. As Alexander suggests, beauty and ugliness are not "mere" psychological phenomena, but rather, manifestations of a deeper order, and of our own innate biological skill at detecting environmental order that will likely be beneficial to us, as well as its opposite. That helps explain why we hunger for beauty, in an almost literal sense. For that reason, the relation of this growing ugliness to a growing crisis of sustainability is not a coincidence. It is a biological warning signal, commanding our attention and response.

Both Alexander and Jacobs recognize the daunting challenges we face in the years ahead — ecological crises, resource crises, and at the heart of it, crises in our technological and cultural systems. They are certainly not alone in these concerns, or in the effort to offer constructive solutions. Their unique contribution, as this book has discussed, may be in the complementary structural outlines they have mapped out for us.

Quite intentionally, this book has not discussed the considerable criticisms that have been made of both Jacobs and Alexander. That is for another book, or perhaps many books. However, it is worth noting one persistent misunderstanding of both of them: that they are in the league of so many other designers and theorists who offer just more *ex cathedra* pronouncements, ideologically laden design theories, and assumptions that must be swallowed whole in cultish fashion. That is indeed a malady of much of the architecture and planning world today — but Jacobs and Alexander are critics from outside of it, not participants within it.

Indeed Jacobs was particularly withering in her criticism of professional ideology, declaring it a "pseudo-science" that "seems almost neurotic in its determination to imitate empiric failure and ignore empiric success." Alexander for his part envisioned patterns as "falsifiable hypotheses," and he acknowledged a strong influence from the empiricist philosopher of science Karl Popper. In fact, throughout his career, he showed a dogged concern with observation and reliable conclusion, and a repeated willingness to make major revisions in his conclusions when the evidence demanded it. (It was Alexander who, in the tenth anniversary of his book *Notes on the Synthesis of Form*, used its new preface to repudiate some of his own ideas in the book in light of subsequent evidence.)

In Alexander's case, this empiricism was sometimes obscured by the poetic (some would say spiritual) quality of his writing, and his tenacious, sometimes pugnacious debating style with colleagues (one that is not uncommon among British empiricists, it should be noted). In Jacobs' case, her methods of observation were only the first step in what could be considered a scientific method (as my colleague Stephen Marshall has noted) — but a remarkable and important first step it was.

Both authors leave us today free to test their ideas, to falsify, modify, combine with others — and then, if we find them useful, proceed to apply the ideas constructively, or alternatively, revise them as needed. Both authors have frequently urged us to follow an evidence-based approach, and continue the journey of learning and growth.

This book has argued that, very usefully, their ideas offer us a kind of working hypothesis, or pair of overlapping hypotheses, that offer "something to go on," as all good science does. Most importantly, I think, they show us that an alternative path is available, and they provide detailed information about the structural nature of the changes needed. I have also argued that, partly as a result of their useful ideas, an urban renaissance is already beginning to be visible, and it awaits further development.

In that sense, they have both offered us a useful road map — and, I think, defined for us a critical choice.

This is the choice that we now face — and it is an increasingly urgent one. As discussed earlier, we are in an unprecedented era of urbanization, very likely producing more sheer area of urban fabric in the first half of the 21st Century than we have produced in all of human history. What will be the model, if not the old 20th Century "business as usual"? How will we transition to another, more durable kind of urbanism, rooted in a more durable kind of technology, economy and culture? How will we avert the catastrophic collapse that seems inevitable without changes to the current unsustainable path?

These are the broader questions that underlie the New Urban Agenda and its implementation, and that connect it to the Sustainable Development Goals, the Paris Agreement on Climate Change, and related initiatives. These are the urgent questions that underlie this young urban renaissance, and underscore its integral role in larger questions of human well-being.

As I asked in Chapter I.2, will we continue to stake our entire future on what I referred to as a kind of economic "crack cocaine high" — a quick and intense economic boost, followed by a planetary hangover — and meanwhile, allow our politics to devolve into ugly shouting matches over who gets the next fix? That way lies a "dark age ahead," as Jacobs put it memorably in her last cautionary book.

Or will we apply the knowledge of how cities (and economies) really can work, at their best? Will we put cities and towns to work as engines of sustainable regeneration, taking the steps needed to unleash their powerful urban dynamics? Will we make the transition to what Jacobs called an "age of human capital?"

While much remains to be done, and this book only begins to explore some of the issues ahead, I think we can — and we must.

REFERENCES AND FURTHER READING

Alexander, Christopher (1964). *Notes on the Synthesis of Form.* Cambridge, MA: Harvard University Press.

Alexander, Christopher (1965). *'A City is Not A Tree'.* Originally published in *Architectural Forum*, Vol. 122, No. 1, April 1965, pp. 58–62 (Part I), Vol. 122, No. 2, May 1965, pp. 58–62 (Part II). Available in Mehaffy, M. (Ed.) (2015), *A City is Not a Tree: 50th Anniversary Edition.* Portland: Sustasis Press.

Alexander, Christopher et al. (1977). *A Pattern Language: Towns, Buildings, Construction.* New York: Oxford University Press.

Alexander, Christopher (1979). *The Timeless Way of Building.* New York: Oxford University Press.

Alexander, Christopher (2003). *The Nature of Order: An Essay on the Art of Building and the Nature of the Universe.* (Vols 1–4). Berkeley, CA: Center for Environmental Structure.

Alexander, Christopher et al. (2012). *The Battle for the Life and Beauty of the Earth.* New York: Oxford University Press.

Aristotle (1933). *Metaphysics.* Greek text with English: Trans. Hugh Tredennick, 1933 Edition. Cambridge MA: Harvard U. Press, Loeb Classical Library.

Buchanan, Peter (2015). "Starchitecture's Swan Song." In Architectural Review, February 2015. Available on the web at https://www.architectural-review.com/rethink/viewpoints/empty-gestures-starchitectures-swan-song/8679010.article (Accessed August 2, 2017).

Carroll, Lewis (1889). "The Man in the Moon." From *Sylvie and Bruno Concluded.* Retrieved from http://www.hoboes.com/FireBlade/Fiction/Carroll/Sylvie/Concluded/Chapter11/, July 13, 2010.

Congress for the New Urbanism (1996). *Charter of the New Urbanism.* Available on the Web at https://www.cnu.org/who-we-are/charter-new-urbanism, (Accessed August 2, 2017.)

Frampton, Kenneth (2005). "The work of Architecture in the Age of Commodification." In *Harvard Design Magazine* No. 23 (2005). Available on the web at http://www.harvard-designmagazine.org/issues/23/the-work-of-architecture-in-the-age-of-commodification (Accessed August 2, 2017).

General Motors (1956). "Design for Dreaming". Featurette. Available on the Web at https://www.youtube.com/watch?v=4_ccAf82RQ8. (Accessed August 2, 2017.)

George, Henry (1879). *Progress and Poverty*. New York: Cosimo Books.

Gödel, Kurt (1931). "On formally undecidable propositions of Principia Mathematica and related systems I.: In *The Collected Works of Kurt Gödel*. 2001. Edited by S. Feferman, J. W. Dawson, S. C. Kleene, G. H. Moore, R. M. Solovay and J. van Heijenoort. New York.

Goodwin, Brian (1994) "A Science of Qualities", in *How the Leopard Changed its Spots: The Evolution of Complexity*. New York: Charles Scribner's Sons.

Jacobs, Jane (1961). *The Death and Life of Great American Cities*. New York: Random House.

Jacobs, Jane (1970). *The Economy of Cities*. New York: Vintage Books.

Jacobs, Jane (1994). *Systems of Survival: A dialogue on the moral foundations of commerce and politics*. New York: Vintage.

Jacobs, Jane (2000). *The Nature of Economies*. New York: Random House.

Jacobs, Jane (2004). *Dark Age Ahead*. New York: Random House.

Koolhaas, Rem (1995). "Whatever Happened to Urbanism?" In Koolhaas, R and Mau, B. *S, M, L, XL*. New York: Monacelli Press.

Laurence, Peter. L. (2016). *Becoming Jane Jacobs*. Philadelphia: University of Pennsylvania Press.

Le Corbusier. (1943). *The Athens Charter*. 1973 edition. New York: Grossman Books.

Le Corbusier. (1924). *Towards a New Architecture.* Translated by Frederick Etchells. 1931. New York: Dover Publications.

Mehaffy, Michael W. (2010). "Horizons of Pattern Languages," In *Patterns, Pattern Languages and Sustainability: Symposium Proceedings,* University of Oregon Foundation (May).

Mehaffy, Michael W. and Salingaros Nikos A. (2015). *Design for a Living Planet.* Portland: Sustasis Press.

Newman, Stuart and Bhat, Ramray (2008). "Dynamical Patterning Modules: a "Pattern Language" for Development and Evolution of Multicellular Form." *International Journal of Developmental Biology.* 53:693-705 (2009)

Ostrom, Elinor (1990). *Governing the Commons: The Evolution of Institutions for Collective Action.* Cambridge, UK: Cambridge University Press.

Plato (1974). *Republic.* Translation by G. M. A.Grube. 1974. Indianapolis: Hackett Publishing.

Piaget, Jean (1970). *Structuralism.* Translated and Edited by C. Maschler. New York: Basic Books.

Simon, Herbert (1962). "The Architecture of Complexity." *Proceedings of the American Philosophical Society.* Vol. 106, No. 6 (Dec. 12, 1962), pp. 467-482.

UN-Habitat (2016). *The New Urban Agenda.* Available on the web at http://habitat3.org/the-new-urban-agenda/ (Accessed August 2, 2017).

United Nations (2015). Sustainable Development Goals. Available on the web at http://www.un.org/sustainabledevelopment/sustainable-development-goals/ (Accessed August 2, 2017).

United Nations Framework Convention on Climate Change (2015). *The Paris Agreement.* Available on the Web at http://unfccc.int/paris_agreement/items/9485.php. (Accessed August 2, 2017).

Whitehead, Alfred North and Russell, Bertrand (1910-1912). *Principia Mathematica.* Cambridge: Cambridge University Press.

Whitehead., Alfred North (1929). *Process and Reality.* London: MacMillan.

Whitehead, Alfred North (1933). *Adventures of Ideas.* New York: MacMillan.

Whitehead, Alfred North (1938). *Modes of Thought.* New York: MacMillan.

Zipp, Samuel and Storring, Nate, Eds. (2016). *Vital Little Plans: The Short Works of Jane Jacobs.* New York: Random House.

ABOUT THE AUTHOR

Michael W. Mehaffy, Ph.D. is Director of the Future of Places Research Network, and Senior Researcher at KTH Royal Institute of Technology in Stockholm. He is also Executive Director of the Sustasis Foundation and Sustasis Press, a research and publication NGO based in Portland, Oregon that is focused on topics of urban sustainability. Dr. Mehaffy has been a consultant to UN-Habitat for the Habitat III conference and its outcome document, The New Urban Agenda. He is also an author, researcher, educator, and practitioner in urban design and strategic urban development with an international practice. He has held teaching and/or research appointments at seven graduate institutions in six countries, and he is on the editorial boards of two international journals of urban design. He was formerly the Director of Education for the Prince's Foundation for the Built Environment in London, and is currently Chair of the College of Chapters of the International Network for Traditional Building, Architecture and Urbanism (INTBAU), a London-based NGO co-founded by the Prince of Wales. He studied philosophy of science at the Graduate School of the University of Texas at Austin, and architecture and planning at the University of California, Berkeley. He received his Ph.D. in architecture at Delft University of Technology in the Netherlands, where his research focused on urban form and greenhouse gas emissions.

INDEX

C

D